CW00539727

FERRIES 2002

BRITISH ISLES AND NORTHERN EUROPE EDITION

ISBN 1 871947 70 7

Ferry Publications, PO Box 33,
Ramsey, Isle of Man IM99 4LP

Email: ferrypubs@aol.com Website: www.ferrypubs.co.uk

europe's **leading** guide to the ferry industry

contents

Lady of Mann, SeaCat Isle of Man and Ben-my-Chree *(IOMSP Co. Ltd)*

europe's **leading** guide to the ferry industry

introduction

THIS is the fifteenth edition of this book, which first appeared in 1983 as the 24 page 'home published' 'Car Ferries from Great Britain and Ireland'. The book aims to list every passenger/vehicle ferry in Great Britain and Ireland, ro-ro freight vessels which operate regular services between Great Britain and Ireland and to nearby continental destinations and major passenger/vehicle ferries in other parts of Northern Europe. The coverage of Northern Europe is not fully comprehensive (to make it so would probably triple the size of the book) and does not include freight-only operations and vessels- although for the first time some freight-only vessels have been included where the operators also run passenger services. Also, ro-ro vessels engaged in 'deep sea' and Mediterranean trade and those operated solely for the carriage of trade cars are not included.

Each operator is listed alphabetically within sections - international and Northern Ireland routes, domestic services, freight-only operations, chain, cable and float ferries, passenger only ferries, other North European passenger operators and vehicle/passenger vessels owned by companies not currently engaged in operating services. After details relating to each company's management, address, telephone numbers, email, web site and services, there is a fleet list with technical data and then a potted history of each vessel with previous names and dates.

After several rather lean years in the wake of the impact of the Channel Tunnel and the loss of duty free, the British Isles saw a number of interesting new ferries on a variety of routes. Most were of the growing breed of 'super ro-pax' configuration - hulls designed to carry vast amount of freight but, on top, passenger accommodation finished to a high standard. The speed of conventional shipping is increasing but, on the other hand, the fast ferry market seems to be stagnant, with little growth and some cut backs. This year promises to be of almost equal interest with Superfast and NorthLink both starting operations and new tonnage for P&O Irish Sea and Brittany Ferries. The ferry business is not easy - and perhaps never will be - but it does seem to be on the up at the moment and long may it continue.

Whitstable, Kent **Nick Widdows**

May 2002

europe's **leading** guide to the ferry industry

foreword

There have been some fairly radical changes in the industry during the last year with many operators becoming increasingly aware that fast craft operations are not entirely the answer to their long term profits. Certainly the industry in Northern Europe is looking more and more to the development of fast conventional ferries or ro-pax vessels instead of the fast craft which made such an impact during the previous decade.

One of the most interesting developments of the 2002 must be the introduction of the Superfast vessels across the Bass Strait. Whilst the Tasmanian Government have been pouring millions of dollars into Robert Clifford's InCat business, right under their noses TT Line in Australia have decided to switch their operation to a conventional operation between Devonport and Melbourne with the acquisition of the two Superfast vessels from Greece. Austal also are in financial trouble and the rest of this sector of the fast craft building industry does not hold well for the next couple of years. Also there are currently a number of fast craft laid-up around ports in Northern Europe as ferry companies are now far more reluctant to use them with their high fuel costs, their unrealiability during bad weather conditions and their high technical running costs. Meanwhile Stena Line remain saddled with their HSS craft on the Irish Sea and North Sea with the fixed infrastructure for them. In the light of high losses in their UK operations, there appears to be no future for these craft. If there is a large rise in oil costs during this year, this will lead to further problems for the Swedish company and possibly the withdrawal of the HSS.

On a positive note as far as new ferries are concerned, the direction appears to be conventional built ships that can operate in most weather conditions at operating speeds of up to 28 knots. The investment that Blue Star Ferries have put into their operations in the Aegean in the last couple of years will pay volumes for them in the long-term. The new Korean-built vessels of Blue Star Ferries will rival those of Hellas Ferries over the next couple of years in Southern Greece - an area which remains saddled with many old vessels from the English Channel and North Sea. Meanwhile Superfast have developed their fast ferry service using conventional ships which can operate up to 28.6 knots. Their futuristic-looking ships are now very much the envy of the industry in Europe. A number of other ferry companies are now developing a strategy of conventional fast ships, which must be the future. Brittany Ferries are due to order a new fast conventional vessel for their operations to Spain and Ireland to replace the *Val de Loire*. Once this new ferry comes into service, not only will she allow the Breton company operate more sailings a week than at present but it will also speed passengers to their destinations faster and in a greater style and comfort than ever seen before.

The industry in Northern Europe has a wealth and variety of different vessels operating and this is richly illustrated in this publication which is now accepted as the ferry industry's 'bible' for information, specification, etc. We do hope that you will enjoy this enlarged version for 2002, which carries additional information requested by readers from the industry. If you have any further comments, or you would like to see further information included within the publication, please do let us know.

Miles Cowsill and John Hendy

Pride of Rotterdam *(Mike Louagie)*

a guide to using this book

Sections Listing is in seven sections ***Section 1*** - Services from Great Britain and Ireland to the continent and between Great Britain and Ireland (including services to/from the Isle of Man and Channel Islands), ***Section 2*** - Domestic services within Great Britain and Ireland, ***Section 3*** - Freight only services from Great Britain and Ireland and domestic routes, ***Section 4*** - Minor vehicle ferries in Great Britain and Ireland (chain and cable ferries etc), ***Section 5*** - Major passenger only operators, ***Section 6*** - Major car ferry operators in Northern Europe, ***Section 7*** - Companies not operating regular services possessing vehicle ferries which may be chartered or sold to other operators.

Order The company order within each section is alphabetical. Note that the definite article and words meaning 'company' or 'shipping company' (eg 'AG', 'Reederei') do not count. However, where this is part of a ship's name it does count. Sorting is by normal English convention eg 'Å' is treated the same as 'A' and comes at the start, not as a separate character which comes the end of the alphabet as is the Scandinavian convention. Where ships are numbered, order is by number whether number is expressed in Arabic or Latin digits or words (eg SUPERSEACAT TWO comes before SUPERSEACAT THREE).

Company information This section gives general information regarding to status of the company ie nationality, whether it is public or private sector and whether it is part of a larger group.

Management The managing director and marketing director or manager of each company are listed. Where these posts do not exist, other equivalent people are listed. Where only initials are given, that person is, as far as is known, male.

Address This is the address of the company's administrative headquarters. In the case of some international companies, a British and overseas address is given.

Telephone and Fax Numbers are expressed as follows + [*number*] (this is the international dialling code which is dialled in combination with the number dialled for international calls (00 in the UK, Ireland and most other European countries); it is not used for calling within the country), ([*number*]) (this is the number which precedes area codes when making long distance domestic calls - it is not dialled when calling from another country or making local calls (not all countries have this)), [*number*] (this is the rest of the number including, where appropriate, the area dialling code). In a few cases free or local call rate numbers are used for reservations; note that these are not available from overseas. Telex numbers are also included where applicable; it should be noted that many operators no longer use this service, its role having largely been taken over by Fax and Email.

Internet Email addresses and Website URLs are given where these are available; the language(s) used is shown. Note that use of the Internet is increasing quickly and new sites may come into use during the currency of this book. If a web site is not shown for a particular operator, it may be worth trying one or more search engines to see if a new site has opened. In a few cases Email facility is only available through the Website. To avoid confusion, there is no other punctuation on the Internet line. All these addresses can be accessed from http://homepages.enterprise.net/nickw00000 and this will be updated at regular intervals as new web sites come on line. It should be noted that some sites are not always up to date and it is disappointing that few operators use this facility for 'real time' data showing day by day service changes. However, the standard is generally much higher than a few years ago and many operators now allow on-line booking, often at a discount over other methods. It is also often possible to find times for freight only sailings.

Routes operated After each route there are, in brackets, details of ***1*** normal journey time, ***2*** regular vessel(s) used on the route (number as in list of vessels) and ***3*** frequencies (where a number per day is given, this relates to return sailings). In the case of freight-only sailings which operate to a regular schedule, departure times are given where they have been supplied. Please note that times are subject to quite frequent change and cancellation.

Winter and Summer In this book, **winter** generally means the period between October and Easter while **summer** means, Easter to October. The **peak summer period** is generally June, July and August. In Scandinavia, the summer peak ends in mid-August whilst in the UK it starts rather later and generally stretches into the first or second week of September. Dates vary according to operator.

Spelling The convention is used in respect of town and country names is that English names are used for towns and areas of countries where such names exist (eg Gothenburg rather than Göteborg) and English names for countries (eg Germany rather than Deutschland). Otherwise local names are used, accented as appropriate. In a few cases, English names have slipped out of common usage and the local name is more commonly used in Britain, ie Dunkerque not Dunkirk, Helsingør not Elsinore and Vlissingen not Flushing. Many towns in Finland have both Finnish and Swedish names; we have used the Finnish name except in the case of Åland which is a Swedish speaking area. In the case of Danish towns, the alternative use of 'å' or 'aa' follows local convention. For technical reasons it is not possible to express some Polish names with the correct accents. The following towns, islands and territories are expressed using their English names; the local name is shown following: Antwerp - Antwerpen/Anvers, Fyn - Funen, Genoa - Génova, Ghent - Gent, Gothenburg - Göteborg, Jutland - Jylland, Copenhagen - København, Ostend - Oostende, Oporto - Porto, Seville - Sevilla, Sealand - Sjælland, Venice - Venezia.

Terms The following words mean ***'shipping company'*** in various languages Redereja (Latvian), Rederi (Danish, Norwegian, Swedish), Rederij (Dutch), Reederei (German), Zegluga (Polish). The following words mean ***'limited company'*** AB - Aktiebolag (Swedish) (Finnish companies who use both the Finnish and Swedish terms sometimes express it as Ab), AG - Aktiengesellschaft (German), AS - Aksjeselskap (Norwegian), A/S - Aktie Selskabet (Danish), BV - besioten vennootschap (Dutch), GmbH - Gesellschaft mit beschränkter Haftung (German), NV - naamloze vennootschap (Dutch), Oy - (Finnish), Oyj - (Finnish (plc)), SA - Société Anonyme (French).

Types of Ferry

These distinctions are necessarily general and many ships will have features of more than one category.

Car Ferry Up until about 1970, most vehicle ferries were primarily designed for the conveyance of cars and their passengers and foot passengers. Little regard was paid to the conveyance of lorries and trailers, since this sort of traffic had not began to develop. Few vessels of this type are still in service.

Multi-purpose Ferry From about 1970 onwards vehicle ferries began to make more provision for freight traffic, sharing the same ship with passengers and cars. Features usually include higher vehicle decks, often with retractable ramps enabling two levels of cars or one level of freight and coaches, and separate facilities (including cabins on quite short crossings) for freight drivers.

Cruise Ferry In the 1980s the idea of travelling on a ferry, not just to get from A to B, but for the pleasure of the travel experience became more and more popular and ferries were built with increasingly luxurious and varied passenger accommodation. Such vessels also convey cars and freight but the emphasis is on passenger accommodation with a high level of berths (sometimes providing berths for all passengers).

Ro-pax Ferry A vessel designed primarily for the carriage of freight traffic but also carry a limited number of ordinary passengers. Features generally include a moderate passenger capacity - up to about 500 passengers - and a partly open vehicle deck. Modern ro-pax vessels are becoming increasingly luxurious with facilities approaching those of a cruise ferry.

Ro-ro Ferry A vessel designed for the conveyance of road freight, unaccompanied trailers and containers on low 'Mafi' trailers. Some such vessels have no passenger accommodation but the majority can take up to 12 passengers - the maximum allowed without a passenger certificate. On routes where there is a low level of driver accompanied traffic (mainly the longer ones), ordinary passengers, with or without cars, can sometimes be conveyed. On routes with a high level of driver accompanied traffic, passenger capacity will sometimes be higher but facilities tend to be geared to the needs of freight drivers eg lounge with video, high level of cabins on routes of three hours or more. Technically such vessels are passenger ferries (having a passenger certificate) but are included in the freight section when exclusively or largely conveying freight drivers.

Fast Ferry Streamlined vessel of catamaran or monohull construction, speed in excess of 30 knots, water jet propulsion, generally aluminium built but some have steel hulls, little or no freight capacity, no cabins.

List of vessels

NO (A)	NAME	GROSS TONNAGE (B)	YEAR BUILT	SERVICE SPEED (KNOTS)	LENGTH OVERALL	NUMBER OF PASSENGERS	VEHICLE (C) DECK CAPACITY		VEHICLE ACCESS DECK (D)	FLAG (E)
1	NAME	‡26433t	87	22k	150m	290P	650C	100L	BA2	UK

(A) » = fast ferry, • = vessel laid up, F = freight only vessel, p = passenger only vessel

(B) '‡' = not measured in accordance with the 1969 Tonnage Convention; c = approximate.

(C) C = Cars, L = Lorries (**15m**), T = Trailers (**13.5m**), r = can also take rail wagons, - = No figure quoted.

(D) B = Bow, A = Aft, S = Side, Q = Quarterdeck, R = Slewing ramp, 2 = Two decks can be loaded at the same time, C = Vehicles must be crane loaded aboard, t = turntable ferry.

(E) The following abbreviations are used:

AT = Antigua & Barbuda
BA = Bahamas
BB = Barbados
BD = Bermuda
BE = Belgium
CI = Cayman Islands
CR = Croatia
CY = Cyprus
DK = Denmark
ES = Estonia
FA = Faroes
FI = Finland
FR = France
GI = Gibraltar
GR = Greece
GY = Germany
IM = Isle of Man
IT = Italy
IR = Irish Republic
KE = Kerguelen Islands (FR)
LB = Liberia
LT = Lithuania
LX = Luxembourg
MA = Malta
NA = Netherlands Antilles
NL = Netherlands
NO = Norway
PA = Panama
PL = Portugal
PO = Poland
RO = Romania
RU = Russia
SI = Singapore
SP = Spain
SV = St Vincent & Grenadines
SW = Sweden
UK = United Kingdom

In the notes ships are in CAPITAL LETTERS, shipping lines and other institutions are in *italics*.

Capacity In this book, capacities shown are the maxima. Sometimes vessels operate at less than their maximum passenger capacity due to reduced crewing or to operating on a route on which they are not permitted to operate above a certain level. Car and lorry/trailer capacities are the maximum for either type. The two figures are not directly comparable; some parts of a vessel may allow cars on two levels to occupy the space that a trailer or lorry occupies on one level, some may not. Also some parts of a vessel with low headroom many only be accessible to cars. All figures have to be fairly approximate.

Ownership The ownership of many vessels is very complicated. Some are actually owned by finance companies and banks, some by subsidiary companies of the shipping lines, some by subsidiary companies of a holding company of which the shipping company is also a subsidiary and some by companies which are jointly owned by the shipping company and other interests like a bank, set up specifically to own one ship or a group of ships. In all these cases the vessel is technically chartered to the shipping company. However, in this book, only those vessels chartered from one shipping company to another or from a ship owning company unconnected with the shipping line, are recorded as being on charter. Vessels are listed under the current operator rather than the owner. Charter is 'bareboat' (ie without crew) unless otherwise stated. If chartered with crew, vessels are 'time chartered'.

Gross Tonnage This is a measure of enclosed capacity rather than weight, based on a formula of one gross ton = 100 cubic feet. Even small alterations can alter the gross tonnage. Under old measurement systems, the capacity of enclosed car decks was not included but, under a 1969 convention, all vessels laid down after 1982 have been measured by a new system which includes enclosed vehicle decks as enclosed space, thereby considerably increasing the tonnage of vehicle ferries. Under this convention, from 1st January 1995, all vessels were due to be re-measured under this system; despite there, there are a number of vessels which have either not been re-registered or the details of the new measurements were not obtainable. All vessels measured by the old system are indicated with a double dagger '‡'. Tonnages quoted here are, where possible, those given by the shipping companies themselves.

The following people are gratefully thanked for their assistance with this publication many people in ferry companies in the UK and abroad, Gary Andrews, Cees de Bijl, Dick Clague, Geoffrey Hamer, Erik B Jonsen, Barry Mitchell, The Ostend Ferry Crew, Jack Phelan, Pekka Ruponen, Christian Schrandt, Michael Speckenbach (FERRYinformation), Mike Louagie, Chris Randall, Matthew Punter, Henk van der Lugt, Ian Smith (Camrose Organisation), Foto Flite, Haven Colourprint and Pat Somner (Ferry Publications).

Whilst every effort has been made to ensure that the facts contained here are correct, Neither the publishers nor the writer can accept any responsibility for errors contained herein. We would, however, appreciate comments from readers, which we will endeavour to incorporate in the next edition which we plan to publish in spring 2003.

Pride of Le Havre *(Chris Randall)*

Caledonian MacBrayne
NO SMOKING
CLANSMAN
GLASGOW

Clansman *(Miles Cowsill)*

the giants of cruiseferries

A PRIDE OF SUPER FERRIES

The ferry world is long used to superlatives. It is in the very nature of public relations, which of course is crucial to the ongoing success of the industry, that the latest arrivals are trumpeted as the largest, fastest, most spectacularly-designed vessels in the world. And of course, to most people they are: it is extremely rare indeed - and is a testament to the never-ending increase in quality over the last 50 years - that a new ferry arrives and fails to impress.

One thinks back over the years as generation has evolved into generation and the superlatives have never ceased to flow. In *A Manx Enterprise* (1985), one of this publishing house's earliest books, editor John Hendy wrote of the newly-arrived *Free Enterprise III* in 1966:

"She was enormous! At that time, the F.E.III was the largest car ferry in the English Channel and what an impression she created with her bright, clean, pale-green hull and its narrow red stripe above. Needless to say, she dwarfed most of the other vessels in the port ... altogether a more elegant and noble ship with a decent, single, funnel placed in the "proper" place."

Of course, these were pioneering days: the Norwegians were once again conquering our coasts and the first North Sea Ferry - another 'jumbo' was also entering service. But the size - and the compliments increased. The *Free Enterprise III* begat the *Free Enterprise IV* and company. The *Spirit of Free Enterprise* begat the *Pride of Dover* whilst on the Irish Sea we witnessed the *St Columba*, the *St Brendan*, the *Felicity* and the *Isle of Inishmore* each out-doing their predecessor.

One could therefore argue that by the time the 1990s drew to a close, our appreciation of truly great ferries was somewhat dulled by the huge advances in size and splendid facilities to match. And so it was one cold January morning that P&O announced that the best was yet to come. Several years in the planning, it was time to declare that they had placed the order for the world's largest ferries. For the company, a massive investment for the nearing new century; for the ferry enthusiast, the welcome return of a trophy not seen in the UK since the *Finnjet* powered off with it in 1977; and for the passenger, another paradigm shift in the whole ferry concept.

SeaFrance Rodin *(John Hendy)*

Ulysses *(Irish Ferries)*

Quatre Saisons a la carte restaurant - **Pride of Rotterdam** *(Mike Louagie)*

Irish Bar - **Pride of Rotterdam** *(Mike Louagie)*

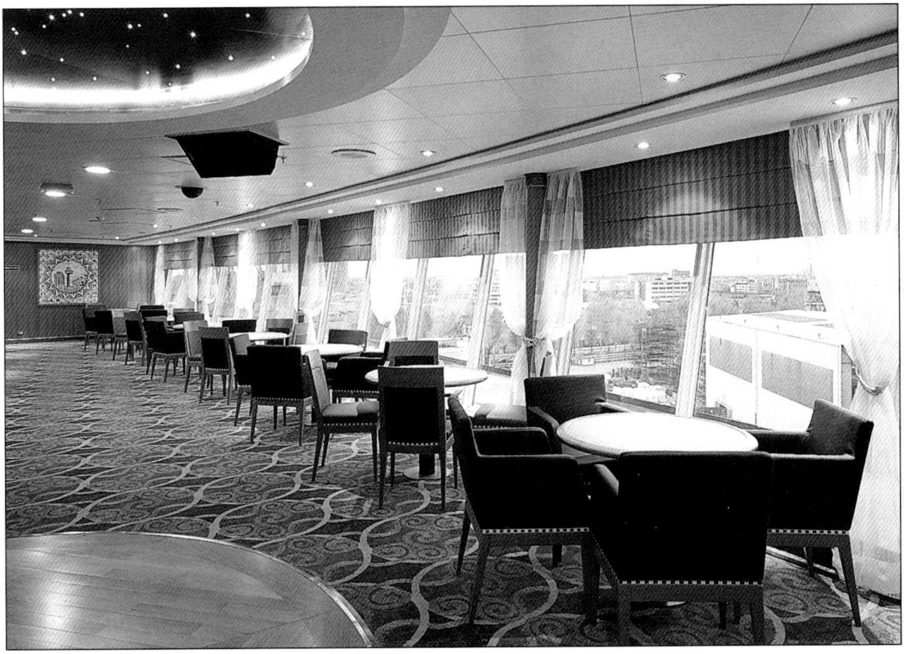

Sky Lounge - **Pride of Rotterdam** *(Mike Louagie)*

Continental Café - **Pride of Rotterdam** *(Mike Louagie)*

FIVE DECADES OF FERRY DESIGN

Not that anyone should have been surprised by either P&O North Sea Ferries' decision or their confident re-establishment of Anglo-Dutch services as pioneers in the ferry world. The company is in its fifth decade at the forefront of ferry evolution, and each succession of design has been internationally significant.

Back in 1965, the decision by the then-styled North Sea Ferries to inaugurate passenger, car and freight services between Hull in Yorkshire and Rotterdam in the Netherlands was itself a bold move, and one very much in tune with the growing pan-European economy. The first ships chosen to inaugurate the service - the purpose built, 4,000 gross tonnes *Norwind* and *Norwave* - were viewed as the ultimate in ferry design. If the *Free Enterprise III* showed all the hallmarks of a worthy 'traditional' design, then the 'Nor' newcomers were something of a revolution, functionally as well as aesthetically.

Essentially, the German-built pair were what we would now call today 'ro-pax' ferries (see *Ferries of the British Isles & Northern Europe 1999*). The vessels' unusual design was principally for the purpose of carrying freight. Their predecessor, Ellerman Wilson Lines' *Sphero* was very much a passenger vessel of the old guard. The new ships could carry 47 trailers and 70 cars but only 250 passengers; this mix has been a feature ever since.

After ten years, such was the success of the service, North Sea Ferries embarked on a major expansion programme that saw not only the opening of a second route into Belgium, but the commissioning of two vastly bigger vessels. NSF returned to the Bremerhaven yard for the construction of the *Norland* and *Norstar*, ships in which the passenger facilities would come into their own, perhaps for the first time.

But how things had changed over the decade. The pair dwarfed pioneers *Norwind* and *Norwave*, which moved to provide rather unequal coverage for the new Zeebrugge route. Interestingly, whilst the company's inaugural sisters were somewhat unique at that time, the second generation vessels were very much ferries of their day. With accommodation for 1,200 and capacity for 500 cars or 134 trailers, the 13,000 gross tonnes *Norland* and *Norstar* were the largest ferries in the world, although only marginally so against a number of Scandinavian contemporaries. Already in service were giants such as the *Dana Regina* (DFDS, 13,000 grt/1974), *Peter Pan/Nils Holgersson* (TT-Linie, 12,500 grt/1974) and the *Bore Star/Wellamo/Svea Corona* (Silja companies, c.12,500 grt/1974-5).

Such was the advance brought by the new vessels, they maintained the Rotterdam service well into the mid-1980s before thought was given to incorporate further advances. This time, the decision was made to ensure both services were far more evenly matched and orders were placed in the UK and Japan for a pair of vessels which, at 31,000 gross tonnes would become the largest in service from Britain and the Netherlands. At the same time, the *Norland* and *Norstar* would be reconstructed, increasing their size to match the latest arrivals.

In 1987, the new *Norsea* and *Norsun* entered service, almost simultaneously. Although their thunder had been stolen a few months earlier by the fractionally smaller *Koningin Beatrix*, the third generation ships still offered some impressive statistics.

Passenger capacity was for 1,250 (a slight increase over their predecessors) and vehicle capacity was for 850 cars or 180 trailers; they were amongst the largest freight carriers of their day. And whilst NSF tried to disguise the continuing freight-dominance of the route with impressive marketing and genuinely attractive facilities both vessels dated quite rapidly against other passenger vessels entering service during the 1990s. By the end of that decade, the discerning passenger would notice that compared to the better offerings on the English Channel and around Scandinavian shores, the passenger areas of *Norsea, Norsun* and their older cousins were increasingly spartan and pokey.

But what could be done? NSF's forward-thinking decision to enlarge *Norland* and *Norstar* on the introduction of the *Norsea* and *Norsun* disrupted the natural cycle of fleet management to some extent. Even if a company's lead ships do not need replacing at a given time, the chances are that older fleet members will and so the arrival of superior tonnage every few years or so ensures that weaker vessels can be 'retired' at the appropriate time. With four equally matched vessels, this impetus was not there. Additionally, passenger demand on the longer routes to the continent was at best static although the freight market was growing.

As an interim measure NSF ordered two purpose-built freight vessels in order to double up capacity between Hull and Rotterdam. Arriving in 1993, the *Norbank* and *Norbay* were also significant in that they necessitated the installation of a river berth in the River Humber. Prior to this, all vessels locked in and out of the dock, a task immensely time-consuming, if no less spectacular for that. Along with some refreshing of the fleet's passenger areas, the services were secure for the 1990s.

However, the abilities of interior designers and the capabilities of the crew in maintaining good standards could not keep up with the needs of the ferry industry. By the late 1990s, the *Norland* and *Norstar* were simply too old to continue operating, against a darkening backdrop of ferry disasters which had the effect of highlighting the inadequacies of designs conceived back in the early days of ro-ro operations. Further reconstruction on *Norland* and *Norstar* would be expensive and anyway, stretching their careers into their fourth decade would be unheard of in modern times. Although the *Norsea* and *Norsun* were still very suited to their Dutch route, new ships had to be found. Here arose the difficulties in such a strategy. Any newcomers would be needed to drive significant efficiency savings in order to pay their way. However the market was static, thereby requiring no major increases in capacity. Lateral thinkers please apply here.

OUT OF THE BOX

The obvious solution was to re-order direct for the Zeebrugge service. However, the severe constraints of Hull docks meant that a new design either had to be inefficiently small in order to use the traditional berths or would necessitate the construction of an additional river berth. And so a cunning plan was devised to move the *Norsea* and *Norsun* to the Belgian route whilst each - along with their partnering freighter - would be replaced by two ferries, but this time built on top of each other! Such a vessel would consist of six decks of *Norbank* freight capacity underneath the car decks of *Norsea* all topped off with the passenger accommodation of a cruiseferry. A pair of these ships would be able to use the river berth and replace four older ferries (in the event *Norland*

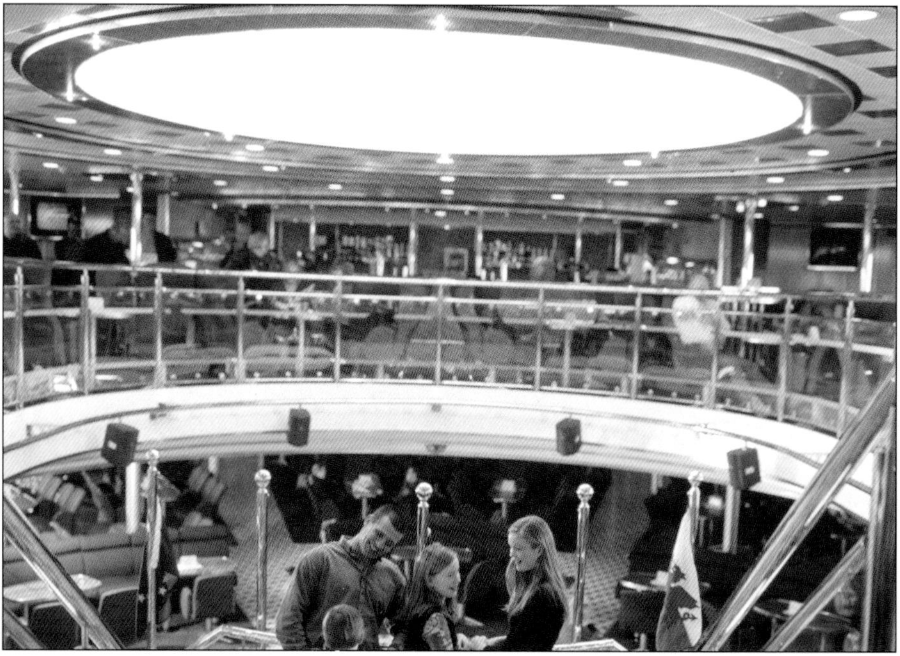

Atrium - **Ulysses** *(Irish Ferries)*

Side Lounge - **Ulysses** *(Irish Ferries)*

Irish Bar - **Ulysses** *(Irish Ferries)*

Observation Lounge - **Ulysses** *(Irish Ferries)*

and *Norstar* as planned, together with *Norbank* and *Norbay*). By now wholly owned by P&O, North Sea Ferries were determined to leave behind their modest passenger areas of the past and create facilities designed to impress, without installing the financial drains which appeared on other ferries during the early 1990s. To be built at Venice by Fincantieri, the names chosen for *Pride of Rotterdam* and *Pride of Hull* reflected not just the new owners, but a completely new attitude to North Sea ferry services. At nearly 60,000 gross tonnes - once again NSF were operating the world's largest - a brand new era in ferry design was beginning.

MEET THE *PRIDE OF ROTTERDAM*

The lead ship *Pride of Rotterdam* arrived in late April 2001, and by then her sister *Pride of Hull* was already at an advanced stage of construction. The arrival of the fourth generation set wholly new standards for UK ferry travel but practically, also brought about a number of important innovations to the service.

Most importantly the ships' distinctive design effectively created a number of separate vehicle decks. This meant that whilst three separate lorry decks were being loaded via the stern ramp, a fourth car deck, accessed through side doors, could be loaded using an additional ramp soaring over the new purpose-built riverside terminal. Not only an efficient use of ship and shore space, enabling cars to park much closer to the passenger areas, this system effectively reinforces the 'two-ships-in-one" aspect of the *Pride of Rotterdam*. Also, the pair are significantly faster than the *Norsea* and *Norsun* and the departure time is now 2100 rather than 1830 whilst maintaining the same arrival time. The shorter crossing time, has, ironically, reduced the 'cruise-like' nature of the trip although P&O have overcome this by allowing passengers to board and use the facilities from late afternoon.

From the exterior, the *Pride of Rotterdam* presents an arresting profile. In order to break up the bulk of such a large ship - which completely dominates much smaller vessels such as the *Pride of Portsmouth* or *Stena Baltica*, the architects have made good use of curves, creating a profile reminiscent of a whale. The abrupt change from fo'c'sle to superstructure is softened by a line sweeping up through the passenger decks and to the lifeboats, themselves incorporated into the rear curve from the skylounge, through the funnel and down to the freight decks.

However, it is once the passenger is inside that the *Pride of Rotterdam* comes into her own, benefiting from managing director Peter van den Brandhof's extensive survey of existing cruiseferries in order to capture the best features from each. Facilities are concentrated on two main decks, entry on deck 8 at the reception providing two main options: shopping and eating aft with entertainment forward. The former consists of two moderately sized outlets aft of which is the Four Seasons Buffet Restaurant. Forward of the foyer is the bar, casino and Sunset Showlounge, a spacious and stylish two-deck high show bar backed by a TV wall. This is linked to the upper tier via a glitzy spiral staircase where two cinemas, video arcade and a second bar are on offer. Further aft on this deck is the Children's World, Continental Café and Cyberzone, linking passengers via satellite to the latest holiday offers on P&ONSF's website in addition to the rest of the internet. The Quatre Saisons à la Carte Restaurant, Quiet Room, Business Lounge & Wine Bar and freight drivers facilities are also in this area.

Cabins are forward on decks 8 and 9 and also occupy the whole of deck 10, through which one accesses the other spectacular design feature of the *Pride of Rotterdam*, the huge panoramic sky lounge. High up above the passing scenery and sea, it is from this vantage point that the true size of the *Pride of Rotterdam* can be truly appreciated.

The panoramic skylounge is also where P&O's step change in passenger comfort and quality can be best appreciated. The area, like the whole of the ship, exudes quality. The skylounge offers not only a bar and coffee shop, with live entertainment provided by a resident pianist. The space is fitted out to very high standards and good use of lighting is made to create an intimate, sophisticated atmosphere by night but a fresh, relaxing ambience by day.

Throughout the rest of the ship, the interior is bright, yet traditional. Warm colours - purples, reds, oranges - are contrasted with abundant wood effects. P&O's quality control has ensured that fittings are designed to last 25 years rather than 5 and this is evident in the standards in the cabins with polished granite vanity tops and Hansgrohe taps.

A WORK OF ART

A key quality measure of the on board experience on the *Pride of Rotterdam* and the *Pride of Hull* is the specially commissioned collection of modern art. These works are a central feature of the public areas and cabins on board both vessels and have been created for P&O North Sea Ferries by renowned British and Dutch artists.

Instrumental in the establishment of such varied collections was P&ONSF Managing Director Peter van den Brandhof who believes that "these works of art will enhance still further the style and quality of the ships. And we attach great importance to the fact that young artists from the two countries which the ferries serve have had this opportunity to show off their considerable talents."

The collection on the *Pride of Rotterdam* is extremely diverse, varying both in terms of subject, medium and size and is an ever present feature in the vessel's public areas. Works range from a five metre high metal and neon sculpture running up the spiral staircase linking the two floors of the Showbar to four enormous depictions of the four seasons on display in the restaurant.

The artworks were commissioned by P&O in partnership with their Amsterdam-based art advisors who selected a number of suitable artists. In conjunction with the designers of the vessel, the selection was short-listed to three potential artists for each on board location. Artists were then given a contract specifying the size, subject, materials and price of each piece, producing preliminary sketches for P&O approval.

The effect of such a major commission has been manifold. Most importantly, not only have P&O further enhanced the sophistication of the on board atmosphere, but many young artists have had the opportunity demonstrate their talents. At the same time, they have been able to create cohesive collections that have - and this is quite rare - been designed to remain in the same location rather than being split up between galleries and other outlets.

Ulysses *(Irish Ferries)*

In the Best of Company

The *Pride of Rotterdam* and *Pride of Hull* are certainly zeitgeist ferries however. Whilst the later 1990s belonged to the Greeks in terms of ferry design, and the previous decade to the Scandinavians, 'conventional' ferry development in the British Isles has been at best rather pedestrian over the last few years, as fast ferries stole the limelight. But the new decade has seen a return to the more adventurous spirit of the early 1980s with a significant number of new designs. Numerically, the purpose-built ro-pax vessels represented by Cenargo's 'Merchant' series and P&O's *European Causeway* trio have been key to the redevelopment of new services. However, in terms of sheer style, 2001-2 is witnessing an historic succession of the highest quality ferries.

First in service was Irish Ferries' massive *Ulysses* which arrived in late March 2001. Although observers have become accustomed to a steady flow of ever-superior ferries for the Irish company, the *Ulysees* has really reached new heights. Passenger facilities are concentrated on one main level with an excellent range of eateries complemented by a stylish shop, large and comfortable bar and family area, all decked out in a fresh and modern décor. On top of this fine selection sits the crowning observation lounge and bar, which, thanks to a difficult access route from the main passenger areas, offers a loftily tranquil place from which to enjoy the passing scenery and access the other facilities below. This feature adds the 5-star element to the *Ulysees*' offer and together with a much smaller but similar feature on fleetmate *Isle of Inishmore*, creates a distinctive alternative to the competition.

At nearly 51,000 grt, the *Ulysses* represents a giant leap for ferrykind on the Irish Sea, and she serves a pure market increase, not just an efficiency drive. What is very distinctive about travelling on board the *Ulysses* is she demonstrates how ferries have 'grown up'. There is an increasing amount of choice as to what to do, what to eat and where to go, but in a much more attractive environment where one is not constantly being bombarded to spend money.

As 2001 closed, the English Channel took delivery of the first of two major vessels. In late November, the *SeaFrance Rodin* was inaugurated, the first purpose-built ferry for the Calais service since the *Pride of Calais* in 1988. The *SeaFrance Rodin* is also the Dover Strait's largest ever passenger ferry and the first newbuild for SeaFrance and its predecessors since the *Champs Elysees*, eighteen years ago.

Whilst at 34,000 gross tonnes the *SeaFrance Rodin* does not represent such a paradigm shift in ferry design on the Channel, she is certainly very much in tune with recent trends. SeaFrance have also gone to great lengths to create a very memorable vessel, most notably through the meandering central aisle, stunningly featuring a two-deck high atrium and glass wall providing an excellent view of the Channel.

Providing something different to the highly - and widely - acclaimed P&O Stena offer is not easy, yet in *SeaFrance Rodin*, her owners have succeeded. Once again, the vessel offers something broadly comparable, yet tangibly different to the competition and represents a gentler, yet fresher approach to ferry interiors, the *pièce de la resistance* of course being the atrium. The 'Rodin's interior retains the same corporate themes as her fleetmates (Le Pub, Le Parisien Café etc.), yet the colour scheme is bright and the general ambience of a very high quality.

Still to come this year is the latest in a slow but steady procession of high quality vessels for Brittany Ferries' Western Channel services. Currently nearing completion at Rotterdam, the 35,000 gross tons *Mont St Michel* enters service in July opposite 1992's *Normandie*. For many years now Brittany Ferries have been seen as one of the highest quality operators and to a degree, the *Mont St Michel* is just the latest in this trend. With the next generation of Brittany Ferries' facilities and services the ferry will provide, she will enable a greater consistency across the fleet which will be completed on the arrival in 2004 of the next ferry under construction in Germany

THE FUTURE'S BRIGHT

The arrival in 2001 and 2002 of *Pride of Rotterdam* and the other new generation superferries - *Pride of Hull, Ulysses, SeaFrance Rodin* and *Mont St Michel* - reaffirmed the strength of services to and from the UK. These five superlative ferries have advanced the industry standards immensely with their stylish interiors and excellent choice of facilities. At no time for maybe decades, the North West European ferry industry can look to the future with an air of confidence.

So is it possible to extrapolate future trends from these recent commissions? What can be stated with confidence is that the cruiseferry is back for good. Despite the extravagance of the 1980s and 1990s when lavish facilities were put before profit, the latest generation - all purpose built - have adopted a more moderate format with carefully designed passenger areas suited to the needs of the route.

The cruiseferry revolution (see *Ferries 2001 British Isles and Northern Europe*) has completed the circle of ferry regeneration over the last ten years and naturally returned to where it all began. Fast ferries now provide express services across the core routes in each sectors, 'ro-pax' looks after the fringe routes and complements fast ferries whilst the cruiseferry has evolved into its modern incarnation as the steward of the high quality 'capital cities' routes.

And long may they continue - the *Pride of Rotterdam* and the *Pride of Hull* are the current champions of a class of many contenders. The *Bretagne, P&OSL Aquitaine, Queen of Scandinavia, Pride of Bilbao* were all extremely noteworthy ferries of their day and in the years to come, replacements will follow to set even greater standards of ferry design. Perhaps when these ferries of the future arrive we will even look back on the P&ONSF 'Prides' as trendsetters of an earlier generation, but for now, their crown as the UK's most exciting new ferries for a generation is most certainly assured.

Matthew Punter

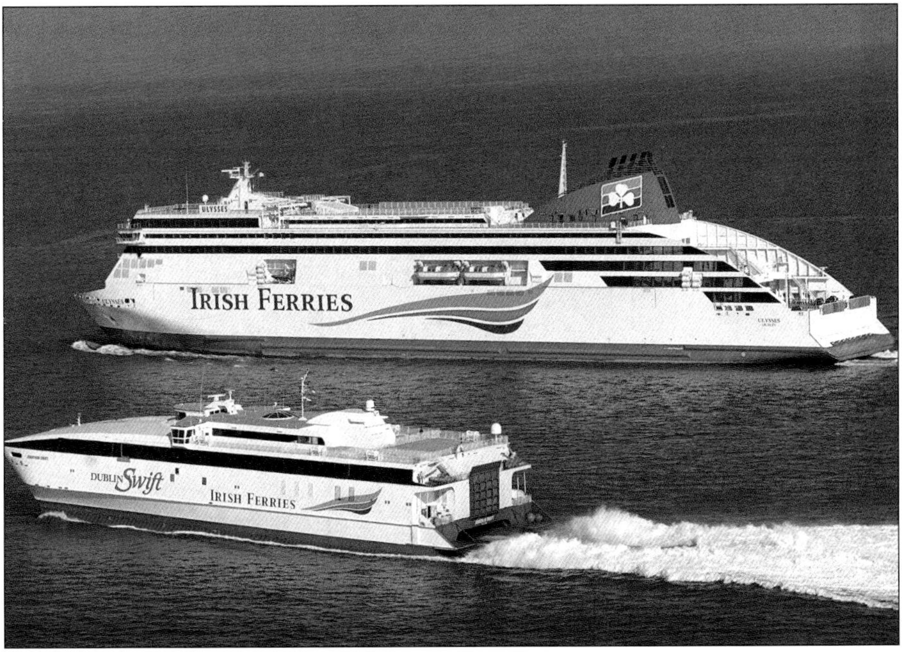

Ulysses and **Johathan Swift** *(Irish Ferries)*

Pride of Hull *(Rob de Visser)*

Fish on Casino Deck 8 - **Pride of Rotterdam** *(P&ONSF)*

Quatre Saisons a la carte restaurant - **Pride of Rotterdam** *(P&ONSF)*

the art of cruiseferries

A unique collection of contemporary artworks is the focus of the interior décor of the Pride of Rotterdam

Art lovers are in for a treat whilst crossing the North Sea. A collection of specially commissioned works of art by renowned Dutch and British artists are a central feature of the décor of the public rooms and passengers' cabins of the *Pride of Rotterdam*. A similar art collection is the focus of the interior décor on the *Pride of Hull*, which entered service in December 2001.

The driving force behind the development of these two exciting collections of onboard art has been Peter van den Brandhof, Managing Director of P&O North Sea Ferries.

According to Peter van den Brandhof, P&O was keen to have specially commissioned art on board because "having such special cruiseferries we wanted some special art works to reflect the quality of our services."

He adds, "these works of art will enhance still further the style and quality of the ships. And we attach great importance to the fact that young artists from the two countries which the ferries serve have had this opportunity to show off their considerable talents."

The works of art, which include not just paintings, prints and drawings on canvas and paper but three-dimensional works, are to be found in many locations all over the *Pride of Rotterdam*. Staircases, restaurants, bars and other public areas, as well as passengers' cabins, all have commissioned art works by artists working in various media. According to David Clixby of SMC Design, project manager of the new ships, the collection of art works is "up-to-the-minute... and can be appreciated on different levels."

The art on board the *Pride of Rotterdam*, along with that to be displayed on the *Pride of Hull*, was chosen under the guidance of Amsterdam art advisors Onderneming and Kunst (Enterprise and Art) along with SMC Design, the interior designers of the ship.

Onderneming and Kunst selected a large number of artists whose work was suitable for various locations on the ship. In conjunction with SMC Design the selection was narrowed down to three proposed artists for each possible location. The final choice of artists was made by representatives of P&O Ferries and SMC Design.

Four Seasons restaurant - **Pride of Rotterdam** *(P&ONSF)*

Each artist received a contract specifying the size, subject, materials and price of each work of art to be produced, as well as a time schedule for delivery and schedule of payments. The artists made preliminary sketches of their works for the ship which were then presented to P&O for approval. Onderneming and Kunst made progress reports at regular intervals until the works were ready for crating and transport.

The collection of paintings, prints and sculptures on the *Pride of Rotterdam* includes works of art both large and small.

One work which is hard to miss is Dutch three-dimensional artist/designer Titia Ex's five-metre high metal and neon sculpture entitled 'The twisting ladder' which is in the well of the spiral stairs in the Show Lounge.

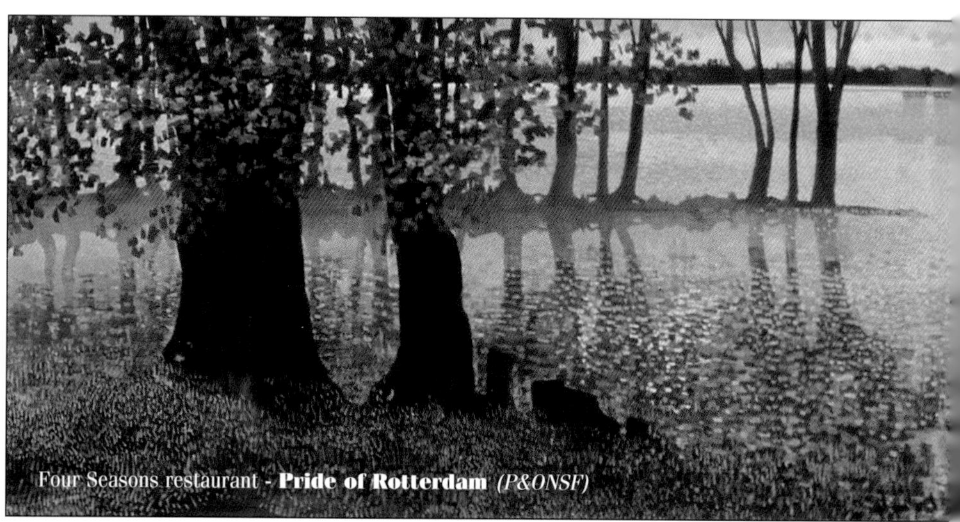

Four Seasons restaurant - **Pride of Rotterdam** *(P&ONSF)*

Another large and very striking work is by Amsterdam artist Barbara Broekman. This is a colourful glass mosaic in the reception lobby of the ship which measures 5.6 x 2.75 metres. This work was a first for Broekman, who as a designer of tapestries had not, up until this commission, produced any glass mosaic work. She felt the chance to work with glass mosaic presented a fascinating challenge. A similar work by Broekman, this time on the theme of 'Hull/Great Britain' will be in the reception lobby of the *Pride of Hull*.

Another large work is to be found in the Irish Bar of the *Pride of Rotterdam*. This is a five-metre long pastel crayon and charcoal work depicting an Irish landscape by Dutch artist Jacobien de Rooy. De Rooy says of her beautiful pastel drawing: "I wanted to draw this landscape in such a fashion that people would want to visit it, I did not make it any prettier than it is." A similar work will adorn the Irish bar of the *Pride of Hull*.

“the collection is up-to-the-minute... and can be appreciated on different levels”

The largest paintings on the ship are to be found in the restaurants. In the buffet restaurant are displayed four vast depictions of the four seasons, the work of Groningen artist Ton Dubbeldam and in the à la carte restaurant is a six-metre flower painting by Tim Maguire. Both these artists find inspiration in the art of the past.

Like the nineteenth-century French Impressionists, Dubbeldam gives light and its reflection in water a central role in his paintings of tranquil natural scenes, whereas for Maguire the starting point for his floral paintings is to be found in seventeenth and eighteenth-century Dutch still-life flower paintings. He uses these as a source of details, details such as individual flowers, which he then enlarges to give each flower new form and significance. His painting demonstrates an interest in the way colour contrasts and transitions from light to dark create an illusion of three dimensionality.

Another artist who uses the art of the past in his work is the Dutch born Hugo Kaagman. From when he was a child, Kaagman has had a fascination with patterns and motifs from folkloristic art from different cultures. He collects and finds new uses for them by combining them with images and icons he takes from everyday life. He has become most well known for his reworking of the images and patterns of the world famous blue and white Delft Blue ceramic ware. Two of Kaagman's 'Delft Ware' paintings can be found in the Sky Lounge on the top deck. These were inspired by Rotterdam and his experiences onboard a P&O ship on a crossing of the North Sea.

Kaagman is a self-taught artist who began his artistic career as a graffiti artist putting his art illegally on hoardings. Now he is a well-established figure in official art circles. He says of his work "A good painting is like a song. My purpose is to modernize traditions giving them a new place in the new millennium."

Life, as opposed to art, is the inspiration for the works of Enric Adserà Riba, a Catalan who has lived in Holland since 1962. His work 'La vida cotidiana'

Lincoln Motel Drivers' restaurant - **Pride of Rotterdam** *(P&ONSF)*

Continental Cafe - **Pride of Rotterdam** *(P&ONSF)*

Pride of Rotterdam *(P&ONSF)*

Pride of Rotterdam *(P&ONSF)*

(Everyday Life) can be found on one wall of the Wine Bar on the *Pride of Rotterdam*, a work that has two themes as it source of inspiration: journeys by ship and wine. This is an unusual work of art as it combines whitewash, *objets trouvés*, pictures which have been stuck on the wall and partly ripped off again, drawings, etchings and sketches to give a sense of a wall on which time has left its traces.

The Mediterranean and the surroundings of his childhood come to life in his work, as he explains: "As a young boy hanging from our family farm's attic all I could see was vineyards basking in the bright sunshine. And in the distance the silvery gleaming Mediterranean with a single ship on the horizon. Wine, sun, sea...for 'La vida cotidiana' inexhaustible sources of inspiration for an entire life every day."

Works on a smaller scale are to be found in the Drivers' Lounge and Restaurant, both reserved for the exclusive use of freight drivers, and in passengers' cabins.

The Drivers' Lounge and Restaurant features a series of eight oil paintings by Araun Gordijn, a Dutch artist. These paintings in a photo-realistic style depict the America of the 'American Dream' and vividly recall the atmosphere of the 1950s: American cars, gas stations, diners, motels and desert landscapes.

A rather interesting detail of his painting 'Lincoln Motel' is the furry dice hanging in the windscreen of the car (see page 31).

Gordijn explains what the P&O commission meant for him: "One whole year working in my workshop is likely to produce a fine cohesive collection. Once the work is exhibited, however, gaps will unfortunately appear with parts of the series being sold. The beauty of this P&O commission is that I could work on a series of eight canvases that are to remain together as a whole at one location."

Thirteen graphic artists from Britain and Holland have produced a collection of 130 limited edition prints for passengers' cabins. Among them are woodcut, linocut, silkscreen and litho prints and colour etchings, all on the theme of nature.

The printmakers have taken a wide variety of starting points for their work: skies, water, landscapes (Tuscany to Scottish coastal towns), flower and leaf forms, animals and birds.

Despite these being smaller works of art than some of the pictures in the public areas of the *Pride of Rotterdam*, the locations that have been chosen for these prints have been very carefully considered. For example, knowing of Dutch artist Joost Minnigh's preference for the theme of birds and water, P&O asked him to produce a work that could be displayed in the windowless inside cabins of the ships.

Commenting on the new ships' collections of onboard art, Managing Director Peter van den Brandhof has this to say: "The result is impressive...the collections are a very special acquisition for both vessels."

round britain review 2001

EAST COAST

Superfast Ferries commenced their overnight Rosyth - Zeebrugge service on 17th May when the industry was carefully looking at ramifications of this bold enterprise to the established English routes to the Low Countries. Many questions were being asked: will the new service generate its own traffic, has Scotland enough traffic of its own to support the link and if so, how will this affect DFDS at Newcastle?

DFDS Seaways introduced their *Queen of Scandinavia* (ex *Finlandia*) onto their North Shields - IJmuiden route on 29th June 2001. Meanwhile the *King of Scandinavia* enjoyed a summer charter to Cotunav of Tunisia but was then ear-marked for a new service linking Copenhagen with the Polish port of Gdynia. However, continued trading losses on the traditional Harwich - Esbjerg route saw the company surprisingly announce that the *Dana Anglia* would switch to their new Baltic service in October 2002. The 'King' was thus spare and was sold for further service in the Mediterranean.

A further DFDS initiative during March 2002 was the switch of the vibratory *Admiral of Scandinavia* from Hamburg to Cuxhaven. Although such a move makes great sense in that it saves both fuel and time at sea, the port Cuxhaven was certainly not prepared for the transfer with foot passengers having to queue for passports and customs on the open quayside. Although road communications to Bremen are excellent, the same cannot be said for those to Hamburg and the city has certainly lost out on the popular mini-cruise market.

P&O North Sea Ferries duly introduced the world's largest ferry the 59,925 gross ton *Pride of Rotterdam* on the overnight service linking Rotterdam (Europort) with Hull on 30th April. After an irritating period of technical troubles with the lead ship, the sistership *Pride of Hull* joined her in service on 2nd December. Meanwhile the second generation NSF vessels *Norstar* and *Norland* were duly sold to Italian owners SNAV.

The company's Felixstowe - Europort freight service has lost money and the *Norbank* and *Norbay* were therefore chartered to the company's Irish Sea services. P&O have announced their intention to sell the Felixstowe- Europort route to Stena who will also take back the elderly trio which they once owned: *Pride of Flanders, European Freeway* and *European Tideway*. We may expect Stena to continue the service but from their own base on the other side of Harwich Harbour. Losses on the Felixstowe service are surprising especially in view of the problems experienced at Hull where the twin new cruise-ferries are frequently capacity constrained. The benefactors of this serious lack of P&O vision are both Cobelfret, Stena Line, Norfolk Line and Dart Line.

Queen of Scandinavia *(Alan Small)*

Pride of Flanders *(Miles Cowsill)*

At Harwich, the Stena Line service linking the Hook of Holland was joined by the second ro-pax *Stena Hollandica* on 9th March. Stena BV's freight service to Immingham has been enjoying brisk patronage, so much so that the *Stena Britannica* is expected to be transferred to the link.

A further service linking Immingham with Ostend commenced on 29th January 2002. Ferryways (operators of the Ipswich - Ostend service) chartered the freighters *Vilja* and *Tango* to open the route.

Cobelfret launched a Purfleet - Rotterdam ro-ro service on 23rd April while across the Thames, a new Dart Line service to Dunkirk commenced on 17th September. Sammarina's attempts to revive the fortunes of Sheerness, firstly to Ostend and then Zeebrugge, sadly came to naught.

EASTERN CHANNEL

The Ramsgate-Ostend operation of the Slovenian company TransEuropa Shipping Lines (TSL) goes from strength to strength although 2001 saw no attempts to reopen the link to passengers. More infrastructure continues to be built in the Belgian port which after many years of decline is at last seeing some significant traffic growth. During April 2001, TSL purchased the P&O Stena Line vessel *P&OSL Picardy* and have renamed her *Oleander*. At the time of writing the vessel remains at Dunkirk but one former Dover Strait ferry that did return to service was the *Laburnum* (ex *Free Enterprise V*) which commenced operations from Ostend in July.

The Dover Strait's first new purpose-built ferry since the opening of the Channel Tunnel duly took up service from Calais to Dover on 29th November. The FFr 611 million *SeaFrance Rodin* replaced the *SeaFrance Renoir* in the fleet. At 34,000 gross tons the new ship is the largest ferry ever to operate across the Strait and with a trials speed of 29 knots, her 53,000 hp Wartsila engines are certainly the most powerful fitted in a local, conventional ferry. A service speed of 25 knots was spoken of although operationally this appeared very unlikely as all ships on the Calais - Dover link are limited by the speed of the vessel ahead of them.

Certainly SeaFrance have been very impressed with their latest acquisition and although it was originally stated that a second ship would not be built, a duplicate of this type could certainly make dramatic inroads into the market. SeaFrance have also indicated that they are assessing the *SeaFrance Nord Pas-de-Calais* for conversion to ro-pax status.

P&O Stena Line introduced a passenger 'no frills, cut-price' service on their three Dover - Zeebrugge freighters as from 1st May 2001. This unexpected move came as a result of continuing progress made by Norfolkline with their chartered freighters *Northern Merchant* and *Midnight Merchant*. Both vessels were modified during April 2002 in order that their sterns could use the double-decked berths at Dover and thereby allow faster turn-rounds.

P&O Stena Line's promised new vessels to replace the *P&OSL Kent* and *P&OSL Canterbury* appear to be further away than ever with the news that the company are seeking to close the Zeebrugge link and modify two of the existing 'European' class

doverport.co.uk
your first port of call

freighters to full multi-purpose status. The 'Burgundy' is proof that this can be done although it is understood that these conversions will not necessarily follow the same plan as before.

At the same time, cash-strapped Stena Line are to shed their 40% interest in the partnership allowing P&O to regain total control of the premier cross-Channel service.

Hoverspeed's erratic use of their fast ferry fleet continues to baffle observers with the first three of their 'SuperSeaCat' mono-hulled craft being switched to the Dover Strait for the 2001 season. As many outside senior Sea Containers management foresaw, this proved to be something of an operational disaster and 2002 sees the sensible return of the 74 metre craft for Calais and an 81 metre craft for Ostend. Sadly, the timetable on the latter service fails to allow a day-trip to the attractive Belgian port.

The Folkestone-Boulogne service, latterly operated by Falcon Marfret's ro-pax *Neptunia,* finally closed on 8th June 2001. The closure was attributed to the success of Norfolkline on the Dover - Dunkirk service and to Sea Containers who failed to develop their remaining port.

At Newhaven, Transmanche Ferries commenced service with the chartered Corsica Ferries' vessel *Sardinia Vera* on 16th April 2001 although there have been problems with her passenger certificate being withdrawn after it was discovered that the crew were unable to launch the lifeboats and that the water-tight doors in the engine room had been left open. Coupled with a serious grounding off the Sussex port in February 2002, it has not been the happiest period for the new company. They have however, acquired their own vessel in the form of the old TT Line ro-pax *Saga Star* which they renamed *Dieppe.* After a refit in Le Havre the ship entered service from Dieppe on 4th March 2002. At 17,672 gross tons she is the largest ever to sail on the most direct route between London and Paris although her length precludes her turning inside the River Ouse at Newhaven. It is thought that this may well cause operational problems during periods of bad weather when the ship, not particularly known for its amazing astern power, will be required to navigate stern first into the Channel before heading for her home port.

Wightlink's Isle of Wight services introduced the new Portsmouth - Fishbourne ferry *St. Clare* on 20th July 2001. The £11.5 million ferry was built in Poland and has capacity for 771 passengers and 142 cars. The largest ferry ever to serve the island is quite non-standard in her design and the operation of a slick five ship schedule has so far been highly problematical.

WESTERN CHANNEL

Following the success of P&O Portsmouth's fast ferry service between Portsmouth and Cherbourg, 2001 saw Brittany Ferries starting their own fast ferry service between Poole and Cherbourg with Condor. The new operation commenced on 22nd May using the *Condor Vitesse* with one round sailing a day between Dorset and Normandy. The service was to prove an overwhelming success and is due to be repeated during 2002.

Work commenced on the building of the new *Mont St. Michel* for Brittany Ferries at the yard of Van der Giessen-de Noord. She was due to enter service on the Caen-Portsmouth route on 5th July 2002 but at the time of going to press she was not due for

P&O SL Burgundy *(Miles Cowsill)*

delivery until the end of July. On her eventual entry into service, she is due to operate in tandem with the *Normandie* while the *Duc de Normandie* will be transferred to the Roscoff-Plymouth route in place of the ageing *Quiberon*, which will be disposed of.

During the latter part of 2001, plans were afoot by Brittany Ferries to build a further new vessel for the company to replace the *Val de Loire* on the Spanish and Irish Sea routes. The vessel is due to enter service during 2004, which will allow Brittany Ferries to re-shuffle their fleet again, possibly introducing two vessels on their very successful St. Malo-Portsmouth route.

P&O Portsmouth operated during 2001 with the same tonnage to that of the previous year. The *Pride of Cherbourg* and *Pride of Hampshire*, with the *Portsmouth Express*, maintained the Cherbourg route. The ageing 'Super Viking's' built in 1975 are due to be replaced on the Cherbourg route in September 2002 by the chartered *Isle of Innisfree*, which will be re-named *Pride of Cherbourg*. It looks likely that the company will possibly employ two fast craft on the Cherbourg route during 2003 following the cascading of the older 'Super Viking's' vessels. On their Le Havre route, P&O Portsmouth renegotiated the charter fees for both ships from their owners TT Line, in the light of the company wishing to reduce their heavy losses during the last couple of years. The *Pride of Bilbao* was re-chartered for a further five year period during early 2002 from Irish Ferries, which now secures the company's operations to Bilbao until 2007.

On the Channel Islands, the *Commodore Clipper* and her freight operating partner, the *Commodore Goodwill*, offered good service to the Channel Islands, as did Condor's

Duc de Normandie *(Chris Randall)*

fast ferry operations using the *Condor Express* and *Condor Vitesse*. *Condor 9* was employed to maintain the St. Malo-Jersey-Guernsey links and will be replaced during 2002 by the larger InCat craft *Condor 10*.

IRISH SEA

Swansea Cork Ferries began their 2001 sailings on 12th March using the former *Saint Patrick II*, one of the most travelled ships on the Irish Sea and recently of the Mediterranean. The vessel was sub-chartered on a bareboat basis from Hellenic Mediterranean and sailed under the name of *City of Cork*. The 28 year old ship, with a berth capacity for 800 passengers, was an ideal replacement for the *Superferry* with her limited 450 bed capacity. However, she was to be faced with a number of teething problems, especially with safety, on numerous occasions, and hit the national headlines. Eventually, the vessel settled down into a regular pattern of sailings between Cork and Swansea and was well received by passengers. The charter of the *City of Cork* has not repeated for 2002 in the light of the Cork-based company purchasing the *Superferry* from Strintzis Line. How long the route between Swansea and Cork will be maintained by the *Superferry* is unknown but it seems likely that the service will remain a marginal operation for the future, compared to the other rivals on the Irish Sea.

At Pembroke Dock, the port goes from strength to strength following the replacement of the *Isle of Innisfree* during May 2001 by the larger *Isle of Inishmore* after the introduction of the *Ulysses* on the Central Corridor. The *Isle of Inishmore* entered service between Rosslare and Pembroke Dock on 22nd May and immediately was to make an impression on the route with increased carryings of freight. Sadly there was to be a decline in passengers on the route, in common with other ferry operators on the Irish Sea, in the wake of the Foot and Mouth disease in the UK.

No immediate work was found for the *Isle of Innisfree* and she was sent to Dublin and later to Le Havre for lay-up. Following numerous parties expressing interest in the vessel, including the Italian company Panadriatic, P&O Stena Line, Norfolkline and P&O Portsmouth, no work was found for the vessel until the announcement of her charter to P&O Portsmouth in February 2002.

At Fishguard, in the light of aggressive marketing and the introduction of the *Isle of Inishmore*, freight carryings, passengers and cars were to decline on this established route. Stena Line announced during the autumn of 2001 that they planned to replace the *Koningin Beatrix* on the route by the *Stena Europe* from the Baltic. The Swedish company claimed that the 'Europe' would be an improvement to the route following her £4 million refit to allow her to carry more freight and the improvement of her passenger facilities for travellers on this three and a half hour service to Ireland. The *Stena Lynx III* continued to operate in tandem during 2001 with the *Koningin Beatrix* and this service will be repeated during 2002 with the *Stena Europe*.

At Holyhead, the big news of 2001 was the introduction of the *Ulysses* by Irish Ferries. This impressive looking vessel, built in Finland, arrived from Scandinavia on 4th March. The new EUR 100 million cruise-ferry currently ranks as the world's largest car capacity vessel at sea. Housed in her gigantic four level car deck are almost three miles of vehicle parking space with room for 1,342 cars or 250 trailers per sailing, enough to double Irish

Ferries' freight/car carrying capacity on their premier Dublin-Holyhead route.

The vessel stands 12 decks high with a keel to mast height of 167.5 ft, just 30 ft shorter than Dublin's Liberty Hall. Many of the features onboard the *Ulysses* are named after the characters and events of James Joyce's epic work. Prior to entering service, the *Ulysses* was officially named in Dublin on 21st March by the swimmer Mairead Berry - Ireland's 25 year old Paralympic Games Gold Medal winner. Also present at the naming ceremony was the Irish Prime Minister, Bertie Aherne TD. The *Ulysses* is driven by four giant engines which can deliver 41,808 hp.

On the delivery of the *Ulysses* and her entry into service, the *Isle of Inishmore* was transferred to the Southern Corridor. Meanwhile, the *Jonathan Swift* continued to operate a fast ferry service for the successful Irish company in tandem with the *Ulysses*.

Stena Line's fortunes at Holyhead continue to be overshadowed by Irish Ferries' successes. The *Stena Challenger* was replaced by the Italian chartered vessel *Stena Forwarder* on the Holyhead-Dublin route. The Italian registered and chartered vessel, whilst offering increased freight capacity, is underpowered for the route and often has to have tugs in attendance at both Dublin and Holyhead during inclement weather. Meanwhile, the fast ferry service operated by the *Stena Explorer* continued to operate to Dun Laoghaire, despite continued high operational costs and increased fuel costs during 2001. Like the Belfast-Stranraer route, Stena are saddled with having to continue to operate the HSS vessels on the Irish Sea as they are reliant upon fixed infrastructure which is not common to other ferry ports in the UK or Europe.

Norse Merchant Ferries continued to have success on their operations during 2001 with their services to Belfast and Dublin from Liverpool. Mid-2002 will see the company transfer across the Mersey to the purpose-built river berth at Birkenhead, which will allow the company to operate a more efficient service to both ports in Ireland.

P&O Irish Sea finally switched the *European Ambassador* and the *European Envoy* from Liverpool to Mostyn on 19th November to provide the main accompanied freight and car passenger route to Dublin from their new all-tide facility at the Welsh port. Hot on the heels of this change, which appeared to leave the Liverpool-Dublin service as the poor relation, P&O announced first that the *Norbay* and *Norbank* would be transferred from the North Sea to the Liverpool-Dublin route and then they re-chartered the *Celtic Star* to reinstate the Liverpool-Larne service as the *Northern Star*.

The all-tidal Mostyn Dock has been filled in, 15 acres of landfill has been undertaken to produce a new general cargo terminal with a minimum 9 metre depth of water for vessels using the port. The work, together with extensive dredging to ensure the 24 hr access to the Welsh port and new buoyage, has cost £17 million. There is a completely new marshalling area for 340 unaccompanied and 50 accompanied vehicles. Commercial vehicle check-in is provided at a new two-storey office building at the entrance to the P&O port, passengers and cars using the port have their own facilities. The new operation from Mostyn got underway, with a number of operational difficulties during the inclement winter, however despite these problems the company is well pleased with its new service from Wales to Ireland.

The introduction of the *Norbank* and *Norbay*, which were originally built at Van der Giessen-de Noord in 1993 and 1994 respectively, started their new role in early January between Liverpool and Dublin. Both vessels are able to carry 114 passengers and have a good turning speed of 22 knots to maintain the route between Liverpool and Dublin. How long both former P&O North Sea Ferries' vessels are maintained on the link is unknown, possibly in the future they may be transferred to the Mostyn link to provide up to three sailings a day between each port.

Meanwhile, as far as continental services to France are concerned, P&O announced a number of changes during 2001/2002. The *European Seafarer* was replaced on the Rosslare-Cherbourg service by the *European Diplomat* (ex *Pride of Suffolk*). The vessel was transferred to a Spanish crew and after an extensive refit is now earmarked to maintain this route in the long-term. The *European Seafarer* was transferred back to the Fleetwood-Larne service on the introduction of the 'Diplomat' at Rosslare. The vessel has also transferred her crewing back to British crews instead of Spanish as when she was on the Rosslare operation.

In another surprise move by P&O during early 2002, the *European Ambassador* is now to be employed on a regular Saturday sailing from Dublin to Cherbourg, returning Sunday with arrival Monday back at Dublin on an all-year-round basis. The introduction of the 'Ambassador' now allows P&O Irish Sea to offer up to four sailings a week between Ireland and Cherbourg.

The effects of the foot and mouth disease and the cancellation of the TT festival in the Isle of Man was to see a drop in traffic levels and profits for the Isle of Man Steam Packet Company during 2001. The 81 metre InCat craft *Rapide* was employed on the Liverpool-Dublin/Douglas service during 2001, with the *Ben-my-Chree* and *SeaCat Isle of Man* supporting the other operations to the Isle of Man. The Heysham-Belfast service was maintained by the veteran *Hoverspeed Great Britain*. For 2002, Sea Containers have transferred the *SuperSeaCat Three* back to the Irish Sea to allow her to maintain the Liverpool-Dublin/Douglas operation. The *Ben-my-Chree* and the *SeaCat Isle of Man* are once again the mainstay of operations to and from the Isle of Man. For 2002, the *Rapide* replaces the *Hoverspeed Great Britain* on the Heysham-Belfast service.

At Cairnryan, P&O Irish Sea continued to aggressively market themselves against their rivals Stena Line. 2002 sees the introduction of a sister to the successful *European Causeway*, the *European Highlander*. On the introduction of the 'Highlander' in July 2002, both she and her near sister the 'Causeway' will be the mainstay of the Larne-Cairnryan service with the fast ferry *Superstar Express*. It seems likely that the *European Endeavour* and *European Pathfinder* will be maintained by P&O on the route in the short-term.

With heavy losses on their Irish Sea operations, Stena Line made further rationalisations on their Stranraer-Belfast service. The *Stena Galloway* was sold by the company to Moroccan interests during early 2002. The route in the future will be maintained by the HSS *Stena Voyager* with the *Stena Caledonia* offering a conventional ferry service. Autumn 2001 saw plans being unveiled by Stena Line to move their operations from Stranraer to north of P&O Irish Sea's terminal at Cairnryan. If the plan, with an EU grant, proceeds it will see two ferry ports established very close to each other at Cairnryan. Long-term, it will see possibly the demise of the railway line to Stranraer and also requirements for improved road links to north of Loch Ryan.

Condor Vitesse *(FotoFlite)*

Barfleur *(John Bryant)*

Continental services from Ireland to France continued to be maintained by Irish Ferries using their *Normandy* serving Cherbourg and Roscoff. Meanwhile, Brittany Ferries' operations between Cork and Roscoff saw further increases in traffic during 2001.

SCOTLAND

Caledonian MacBrayne introduced two new ferries during 2001. The first of these vessels was the *Hebrides* for the Uig-Tarbert/Lochmaddy links in March. The new ferry with a service speed of 16.5 knots is able to cut the crossing times to North Uist and Harris, and offers a greater capacity for both passengers and cars to that of the previous vessel. The second new ferry to join the ranks of the CalMac fleet was the *Lochnevis* for the passenger operations to Eigg, Muck and Rhum.

A new freight ro-ro service between Ullapool and Stornoway commenced on 8th March against the established operations Caledonian MacBrayne. The service was operated by Taygran Shipping Limited and using the ro-ro freighter *White Sea*, registered in Bergen and manned by a Polish crew. In June she was replaced by the *Taygran Trader* (ex *European Trader*). The new service was not to last long and in spite of good initial trade, but the company hit financial diffuculties during the summer and the operation closed.

The latter part of the year saw Caledonian MacBrayne making further annoucements of new tonnage for their fleet; two new ferries will be built at the cost of £12.6 million. Both new ships are due to enter service by summer of 2003.

Work started at the yard of Aker Finnyards on the construction of the three new ferries for Northlink, who take-over the Orkney and Shetland services from P&O Scottish Ferries in October 2002. The first steel for the new Northlink vessels was cut by Chief Executive John Horton at Aker Finnyards Rauma yard on Monday 20th August. The first of the larger Aberdeen - Kirkwall - Lerwick vessels is due to be completed by July 2002, the other about a month later and the 110 metre Pentland Firth vessel by the end of September 2002.

Northlink have made a complete break from tradition in the names for their new vessels which were chosen as a result of a competition run through the local newspapers and radio stations in both Orkney and Shetland with prizes of trips to Finland for the launch and a trip on the inaurgural voyage to the islands for the winners. The two 125 metre vessels will be called *Hrossey* (old Norse name for mainland of Orkney - Horse Island) and *Hjaltland* (old Norse name for Shetland) respectively. The 110 metre Pentland-Firth vessel will be called *Hamnavoe* (old name for Stromness - her home port).

Miles Cowsill & John Hendy

Seacat Danmark

SeaCat Danmark *(FotoFlite)*

scandinavia & northern review

review 2001

The year 2001 was another year of takeovers. Following their acquisition of Swedish Scandlines in 2000, Stena Line agreed a takeover of HH Ferries, who operate between Helsingør and Helsingborg using two Superflex vessels. Since HH Ferries and Scandlines are in competition, the agreement of the competition authorities was needed before the takeover was agreed but the argument is similar to that of the P&O/Stena Line merger on Dover - Calais - the fixed link is the main competitor and with that in existence, competition between ferry operators is no longer necessary. Final agreement was given in March 2002. Scandlines AG attempted to take over freight operator Nordö Link between Travemünde and Malmö but after considering the conditions imposed by the authorities, the plan was abandoned. The charter of the Ask to that company went ahead however in early 2002. A more successful take-over was that of the Lithuanian state shipping operator Lisco which was partly acquired by DFDS during the year. The purchase included three ro-pax and three ro-ro vessels plus six multi-purpose container ships. Their route network included Klaìpeda - Karlshamn (Sweden) (which recently replaced the Stockholm service), Klaìpeda - Kiel (joint with Scandlines Euroseabridge under the Kiel-Klaìpeda-Express name) and Klaìpeda - Sassnitz (Germany) (also joint service with Scandlines Euroseabridge). The new operation now trades as Lisco Baltic Service. The rest of the Lisco fleet - bulkers and other cargo ships - was transferred to a new state-owned company.

The other most notable event of 2001 was the arrival of Superfast Ferries in the Baltic - an event which has implications for almost all Baltic Ferry operations. With the opening of their service to Södertälje in Sweden in 2002 - the first service from Germany to the east coast of Sweden for many years - the effects are likely to be even greater.

The following geographical review again takes the form of a voyage along the coast of The Netherlands and Germany, round the southern tip of Norway, down the Kattegat, through the Great Belt and into the Baltic (with a side journey to the Oresund) then up to the Gulf of Finland and Gulf of Bothnia.

The Cuxhaven - Brunsbüttel service operated by Elbe-Ferry ceased operations in the spring following heavy losses, attempts to secure subsidies from the local authorities involved proving unsuccessful. German Frisian Islands operator AG Ems introduced a new Oceanfast Ferries (Australia) 45m passenger-only catamaran Polarstern for their services between Emden and Borkum.

'Traditional' Hurtigruten ships *Harald Jarl* and *Lofoten* spent their last full year on the route, with both being replaced by newbuildings in 2002. However, it is not the end for the latter ship, now declared a Norwegian national monument. She continues to operate short cruises and is to substitute on the Hurtigruten for the Nordnorge during winter

2002/3 when she goes to Chile to operate cruises along the coast and to Antarctica in conjunction with a local company. Although the *Harald Jarl* is the older of the two traditional ships, she is in less authentic original condition.

Color Line pulled out of the port of Moss, on the Eastern side of Oslofjord and scrapped both their Moss - Hirtshals and Moss - Larvik - Frederikshavn services. The former was operated by the former Fred. Olsen lines train ferry *Skagen* and she continued to operate between Hirtshals and Kristiansand until the fast ferry *Silvia Ana L* came into service on 5th April. She then moved to the Larvik - Frederikshavn route as freight back-up to the *Peter Wessel.* The Moss - Larvik - Frederikshavn route was a recent extension to the long established Larvik - Frederikshavn service and has now reverted to its traditional form. The Sandefjord - Strömstad service was, from the start of the year, no longer marketed as Color Scandi Line, completing the full integration of Color Line, Larvik Line and Scandi Line as a single brand. The *Color Viking,* chartered from P&O Stena Line, was purchased during the year. The chartered ferry *Silvia Ana L* in 2001 was sold by South American owners to MDFC Aircraft of the Irish Republic (a subsidiary of the Boeing Aircraft Corporation) and chartered to Color Line for four years. No longer returning to South America in the European winter, she is now in Color Line colours.

Stena Line's Gothenburg - Frederikshavn service operated much as before except that the fast ferry sailings by the HSS *Stena Carisma* between Göteborg and Frederikshavn were reduced to two per day during the winter period. However, unlike previous years, the *Stena Jutlandica* continued to operate in passenger mode throughout the winter giving, with the *Stena Danica,* six conventional ferry sailings per day (except during refit periods). On the more southerly Grenaa - Varberg route it was reported earlier in the year that Stena Line were looking for a new ship which would give greater freight capacity. In the event it was decided to rebuild the *Stena Nautica* to enable freight to be carried on the upper vehicle deck; the rebuilt ship entered service during spring 2002.

Stena Line appeared to face new competition in the spring when Transocean Line of Denmark, operating between Århus (Denmark) and Halmstad (Sweden), with two 12 passenger trailer ferries, chartered the 120 passenger *Greifswald* for the route. The aim was to attract more driver accompanied freight and there was talk of taking cars and their passengers. However, traffic levels were poor and the service ceased after about a month.

Mols-Linien's fast ferry *Max Mols* was chartered to Scandlines for their Sassnitz - Rønne (Bornholm) service in July to replace the conventional ship *Rügen,* which was initially moved to the Sassnitz - Trelleborg route to replace the *Sassnitz* (which was damaged by an engine room fire on 1st July) and was then briefly out of service herself following a small electrical fire. The *Sassnitz* returned on 14th July, enabling the fast ferry charter to be ended. The chartered *Mads Mols* substituted on the Århus - Odden service.

DFDS replaced the *Queen of Scandinavia* on their Copenhagen - Helsingborg - Oslo service with the *Pearl of Scandinavia,* formerly the *Athena* of Viking Line but having been used as a cruise ship in the Far East for the last eight years. This enabled the *Queen of Scandinavia* to be moved to the Newcastle - IJmuiden route.

Scandlines' fast passenger services between Denmark and Sweden were drastically

Color Festival *(Miles Cowsill)*

Robin Hood (Mike Louagie)

curtailed in the light of competition from direct rail service operating across the Oresundsbron fixed link. The København - Landskrona and the recently introduced Copenhagen - Helsingborg services (which only attracted a third of the projected travel levels) were axed leaving a basic hourly service between Copenhagen and Malmö, operated by the Swedish registered *Sælen* and *Sjöbjörnen* and all control transferred to Malmö. Several vessels were disposed of. All services ceased in April 2002

Things were brighter on the Gedser - Rostock route where, following the ending of the Easy Line service in December 2000, Scandlines brought the former Great Belt train ferry *Prins Joachim* onto the route, converted to carry road vehicles in a similar way to her sister, *Kronprins Frederik*. She did not, as expected, replace the older *Dronning Margrethe II* but operated as an additional ship, allowing a departure on the route every two hours.

Services between Germany and Sweden continued to show growth, despite the option of the land bridge through Denmark and the Oresundsbron. Swedish Scandlines' Trelleborg - Travemünde freight service, operated by the *Götaland* (and not part of the Scandlines pool) was boosted in the summer by the arrival of a second vessel, Levantina Transport's *Alyssa*, renamed the *Svealand*. TT-Line introduced two brand new ships for their Travemünde - Trelleborg route - the new *Nils Holgersson* and *Peter Pan*, with less passenger capacity but more space for commercial vehicles than their predecessors. The previous generation ships, originally converted from ro-pax vessels, were converted to a condition close to their original specification (but not quite the same), renamed Tom *Sawyer* and *Huckleberry Finn* respectively and placed on the secondary but fast growing Rostock - Trelleborg route.

Scandinavia - Poland traffic also continued to grow - although the bulk of the changes to take account of this growth will take place in 2002. Stena Line's Karlskrona - Gdynia service will receive a boost on the passenger side when the Stena Europe is replaced by the *Stena Baltica*, formerly the *Koningin Beatrix*, and the freight side through the introduction of a second ship, the ro-pax *Stena Traveller*, formerly the *TT-Traveller*. Additionally, DFDS's new Copenhagen - Gdansk service with the *Dana Anglia* will also provide additional capacity. There was also talk of a second vessel for Unity Line, operating between Swinoujscie and Ystad, although nothing has yet happened. Polferries, with their increasingly ageing fleet and insufficient profits for newbuildings, seem to have been unable to benefit from this growth and will face increasing problems unless they are able to secure more up-to-date tonnage. The fast ferry *Boomerang* did not prove a commercial success and was sold to Tallink in the spring.

Services to the Lithuania and Latvia continued slow development but freight continued to dominate. New operator Latlines started a new Lübeck - Riga service using the Cypriot registered ro-pax *Sea Symphony* on a twice weekly schedule. At the beginning of the year Scandlines ended the charter of the *Greifswald*, when sister vessel the *Petersburg* was transferred from the Sassnitz - Klaìpeda to the Kiel - Klaìpeda route, leaving only the 12 passenger Lisco vessel *Klaìpeda* to operate this service. However, in the autumn, the *Greifswald* returned (operating this time for Lisco) and the Kiel - Klaìpeda service was upped to four sailings per week. Scandlines' Rostock - Liepaja (Latvia) vessel, the *Ask*, was lengthened by 20m during the year and her passenger capacity increased. In early 2002 she was replaced by sister vessel the *Urd* which had

been similarly converted.

Between her time with Transocean Line and her return to Scandlines, the Greifswald spent a brief period on charter to TransRussia Express, a freight operator between Kiel, Sassnitz and St Petersburg, partly owned by Finnlines. With their other vessel the 84 passenger *Translubeca*, it appeared that a greater passenger emphasis could be in the offing. However, the departure of the *Greifswald* and her replacement by a 12 passenger vessel suggests that this in not imminent.

Finnlines daily ro-pax service from Lübeck to Helsinki moved to Travemünde during October, saving about two hours sailing time; however the twice weekly sailings between the same ports by the 440 passenger *Finnclipper* continued unchanged - although the original concept of utilising her sister, the *Finneagle* on the same route never materialised and she remained on the six hour FinnLink Kapellskär (Sweden) - Naantali (Finland) service. There are plans to double the 90 passenger capacity of the ships used on the daily service and in the longer term the *Finnclipper's* role may well change - she has in fact received similar modifications to her sister allowing bow access to the upper vehicle deck, a facility not used on her current route.

Most spectacular development on Germany - Finland services was however the arrival of the Greek owned Superfast Ferries, operating at speeds approaching that of Silja Line's gas turbined *Finnjet* but, with two ships, more frequently. The Rostock - Hanko route adopted is the shortest crossing between the two countries but the 22 hour crossing time allows six departures per week. The *Superfast VII* entered service on 17th May, followed by the *Superfast VIII* on 16th July. The complimentary service from Rostock to Södertälje in Sweden, operated by the *Superfast IX* and *Superfast X* did not start until January 2002 but closed in April.

VV-Line continued to operate their service from the small Swedish port of Västervik to Ventspils in Latvia and Tallinn in Estonia. They purchased the former Finnlines ship the *Finnmaid* from her Finnish owners and renamed her the *Mermaid II*.

The first of the new ro-pax ferries under construction for Rederi AB Gotland for their subsidiary Destination Gotland was launched (but not named) at the Goangzhou Shipyard in China on 3rd July. Originally due to enter service in 2001, work was affected by floods and other bad weather conditions and they will not now enter service until later this year.

Finland - Estonia traffic continued to boom with Tallink replacing their passenger fast ferry *Tallink Express I* with a second car carrier - the *Tallink Autoexpress 2*, formerly Polferries' *Boomerang*. This enabled Tallink to match the frequency of Nordic Jet Line who operate two smaller vessels. There were strong rumours at the beginning of the year that Silja Line SeaCat would have to surrender the newest of the four SuperSeaCats, the *SuperSeaCat Four* to enable three such vessels to operate from Dover. The expected replacement was the *Hoverspeed Great Britain*, one of the oldest of the 74m InCats. One can imagine that local management were not best pleased at the prospect of having to compete with a vessel older and slower than the competition and in the event it was the Irish Sea operation which had to make the sacrifice. On the conventional ferry side there was little change, although Tallink's new *Romantika*, the first new cruise ferry of the type built in the late eighties and early nineties to be delivered to the Baltic for several years is eagerly awaited.

Transeuropa *(Mike Louagie)*

Stena Saga (Miles Cowsill)

At the beginning of the year, Tallink took over EstLine's Stockholm - Tallinn business. Tallink immediately reduced the frequency - increased to daily in 1998 - back to alternate days and transferred the *Baltic Kristina* to their shorter freight orientated Kapellskär - Paldiski route, enabling frequency to be doubled. However, when the new ship is delivered, it is planned to move the *Fantaasia* to the route between the two capitals enabling a daily service again. It is also likely that the *Vana Tallinn* will move to the shorter route in October, replacing the smaller *Baltic Kristina*.

Silja Line subsidiary SeaWind Line continued to operate a single daily passenger crossing each day as plans to rebuild the *Star Wind*, the former German train ferry the *Rostock*, to full passenger specification were shelved. In the autumn it was announced that majority shareholder, Sea Containers, had purchased the Scandlines train ferry *Öresund*, previously used on the DanLink service between Copenhagen and Helsingborg until the fixed link opened in 2000, and were to have her converted a passenger ferry for the Stockholm - Turku route. She is to be named the *Sky Wind* and is expected to enter service later this year.

Silja Line cut back the night sailing from Turku, operated by the *Silja Europa*, to the port of Kapellskär, at the mouth of the Stockholm archipelago during the off peak period. Most 'mini-cruise' traffic is night out/day back so the majority of round trip customers on this ship are from Finland. Cutting back the sailings enabled more attractive departure and arrival times to be offered and reduced fuel costs. During the summer the service reverted to serving Stockholm. This pattern will be repeated in 2002.

When Silja Line gave up the Vaasa - Umeå service at the end of 2000 the service was put out for franchise again and there were two main bidders. Botnia Link, who were already operating a freight service, offered an all year round ro-pax service backed up by a summer fast ferry service in cooperation with Helsinki based Nordic Jet Line. A new operator, RG Line, offered a year round passenger and freight service using the former Silja Line ferry *Fennia*. In the event it was RG Line - named after Vaasa based pizza chain owner Rabbe Grönblom - which won the contest and their service started in the spring. The *Fennia* was purchased from Silja Line and renamed the *Casino Express*, the emphasis being placed on the gambling opportunities available on the service - even if there were no duty-free sales. However, Botnia Link did not give up - despite financial problems which at one stage led to the deferral of harbour dues - and introduced a larger ferry with more passenger facilities. This was the 63 passenger *Transparaden* - formerly the *Rosebay* used by Stena Line on their Harwich - Hoek van Holland freight service. They also opened a service between Vaasa and the more southerly port of Härnösand using the same ship.

Nick Widdows

BRITISH ISLES
Scrabster
Stornoway
Ullapool
Aberdeen
Castlebay
Mallaig
Oban
Rosyth
Gourock
Largs
Troon
Cairnryan
Stranraer
Newcastle
Middlesbrough
Arranmore
Larne
Belfast
Douglas
Heysham
Fleetwood
Hull
Portaferry
Killingholme
Immingham
Warrenpoint
Holyhead
Liverpool
Mostyn
Dublin
Dun Laoghaire
Tarbert
Felixstowe
Rosslare
Fishguard
Harwich
Castletownbere
Passage East
Cork
Pembroke Dock
Purfleet
Sheerness
Dartford
Ramsgate
Dover
Southampton
Portsmouth
Newhaven
Weymouth
Poole
Fowey
Dartmouth
Penzance

Bergen
Stavanger
Egersund
Kristiansand
North Sea
Hanstholm
Kalundb
Esbjerg
U. K.
Cuxhaven
Norddeich
Harlingen
Emden
IJmuiden
Harwich
Scheveningen
Hoek van Holland
NETH.
Plymouth
Portsmouth
Ramsgate
Dover
Vlissingen
Rotterdam
Ostend
Zeebrugge
Newhaven
Calais
Dunkerque
English Channel
Cherbourg
BELGIUM
Dieppe
Roscoff
Le Havre
Caen
LUX.
St Malo
FRANCE

FINLAND
Rauma
Naantali
Turku
Kotka
ÅLAND
Helsinki
Mariehamn
Långnäs
Hanko
Oslo
SWEDEN
Tallinn
Kapellskär
Paldiski
Moss
Stockholm
Södertälje
ESTONIA
Strömstad
Nynäshamn
Västervik
othenburg
Visby
Ventspils
Oskarshamn
Riga
havn
Varberg
GOTLAND
LATVIA
ÖLAND
Liepaja
toft
Helsingborg
Karlskrona
singør
Klaìpeda
Karlshamn
Malmö
LITHUANIA
penhagen
Ystad
Trelleborg
Rønne
BORNHOLM
Tars
Gedser
Sassnitz
Gdynia
Gdansk
den
Rostock
avemünde
BYEL
eck
Swinoujscie
POLAND
UKR
CZECH
SLOVAKIA

NORMANDIE

Normandie *(Chris Randall)*

section I northern review

gb & ireland

BRITTANY FERRIES

THE COMPANY *Brittany Ferries* is the trading name of *BAI SA*, a French private sector company and the operating arm of the *Brittany Ferries Group*. The UK operations are run by *BAI (UK) Ltd*, a UK private sector company, wholly owned by the *Brittany Ferries Group*.

MANAGEMENT Group Managing Director Michel Maraval, **Managing Director UK & Ireland** David Longden.

ADDRESS Millbay Docks, Plymouth, Devon PL1 3EW.

TELEPHONE Administration +44 (0)1752 227941, **Reservations *All Services*** 08705 360360 (UK only), ***Portsmouth*** +44 (0)8709 011300, ***Plymouth*** +44 (0)8709 010500.

FAX Administration & Reservations +44 (0)1752 600698, **Telex** 86878.

INTERNET Website www.brittanyferries.com *(English, French)*

ROUTES OPERATED Conventional Ferries *All year* Roscoff - Plymouth (6 hrs (day), 6 hrs - 7 hrs 30 mins (night); *(7, until July:6, from July: 3)*; up to 3 per day (summer), 1 per week (winter)), St Malo - Portsmouth (8 hrs 45 mins (day), 10 hrs 30 mins - 11 hrs 30 mins (night); *(2 (summer),2,4 (winter))*; 1 per day), Caen (Ouistreham) - Portsmouth (6 hrs (day), 6 hrs 15 mins - 8 hrs (night); *(5, until July: 3, from July: 4)*; 3 per day), Plymouth - Santander (Spain) (24 hrs; *(7)*; 2 per week (March - November)), Cherbourg - Poole (4 hrs 15 mins; *(1)*; up to 2 per day), ***Summer only*** Roscoff - Cork (14 hrs; *(7)*; 1 per week), ***Jan/Feb only*** St Malo - Plymouth (8 hrs; *(5,6)*; 1 per week. **Fast Ferry** Poole - Cherbourg (2 hrs 15 mins; *(CONDOR VITESSE of Condor Ferries)*; 1 per day). Note The Cherbourg- Poole fast ferry service is operated by *Condor Ferries* jointly with *Brittany Ferries*.

1	BARFLEUR	20133t	92	19k	157.6m	1173P	550C	112T	BA	FR
2	BRETAGNE	24534t	89	21k	152.8m	2030P	580C	84T	BA	FR
3	DUC DE NORMANDIE	13505t	78	21k	131.6m	1500P	350C	38T	BA	FR
4	MONT ST MICHEL	34800t	02	21.2k	173.4m	2120P	600C	166T	BA	FR
5	NORMANDIE	27541t	92	20k	161.4m	2263P	630C	126T	BA	FR
6	QUIBERON	11813t	75	20k	129.0m	1302P	300C	40T	BA2	FR
7	VAL DE LOIRE	31395t	87	21k	161.0m	1800P	550C	104T	BA	FR

BARFLEUR Built at Helsinki for the *Truckline* Cherbourg - Poole service to replace two passenger vessels and to inaugurate a year round passenger service. In 1999 the *Truckline* brand was dropped for passenger services and she was repainted into full *Brittany Ferries* livery.

BRETAGNE Built at St Nazaire for the Santander - Plymouth and Roscoff - Cork services (with two sailings per week between Roscoff and Plymouth). In 1993 she was transferred to the St Malo - Portsmouth service but she operates on the Santander service during the winter.

DUC DE NORMANDIE Built at Heuseden, Netherlands as the PRINSES BEATRIX for *Stoomvaart Maatschappij Zeeland (Zeeland Steamship Company)* of The Netherlands for their Hoek van Holland - Harwich service. In September 1985 sold to *Brittany Ferries* and chartered back to *SMZ*, continuing to operate for them until the introduction of the KONINGIN BEATRIX (see STENA BALTICA) in May 1986. In June 1986 delivered to *Brittany Ferries* and inaugurated the Caen - Portsmouth service. From July 2002 she will move to the Plymouth - Roscoff route.

MONT ST MICHEL Under construction at Krimpen an der IJssel, Rotterdam for *Brittany Ferries* to replace the DUC DE NORMANDIE on the Caen - Portsmouth route. The DUC DE NORMANDIE will

be transferred to the Roscoff - Plymouth route, replacing the QUIBERON. Due to enter service July 2002.

NORMANDIE Built at Turku, Finland for the Caen - Portsmouth route.

QUIBERON Built at Rendsburg, Germany. Ordered by *Lion Ferry AB* of Sweden. The contract was sold to *Svenska Lastbils AB (Svelast)* of Sweden (a subsidiary of *Statens Järnvägar (SJ), Swedish State Railways*) before delivery and she was delivered to them as the NILS DACKE. She was initially chartered to *Svenska Rederi AB Öresund* (another *SJ* subsidiary) for their service between Malmö (Sweden) and Travemünde (Germany). Sister vessel the GUSTAV VASA (now NORRÖNA of *Smyril Line*) was owned by *Lion Ferry AB* of Sweden and was also chartered to *SRÖ*. In 1976, *Svelast* took over the marketing of the service and it was operated under the name *Malmö-Travemünde Linjen*, with *Lion Ferry AB* operating it as agents. Later in 1976, *Svelast* and *Linjebuss International* (a subsidiary of *Stockholms Rederi AB Svea*) formed a jointly owned subsidiary called *Saga-Linjen* and *Lion Ferry AB* continued as administrative operator. In 1981 a joint marketing agreement was reached with the rival German owned *TT-Linie*, (running between Travemünde and Trelleborg (Sweden)) and the two services were marketed as *TT-Saga-Line*. In April 1982 the NILS DACKE was chartered to *Brittany Ferries* with an option to purchase. She was renamed the QUIBERON and placed on the Santander - Plymouth and Roscoff - Cork services; she also operated between Roscoff and Plymouth. In 1984 she was purchased by *Brittany Ferries* and re-registered in France. Following the delivery of the BRETAGNE in July 1989, she was transferred to the Roscoff - Plymouth service. In 2002 she will operate Plymouth - Roscoff until the July arrival of the MONT SAINT MICHEL; she will then be replaced by the DUC DE NORMANDIE.

VAL DE LOIRE Built at Bremerhaven, Germany as the NILS HOLGERSSON for *TT-Line* of Sweden and Germany for their service between Travemünde and Trelleborg. In 1992 purchased by *Brittany Ferries* for entry into service in spring 1993. After a major rebuild, she was renamed the VAL DE LOIRE and introduced onto the Plymouth - Santander and Roscoff - Plymouth/Cork service.

On Order

8	PONT-AVEN	-	04	26k	180.0m	2250P	700C	85L	BA	FR

PONT-AVEN To be built at Papenburg, Germany to replace the DUC DE NORMANDIE. Will operate on the current roster of the VAL DE LOIRE, with that ship taking over the roster of another vessel.

COMMODORE FERRIES

THE COMPANY *Commodore Ferries (CI) Ltd* is a private sector company owned by *Commodore Shipping*, Guernsey.

MANAGEMENT Managing Director Jeff Vidamour, **Commercial Manager** Len Le Page.

ADDRESS PO Box 10, New Jetty Offices, White Rock, St Peter Port, Guernsey GY1 3AF.

TELEPHONE Administration +44 (0)1481 728620, **Reservations (Passenger)** See *Condor Ferries*.

FAX Administration & Reservations +44 (0)1481 728521.

INTERNET Email jvidamour@comferries.com

ROUTE OPERATED ***All year*** Portsmouth - St Peter Port (Guernsey) (6 hrs 30 mins) - St Helier (Jersey) (10 hrs 30 mins) - Portsmouth (8 hrs 30 mins) (return Guernsey via Jersey, 12 hrs 30 mins); *(1)*; 6 per week, ***Summer only*** Portsmouth - Cherbourg (France) (5 hrs; *(1)*; 1 per week).

1	COMMODORE CLIPPER	14000t	99	18.25k	129.1m	500P	100C	92T	A	BA

COMMODORE CLIPPER Ro-pax vessel built at Krimpen an der IJssel, Rotterdam to operate between Portsmouth and the Channel Islands. She replaced the ISLAND COMMODORE, a freight only vessel. Her passenger services are operated as part of the *Condor Ferries* network and she carries the logos of both companies. Her passenger capacity is normally restricted to 300 but is increased to 500 when the *Condor Ferries'* fast ferries are unable to operate.

Mont St Michel *(Mike Louagie)*

Solidor 5 *(Miles Cowsill)*

CONDOR FERRIES

THE COMPANY *Condor Ferries Ltd* is a Channel Islands private sector company owned by *Commodore Shipping*, Guernsey.

MANAGEMENT Managing Director Robert Provan, **General Manager, Sales & Marketing** Nicholas Dobbs.

ADDRESS Condor House, New Harbour Road South, Hamworthy, Poole, Dorset BH15 4AJ.

TELEPHONE Administration +44 (0)1202 207207, **Reservations** +44 (0)1305 761551.

FAX Administration +44 (0)1202 685184, **Reservations** +44 (0)1305 760776.

INTERNET Email sales@condorferries.co.uk **Website** www.condorferries.co.uk *(English)*

ROUTES OPERATED Fast Car Ferries ***Winter Only*** Weymouth - St Peter Port (Guernsey) (2 hrs 15 mins) - St Helier (Jersey via Guernsey) (3 hrs 35 mins); *(3)*; up to 5 per week), ***Spring and Autumn*** Weymouth - St Peter Port (Guernsey) (2 hrs) - St Helier (Jersey via Guernsey) (3 hrs 15 mins); *(3)*; 1 per day, Poole - St Peter Port (Guernsey) (2 hrs 30 mins) - St Helier (Jersey via Guernsey) (3 hrs 50 mins); *(4)*; up to 4 per week, ***Summer*** Weymouth - St Peter Port (Guernsey) (2 hrs) - St Helier (Jersey via Guernsey) (3 hrs 15 mins); *(3)*; 1 per day, Poole - St Peter Port (Guernsey) (2 hrs 30 mins) - St Helier (via Guernsey 3 hrs 50 mins, direct 3 hrs) - St Malo (4 hrs 35 min) ; *(4)*; up to 2 per day to Jersey and Guernsey, 1 per day to St Malo (***Note*** Poole - St Malo service operates via either Guernsey or Jersey), St Malo - St Peter Port (Guernsey) (2hrs 55 mins via Jersey, 1hr 45 mins direct; *(2)*; 2 per day), St Malo - St Helier (Jersey) (1 hr 10 mins; *(2)*; 1 per day - no cars conveyed on this service), Poole - Cherbourg (2 hrs 15 mins; *(3)*; 1 per day (service operated jointly with *Brittany Ferries)*). **Ro-pax Ferry** All year The car and passenger facilities on the ro-pax service between Portsmouth and The Channel Islands and Portsmouth and Cherbourg operated by *Commodore Ferries* (see above) are marketed by *Condor Ferries*.

1»p	●CONDOR 9	752t	90	30k	48.4m	450P	0C	0L	-	UK
2»	CONDOR 10	3241t	93	37k	74.3m	580P	80C	-	BA	SI
3»	CONDOR EXPRESS	5005t	96	39k	86.6m	774P	185C	-	A2	BA
4»	CONDOR VITESSE	5005t	97	39k	86.6m	774P	185C	-	A2	BA

CONDOR 9 FBM Marinteknik catamaran built at Fareham, UK for *Condor Ferries* and initially mainly used between the Channel Islands and Weymouth. In spring 1994, she was chartered to *Viking Line* and operated between Helsinki and Tallinn as the 'VIKING EXPRESS' (although not officially renamed). During winter 1994/95 she went on charter to the Caribbean. On return in mid 1995 she was laid up for a period before starting a new service between the Channel Islands and Torquay. She operated on this route during summer 1996. In 1997 she operated between Jersey and Poole and Jersey and St Malo. From 1998 she operated between St Malo, Jersey and Guernsey. In 2001 operated between St Malo and Jersey only. In 2002 replaced by the CONDOR 10 and laid up.

CONDOR 10 InCat 74m catamaran. Built at Hobart, Australia for the *Holyman Group* for use by *Condor Ferries*. In summer 1995 she was chartered to *Viking Line* to operate between Helsinki and Tallinn under the name 'VIKING EXPRESS II' (although not officially renamed). In summer 1996 she was chartered to *Stena Line* to operate between Fishguard and Rosslare. During northern hemisphere winters she served for *TranzRail* of New Zealand for the service between Wellington (North Island) and Picton (South Island). In May 1997 she was transferred to *Holyman Sally Ferries* and inaugurated a new Ramsgate - Dunkerque (Est) service, replacing the Ramsgate - Dunkerque (Ouest) service of *Sally Ferries*. After further service in New Zealand during winter 1997/98, in summer 1998 she was due to operate between Weymouth, Guernsey and St Malo, but, in the event, the CONDOR VITESSE was chartered for that route and she was laid up in Australia. Refurbished during 2001, she returned to the UK in spring 2002 replacing the passenger-only CONDOR 9 between St Malo and Guernsey and Jersey.

CONDOR EXPRESS InCat 86m catamaran built at Hobart, Tasmania, Australia. She was delivered December 1996 and entered service in 1997.

CONDOR VITESSE InCat 86m catamaran built at Hobart. Built speculatively and launched as the

INCAT 044. Moved to Europe in summer 1997 and spent time in the both the UK and Denmark but was not used. In 1998, she was chartered to *Condor Ferries* and renamed the CONDOR VITESSE. During winter 1999/2000 she was chartered to *TranzRail* of New Zealand. Returned to UK in spring 2000.

DFDS SEAWAYS

THE COMPANY *DFDS Seaways Group A/S* is the passenger division of the *DFDS Group*, a Danish private sector company. *DFDS Seaways Ltd* is a UK subsidiary.

MANAGEMENT Managing Director *(DFDS Seaways Ltd)* John Crummie.

ADDRESS Scandinavia House, Parkeston, Harwich, Essex CO12 4QG.

TELEPHONE Administration +44 (0)1255 243456, **Reservations *National*** 08705 333000 (from UK only), ***Harwich*** +44 (0)1255 240240, ***Newcastle*** +44 (0)191-293 6283.

FAX Administration & Reservations *Harwich* +44 (0)1255 244370, ***Newcastle*** +44 (0)191-293 6245.

INTERNET Email john.crummie@dfds.co.uk **Website** www.dfdsseaways.co.uk *(English)*

www.dfdsseaways.com *(Danish, Dutch, German, Norwegian, Swedish)*

ROUTES OPERATED *All year* Harwich - Esbjerg (Denmark) (19 hrs; *(Until September 2002: 2, from September 2002: ANOTHER SHIP)*; 3 per week or alternate days), Kristiansand (Norway) - Gothenburg (Sweden) (7 hrs (day), 13 hrs 30 min (night); *(4)* 1 per week (spring, summer and autumn), 3 per week (winter)), Harwich - Cuxhaven (Germany) (16 hrs; *(1)*; 3 per week (winter), every 2/4 days (summer), Newcastle (North Shields) - IJmuiden (near Amsterdam, Netherlands) (15 hrs; *(3,5)*; daily), ***Spring, Summer and Autumn only*** Newcastle - Kristiansand - Gothenburg (25 hrs; *(4)*; 2 per week).

1	ADMIRAL OF SCANDINAVIA	19292t	76	21.5k	156.4m	1135P	294C	50T	BA	BA
2	DANA ANGLIA	19589t	78	21k	152.9m	1120P	416C	60T	BA	DK
3	PRINCE OF SCANDINAVIA	22528t	75	26k	182.3m	1692P	379C	35T	AS	DK
4	PRINCESS OF SCANDINAVIA	22528t	76	26k	182.3m	1572P	365C	34T	AS	DK
5	QUEEN OF SCANDINAVIA	33770t	81	21k	166.1m	1624P	360C	70T	BA	DK

ADMIRAL OF SCANDINAVIA Built at Rendsburg, Germany as the KRONPRINS HARALD for *Jahre Line* of Norway and used on their service between Oslo and Kiel (Germany). Acquired by *DFDS* in 1987, renamed the HAMBURG, re-registered in the Bahamas and replaced the PRINS HAMLET (see the NIEBOROW, *Polferries*) on the Harwich - Hamburg service. In March 1997 she was transferred to the Newcastle - IJmuiden and Newcastle - Hamburg services and renamed the ADMIRAL OF SCANDINAVIA. During winter 1997/98 she was temporarily transferred back to the Harwich - Hamburg service; this also happened during winter 1999/2000. For most of 2000 she operated between Newcastle and IJmuiden, the Hamburg service having ceased. In 2001 she returned to the Harwich - Hamburg route. In 2002 the German terminal moved to Cuxhaven.

DANA ANGLIA Built at Aalborg, Denmark for the Harwich - Esbjerg service and has seldom operated elsewhere. On 1st October 2002 to inaugurate a new Copenhagen - Trelleborg - Gdansk (Poland) service and to be replaced by another ship.

PRINCE OF SCANDINAVIA Built at Lübeck, Germany as the TOR BRITANNIA for *Tor Line* of Sweden for their Amsterdam - Gothenburg and Felixstowe - Gothenburg services. She was acquired by *DFDS* in 1981 and subsequently re-registered in Denmark. From winter 1983/4 she also operated on the Harwich - Esbjerg service with the DANA ANGLIA. She has also operated Newcastle - Esbjerg and Amsterdam - Gothenburg. During winter 1989/90 she was used as an accommodation ship for refugees in Malmö. In 1991 renamed the PRINCE OF SCANDINAVIA following a major refurbishment. In summer 1994 and 1995 she operated on the IJmuiden (Netherlands) - Gothenburg (Sweden) and IJmuiden - Kristiansand (Norway) service and did not serve the UK. In 1996 she was chartered to *CoTuNav* of Tunisia for service between Tunisia and Italy. In March 1997 she was transferred to the Harwich - Hamburg route. During winter 1997/98 she covered for other ferries which were being refitted, including the Copenhagen - Oslo vessels, and had major modifications made at Gdansk. In summer 1998 she operated every third trip from Hamburg to Newcastle instead of Harwich; this was repeated in 1999 but in summer 2000 she operated solely between Harwich and Hamburg. In 2001 she was transferred to the Newcastle - IJmuiden route.

PRINCESS OF SCANDINAVIA Built at Lübeck, Germany as the TOR SCANDINAVIA for *Tor Line* of Sweden for their Amsterdam - Gothenburg and Felixstowe - Gothenburg services. In 1979 she was used on a world trade cruise and was temporarily renamed the HOLLAND EXPO. Similar exercises were undertaken in 1980, 1982 and 1984, but on these occasions her temporary name was the WORLD WIDE EXPO. She was acquired by *DFDS* in 1981 and subsequently re-registered in Denmark. She has also operated on the Harwich - Esbjerg service. Between 1989 and 1993 she also operated Newcastle - Esbjerg and Amsterdam - Gothenburg services. In 1991, following a major refurbishment, she was renamed the PRINCESS OF SCANDINAVIA. Since 1994, she generally operated on the Harwich - Gothenburg and Newcastle - Gothenburg routes. During winter 1998/1999 she had major modifications made at Gdansk and during winter 1999/2000 she had a major engine rebuild. She now operates between Newcastle and Gothenburg via Kristiansand.

QUEEN OF SCANDINAVIA Built at Turku, Finland as the FINLANDIA for *EFFOA* of Sweden for *Silja Line* services between Helsinki and Stockholm. In 1990 she was sold to *DFDS*, renamed the QUEEN OF SCANDINAVIA and introduced onto the Copenhagen - Helsingborg - Oslo service. In 2001 transferred to the Newcastle - IJmuiden route.

EMERAUDE LINES

THE COMPANY *Emeraude Lines* is a French private sector company.

MANAGEMENT Managing Director (Channel Islands) Gordon Forrest, **Brittany and Normandy Office Manager** Jean-Luc Griffon.

ADDRESS Terminal Ferry du Naye, PO Box 16, 35401, St Malo Cedex, France.

TELEPHONE Administration & Reservations *St Malo* +33 (0)2 23 180 180, ***Jersey*** +44 (0)1534 766566.

FAX Administration & Reservations *St Malo* +33 (0) 2 23 181 500, ***Jersey*** +44 (0)1534 768741.

INTERNET Email sales@emeraude.co.uk **Website** www.emeraude.co.uk *(English)*

ROUTES OPERATED Fast Car Ferries St Malo (France) - St Helier (Jersey) (1 hr 10 mins; *(2,3)*; up to 4 per day), St Malo - St Peter Port (Guernsey) (1 hr 50 mins; *(2,3)*; up to 3 per day), St Helier - St Peter Port (1 hr; *(2,3)*; 1 per day). **Fast Passenger Ferry** St Helier - Sark (45 mins; *(1)*; 1 per day), Granville (France) - St Helier (1 hr; *(1)*; 1 per day), Carteret (France) - St Helier (50 mins; *(1)*; see note). Note on most days through the summer there is either a Carteret - Jersey or Granville - Jersey service; the timetable varies according to the tidal conditions at the French ports.

1»p	NORMANDIE EXPRESS	449t	88	38k	41.6m	306P	0C	0L	-	FR
2»	SOLIDOR 4	1064t	87	30k	49.5m	302P	36C	-	A	FR
3»	SOLIDOR 5	2300t	01	38k	60.0m	450P	60C	-	A	FR

NORMANDIE EXPRESS Marinteknik 41 CPV, built at Öregrund, Norway as the ÖREGRUND for the *Hong Kong Macao Hydrofoil Company* and operated between Hong Kong and Macao. In 1995 she was chartered to *Universal Aboit* of the Philippines, renamed the SUPERCAT 1 and used on inter island services. In 1999 she was chartered to *Emeraude Lines* and renamed the NORMANDIE EXPRESS. Used on the Carteret/Granville - St Helier - Sark service. She was purchased by *Emeraude Lines* at the end of 2001.

SOLIDOR 4 Westamarin W5000CF catamaran, built at Mandal, Norway. Built for *Gods Trans* of Norway as the ANNE LISE, a high speed frozen fish carrier and used in the North Sea. In 1993 the fish hold was converted to a vehicle deck and an additional passenger accommodation was provided. She was sold to *Brudey Frères* of Guadeloupe renamed the MADIKERA. In 1995 she was sold to *Elba Ferries* and renamed the ELBA EXPRESS; she operated a summer service between Piombino (Italy) and Portoferráio (Elba). In 1999 sold to *Emeraude Lines* and renamed the SOLIDOR 4. After

Commodore Clipper *(Mike Louagie)*

Midnight Merchant *(Mike Louagie)*

refurbishment, entered service in spring 1999.

SOLIDOR 5 Fjellstrand JumboCat 60m catamaran, built at Omastrand, Norway for *Emeraude Lines* to replace the SOLIDOR 3. Entered service in January 2001.

FJORD LINE

THE COMPANY *Fjord Line* is a Norwegian company, 100% owned by *Bergen-Nordhordland Rutelag AS (BNR).* It took over the Newcastle - Norway service from *Color Line* in December 1998.

MANAGEMENT Managing Director (UK) Dag Romslo, **Sales Director (UK)** Mike Wood.

ADDRESS Royal Quays, North Shields NE29 6EG.

TELEPHONE Administration +44 (0)191-296 1313, **Reservations** +44 (0)191-296 1313.

FAX Administration & Reservations +44 (0)191-296 1540, **Telex** 537275.

INTERNET Email fjordline.uk@fjordline.com **Website** www.fjordline.com *(English)*

ROUTES OPERATED Bergen (Norway) - Haugesund (Norway) - Stavanger (Norway) - Newcastle - Bergen (triangular route), Bergen - Haugesund - Stavanger - Newcastle (Bergen - Stavanger (via 6 hrs), Stavanger - Newcastle (direct 18 hrs 30 mins, via Bergen 29 hrs 30 mins), Bergen - Newcastle (21 hrs 15 mins); *(1)*; 3 sailings Norway - Newcastle per week).

Fjord Line also operates between Norway and Denmark; see Section 6.

1	JUPITER	20581t	75	21k	175.3m	1250P	285C	40T	BA	NO

JUPITER Built at Nantes, France as the WELLAMO for *EFFOA* of Finland for *Silja Line* services between Helsinki and Stockholm. In 1981 sold to *DFDS*, renamed the DANA GLORIA and placed onto the Gothenburg - Newcastle and Esbjerg - Newcastle services. In 1983 she was moved to the Copenhagen - Oslo service. In 1984 she was chartered to *Johnson Line* of Sweden for *Silja Line* service between Stockholm and Turku and renamed the SVEA CORONA - the name previously born by a sister vessel, which had been sold. This charter ended in 1985 and she returned to the Copenhagen - Oslo service and resumed the name DANA GLORIA. During winter 1988/89 she was lengthened in Papenburg, Germany and in early 1989 she was renamed the KING OF SCANDINAVIA. She returned to the Copenhagen - Oslo route; in 1990 a Helsingborg call was introduced. In 1994 she was sold to *Color Line* (as part of a deal which involved *DFDS* buying the VENUS from *Color Line*) and renamed the COLOR VIKING. In 1998 she was sold to *Fjord Line* and renamed the JUPITER.

IRISH FERRIES

THE COMPANY *Irish Ferries* is an Irish Republic private sector company, part of the *Irish Continental Group*. It was originally mainly owned by the state owned *Irish Shipping* and partly by *Lion Ferry AB* of Sweden. *Lion Ferry* participation ceased in 1977 and the company was sold into the private sector in 1987. Formerly state owned *B&I Line* was taken over in 1991 and from 1995 all operations were marketed as *Irish Ferries*.

MANAGEMENT Group Managing Director Eamon Rothwell, **Group Marketing Director** Tony Kelly.

ADDRESS 2 Merrion Row, Dublin 2, Republic of Ireland.

TELEPHONE Administration +353 (0)1 855 2222, **Reservations *Dublin*** +353 (0)1 638 3333, ***Cork*** +353 (0)21 455 1995, ***Rosslare Harbour*** +353 (0)53 33158, ***Holyhead*** 0990 329129 (from UK only), ***Pembroke Dock*** 0990 329543 (from UK only), ***National*** 08705 171717 (from UK only), ***24 hour information*** +353 (0)1 661 0715.

FAX Administration & Reservations *Dublin* +353 (0)1 661 0743, ***Cork*** +353 (0)21 450 4651, ***Rosslare*** +353 (0)53 33544.

INTERNET Email info@irishferries.com **Website** www.irishferries.com *(English)*

ROUTES OPERATED Conventional Ferries Dublin - Holyhead (3 hrs 15 mins; *(4)*; 2 per day),

Rosslare - Pembroke Dock (3 hrs 45 mins; *(1)*; 2 per day), Rosslare - Cherbourg (France) (17 hrs 30 mins; *(3)*; 1 or 2 per week), Rosslare - Roscoff (France) (16 hrs; *(3)*; 1 or 2 per week) Note the Rosslare - Cherbourg/Roscoff service operates on a seasonal basis. **Fast Ferry** Dublin - Holyhead (1 hr 49 min; *(2)*; up to 4 per day). Marketed as 'DUBLIN*Swift*'.

1	ISLE OF INISHMORE	34031t	97	21.5k	182.5m	2200P	802C	152T	BA2	IR
2»	JONATHAN SWIFT	5989t	99	39.5k	86.6m	800P	200C	-	BA	IR
3	NORMANDY	24872t	82	19k	149.0m	1526P	420C	62L	BA2	IR
4	ULYSSES	50938t	01	22k	209.0m	1875P	1342C	300T	BA2	IR

ISLE OF INISHMORE Built at Krimpen an der IJssel, Rotterdam for *Irish Ferries* to operate on the Holyhead - Dublin service. In 2001 replaced by the ULYSSES and moved to the Rosslare - Pembroke Dock route.

JONATHAN SWIFT Austal Auto-Express 86 catamaran built at Fremantle, Australia for *Irish Ferries* for the Dublin - Holyhead route.

NORMANDY Built at Gothenburg, Sweden. One of two vessels ordered by *Göteborg-Frederikshavn-Linjen* of Sweden (trading as *Sessan Linjen*) before the take over of their operations by *Stena Line AB* in 1981. Both were designed for the Gothenburg - Frederikshavn route (a journey of about three hours). However, *Stena Line* decided in 1982 to switch the first vessel, the KRONPRINSESSAN VICTORIA (now the STENA EUROPE of *Stena Line AB*), to their Gothenburg - Kiel (Germany) route since their own new tonnage for this route, being built in Poland, had been substantially delayed. She was modified to make her more suitable for this overnight route. Work on the second vessel - provisionally called the DROTTNING SILVIA - was suspended for a time but she was eventually delivered, as designed, in late 1982 and introduced onto the Gothenburg - Frederikshavn route on a temporary basis pending delivery of new *Stena Line* ordered vessels. She was named the PRINSESSAN BIRGITTA, the existing ex *Sessan Linjen* vessel of the same name being renamed the STENA SCANDINAVICA . In early 1983 she was substantially modified in a similar way to her sister. In June 1983 she was renamed the ST NICHOLAS, re-registered in Great Britain and entered service on five year charter to *Sealink UK* on the Harwich - Hoek van Holland route. In 1988 she was purchased and re-registered in The Bahamas. In 1989 she was sold to *Rederi AB Gotland* of Sweden and then chartered back. In 1991 she was renamed the STENA NORMANDY and inaugurated a new service between Southampton and Cherbourg. She was withdrawn in December 1996, returned to *Rederi AB Gotland* and renamed the NORMANDY. In 1997 she was chartered to *Tallink* and operated between Helsinki and Tallinn; this charter ended at the end of the year. In 1998 she was chartered to *Irish Ferries*. She briefly operated between Rosslare and Pembroke Dock before switching to the their French services. In 1999 she was purchased by *Irish Ferries*. She also operates between Rosslare and Pembroke Dock when the regular vessel is away on overhaul.

ULYSSES Built at Rauma, Finland for *Irish Ferries* for the Dublin - Holyhead service.

NORFOLKLINE

THE COMPANY *Norfolkline* (before 1 January 1999 *Norfolk Line*) is a Dutch private sector company owned by *A P Møller Finance* of Denmark.

MANAGEMENT Managing Director D G Sloan, **Deputy Managing Director** J Al-Erhayen, **Marketing Manager** R A Meijer, **Managing Director UK** E J Green, **Manager Dover - Dunkerque** Wayne Bullen.

ADDRESS *Netherlands* Kranenburgweg 180, 2583 ER Scheveningen, Netherlands. ***UK*** Norfolk House, The Dock, Felixstowe, Suffolk IP11 8UY, ***Dover*** Export Freight Plaza, Eastern Docks, Dover, Kent CT16 1JA.

TELEPHONE Administration *Netherlands* +31 (0)70 352 74 00, ***UK*** +44 (0)1394 673676, **Reservations** +44 (0)1304 225151.

FAX Administration & Reservations *Netherlands* +31 (0)70 352 74 35, ***Felixstowe*** +44 (0)1394 603673, ***Dover*** +44 (0)1304 208517.

INTERNET Email info@norfolkline.com dover@norfolkline.com dunkerque@norfolkline.com **Website** www.norfolkline.com *(English)*

ROUTE OPERATED Dover - Dunkerque (France) (2 hrs; *(1,2)*; up to 7 per day).

1	MIDNIGHT MERCHANT	22152t	00	22.5k	180.0m	300P	-	144T	BA2	UK
2	NORTHERN MERCHANT	22152t	00	22.5k	180.0m	250P	-	144T	BA2	UK

MIDNIGHT MERCHANT Built at Seville, Spain for *Cenargo* (owners of *NorseMerchant Ferries*). On delivery, chartered to *Norfolkline* to operate as second vessel on the Dover - Dunkerque (Ouest) service. In 2002 modified to allow two deck loading.

NORTHERN MERCHANT Built at Seville, Spain for *Cenargo* (owners of *NorseMerchant Ferries*). On delivery, chartered to *Norfolkline* to inaugurate a Dover - Dunkerque (Ouest) service in March 2000. In 2002 modified to allow two deck loading.

NORSEMERCHANT FERRIES

THE COMPANY *NorseMerchant Ferries* is a British private sector company, owned by *Cenargo*. In 1999 the operations of *Belfast Freight Ferries* were integrated into *Merchant Ferries plc* and *Norse Irish Ferries Ltd* was acquired. In January 2001 *Merchant Ferries plc* and *Norse Irish Ferries Ltd* started trading as *NorseMerchant Ferries*.

MANAGEMENT Managing Director Philip Shepherd, **Commercial Director** Richard Harrison, **Freight Sales Director** Declan Cleary.

ADDRESS Victoria Terminal 2, West Bank Road, Belfast BT3 9JN.

TELEPHONE ***Administration*** +44 (0)28 9077 9090, ***Reservations UK*** 08706 004321, ***Irish Republic*** +353 (0)1 819 2999.

FAX Administration +44 (0)28 9078 1599.

INTERNET Email enquiries@norsemerchant.com **Website** www.norsemerchant.com *(English)*

ROUTES OPERATED ***From April 2002*** Port of Liverpool (Twelve Quays River Terminal, Birkenhead) - Belfast (8 hrs; *(3,4)*; 1 per day (Sun, Mon), 2 per day (Tue-Sat)), ***Until July 2002*** Port of Liverpool (Canada Dock No 3, Liverpool) - Dublin (7 hrs; *(1,2)*; 1 per day (Sun, Mon), 2 per day (Tue-Sat)), ***From July 2002*** Port of Liverpool (Twelve Quays River Terminal, Birkenhead) - Dublin (6 hrs; *(1,2)*; 1 per day (Sun, Mon), 2 per day (Tue-Sat)).

NorseMerchant Ferries also operate a freight-only services between Heysham and Dublin and Heysham and Belfast; see Section 3.

1	BRAVE MERCHANT	22046t	98	22.5k	180.0m	250P	-	144T	BA	IM
2	DAWN MERCHANT	22152t	98	22.5k	180.0m	250P	-	144T	BA	IM
3	LAGAN VIKING	21856t	97	24k	186.0m	340P	100C	170T	A	UK
4	MERSEY VIKING	21856t	97	24k	186.0m	340P	100C	170T	A	UK

BRAVE MERCHANT Built at Seville, Spain for parent company *Cenargo* and chartered to *Merchant Ferries*. In February 1999 she inaugurated a new service between Liverpool and Dublin.

DAWN MERCHANT Built at Seville, Spain for parent company *Cenargo* and chartered to *Merchant Ferries*. On delivery in autumn 1998, chartered to *UND RoRo Isletmeri* of Turkey to operate between Istanbul and Trieste. Returned to *Merchant Ferries* in late 1998 and in February 1999, inaugurated a new service between Liverpool and Dublin.

LAGAN VIKING, MERSEY VIKING Built at Donada, Italy for *Levantina Transporti* of Italy and chartered to *Norse Irish Ferries*. In 1999 charter was taken over by *Merchant Ferries*. Purchased by *NorseMerchant Ferries* in 2001.

Normandy *(Rob de Visser)*

Norbay *(Gordon Hislip)*

P&O IRISH SEA

THE COMPANY *P&O Irish Sea* is the trading name of *P&O European Ferries (Irish Sea) Ltd*, a British private sector company and a subsidiary of the *Peninsular and Oriental Steam Navigation Company*. It was formed in 1998 by the merger of the shipping activities *Pandoro Ltd* and the Cairnryan - Larne services of *P&O European Ferries (Felixstowe) Ltd*.

MANAGEMENT Chairman Graeme Dunlop, **Managing Director** J H Kearsley, **Passenger Services – Sales and Marketing Manager** James Essler.

ADDRESS Compass House, Dock Street, Fleetwood, Lancashire FY7 6HP.

TELEPHONE Administration +44 (0)1253 615700, **Reservations *UK*** 08702 424777, ***Irish Republic*** 1 800 409 049.

FAX Administration & Reservations +44 (0)1253 615740.

INTERNET Email **Website** www.poirishsea.com *(English)*

ROUTES OPERATED Conventional Ferries *From July 2002* Cairnryan - Larne (1 hr 45 min; *(2,4)*; 6 per day), Mostyn - Dublin (5 - 6 hrs, *(1,3)*; Mostyn to Dublin - 1 per day (Sun, Tue-Sat), Dublin to Mostyn, 2 per day (Tue-Sat) (5-6 hrs) (note the EUROPEAN ENVOY does not convey ordinary passengers on night crossings except on Sunday nights when she operates Mostyn - Dublin), ***Summer only*** Dublin - Cherbourg (18 hrs; *(1)*; 1 per week). **Fast Ferry (March - November)** Cairnryan - Larne (1 hr; *(5)*; 6 per day). Note: some private cars and their passengers are conveyed on some (mainly daytime) sailings on the Fleetwood - Larne, and all sailings on the Rosslare - Cherbourg, Troon - Larne and Liverpool - Dublin routes. However, as these are primarily freight services, the vessels are shown in Section 3. Passengers have also been carried on the freight services between Cairnryan and Larne - at times on a scheduled basis and at other times on an unscheduled basis. Passengers are not conveyed on the Liverpool - Larne freight service.

1	EUROPEAN AMBASSADOR	24500t	01	25k	169.8m	405P	375C	122T	BA2	BA
2	EUROPEAN CAUSEWAY	20800t	00	23k	159.5m	410P	375C	107T	BA2	BA
3	EUROPEAN ENVOY	18653t	79	18.2k	150.0m	107P	-	142T	A	BD
4	EUROPEAN HIGHLANDER	20800t	02	23k	159.5m	410P	375C	107T	BA2	BA
5»	SUPERSTAR EXPRESS	5517t	97	36k	82.3m	900P	175C	-	A	BB

EUROPEAN AMBASSADOR Built at Shimonoeki, Japan for *P&O Irish Sea* for the Liverpool - Dublin service. Service transferred to Mostyn in November 2001.

EUROPEAN CAUSEWAY Built at Shimonoeki, Japan for *P&O Irish Sea* for the Cairnryan - Larne service.

EUROPEAN ENVOY Built at Tamano, Japan as the IBEX for *P&O* for *Pandoro* Irish sea services. In 1980 chartered to *North Sea Ferries*, renamed the NORSEA and used on the Ipswich - Rotterdam service. In 1986 she was renamed the NORSKY. In 1995 she returned to *Pandoro* and was re-registered in Bermuda. Later in 1995 she resumed her original name of IBEX. An additional deck was added in 1996. In late 1997 she was renamed the EUROPEAN ENVOY. Operates on the Mostyn - Dublin service.

EUROPEAN HIGHLANDER Built at Shimonoeki, Japan for *P&O Irish Sea* for the Cairnryan - Larne service.

SUPERSTAR EXPRESS Austal Ships 82 catamaran, built at Fremantle, Australia for *Star Cruises* of Malaysia for their service between Butterworth and Langkawi. Built as the SUPERSTAR EXPRESS, she was renamed the SUPERSTAR EXPRESS LANGKAWI later in 1997. She was due, in 1998, to circumnavigate the world and to seek to take the Hales Trophy from HOVERSPEED GREAT BRITAIN. However, these plans did not materialise and instead she was chartered to *P&O European Ferries (Portsmouth)* and placed on the Portsmouth - Cherbourg route. She resumed the name SUPERSTAR EXPRESS. In April 2000 she was transferred to *P&O Irish Sea*. She is chartered during the summer period.

P&O NORTH SEA FERRIES

THE COMPANY *P&O North Sea Ferries Ltd* is a private sector company, a subsidiary of the *Peninsular and Oriental Steam Navigation Company* of Great Britain. Joint ownership with *The Royal Nedlloyd Group* of The Netherlands ceased in 1996 and the name was changed from *North Sea Ferries* to *P&O North Sea Ferries*. The Felixstowe freight-only operations of *P&O European Ferries* were incorporated into this new company.

MANAGEMENT Managing Director Peter van den Brandhof, **Passenger Managers *UK*** Tony Farrell, ***Benelux*** Michael Amerlaan, ***Germany*** Peter Blomberg.

ADDRESS *UK* King George Dock, Hedon Road, Hull HU9 5QA, ***Netherlands*** Beneluxhaven, Rotterdam (Europoort), Postbus 1123, 3180 Rozenburg ZH, Netherlands, ***Belgium*** Leopold II Dam 13, Havendam, B-8380 Zeebrugge, Belgium.

TELEPHONE Administration *UK* +44 (0)1482 795141, ***Netherlands*** +31 (0)181 255500, ***Belgium*** +32 (0)50 54 34 11, **Reservations *UK*** 08701 296002, ***Netherlands*** +31 (0)181 255555, ***Belgium*** +32 (0)50 54 34 30.

FAX Administration & Reservations *UK* +44 (0)1482 706438, ***Netherlands*** +31 (0)181 255215, ***Belgium*** +32 (0)50 54 71 12.

INTERNET Website www.mycruiseferries.com *(English)*

ROUTES OPERATED Hull - Rotterdam (Europoort) (Netherlands) (10 hrs - 12 hrs; *(3,4)*; 1 per day), Hull - Zeebrugge (Belgium) (12 hrs 30 mins - 14 hrs 30 mins); *(1,2)*; 1 per day).

1	NORSEA	31785t	87	18.5k	179.0m	1000P	850C	166T	A	UK
2	NORSUN	31598t	87	18.5k	179.0m	1000P	850C	166T	A	NL
3	PRIDE OF HULL	59925t	01	22k	215.1m	1360P	250C	400T	AS	UK
4	PRIDE OF ROTTERDAM	59925t	01	22k	215.1m	1360P	250C	400T	AS	NL

NORSEA Built at Glasgow, UK for the Hull - Rotterdam service. In December 2001, she was replaced by the new PRIDE OF HULL and, after a two month refurbishment, in 2002 transferred to the Hull - Zeebrugge service, replacing the NORLAND (26290t, 1974).

NORSUN Built at Tsurumi, Japan for the Hull - Rotterdam service. She was owned by *Nedlloyd* and was sold to *P&O* in 1996 but retains Dutch crew and registry. In May 2001 replaced by the PRIDE OF ROTTERDAM and in July 2001, after a major refurbishment, she was transferred to the Hull - Zeebrugge service, replacing the NORSTAR (26919t, 1974).

PRIDE OF HULL Built at Venice, Italy for *P&O North Sea Ferries* to replace (with the PRIDE OF ROTTERDAM) the NORSEA and NORSUN plus the freight vessels NORBAY and NORBANK on the Hull - Rotterdam service. She can also accommodate 125 x 12 metre double stacked containers.

PRIDE OF ROTTERDAM Built at Venice, Italy. Keel laid as the PRIDE OF HULL but launched as the PRIDE OF ROTTERDAM. Further details as the PRIDE OF HULL.

P&O PORTSMOUTH

THE COMPANY *P&O Portsmouth* is the trading name of *P&O European Ferries (Portsmouth) Ltd*, (until start of 1999 trading as *P&O European Ferries*) a British private sector company, a subsidiary of the *Peninsular and Oriental Steam Navigation Company*.

MANAGEMENT Chairman Graeme Dunlop, **Managing Director** Simon Edsall, **Head of Passenger Marketing & Sales** Paul Barringer, **Head of Freight Sales & Marketing** Phil Garrett.

ADDRESS Peninsular House, Wharf Road, Portsmouth PO2 8TA.

TELEPHONE Administration +44 (0)23 9230 1000, **Reservations** 0870 2424999 (from UK only).

FAX Administration & Reservations +44 (0)23 9230 1134.

INTERNET Email media@poportsmouth.com **Website** www.poportsmouth.com *(English)*

ROUTES OPERATED Conventional Ferries ***Until end of September 2002*** Portsmouth - Cherbourg (5 hrs (day), 7 hrs - 8 hrs 15 mins (night); *(2,3,4 (2 once weekly))*; 2 day crossings, one night crossing per day), ***From end of September 2002*** Portsmouth - Cherbourg (4 hrs 30 mins (day), (longer at night); *(2,7 (2 once weekly))*; 2 per day), ***All year*** Portsmouth - Le Havre (5 hrs 30 mins (day), 7 hrs 30 mins - 8 hrs (night); *(5,6)*; 2 day crossings, one night crossing per day), Portsmouth - Bilbao (Santurzi) (35 hrs (UK - Spain), 30 hrs (Spain - UK); *(2)*; 2 per week). **Fast Ferry** ***Summer only*** Portsmouth - Cherbourg (2 hrs 45 mins; *(1)*; 2 per day).

1»	PORTSMOUTH EXPRESS	5902t	98	41k	91.3m	920P	225C	-	A	
2	PRIDE OF BILBAO	37583t	86	22k	177.0m	2553P	600C	77T	BA	UK
3	PRIDE OF CHERBOURG	14760t	75	18k	143.7m	713P	380C	66T	BA2	UK
4	PRIDE OF HAMPSHIRE	14760t	75	18k	143.7m	713P	380C	66T	BA2	UK
5	PRIDE OF LE HAVRE	33336t	89	21k	161.2m	1600P	575C	91T	BA	UK
6	PRIDE OF PORTSMOUTH	33336t	90	21k	161.2m	1600P	575C	91T	BA	UK

PORTSMOUTH EXPRESS InCat 91m catamaran. Built at Hobart Australia as the CATALONIA for *Buquebus* of Argentina and used by *Buquebus España* on their service between Barcelona (Spain) and Mallorca. In April 2000 chartered to *P&O Portsmouth* and renamed the PORTSMOUTH EXPRESS. During winter 2000/2001 she operated between Buenos Aires (Argentina) and Piriapolis (Uruguay). Returned to *P&O Portsmouth* in spring 2001 and again in spring 2002.

PRIDE OF BILBAO Built at Turku, Finland as the OLYMPIA for *Rederi AB Slite* of Sweden for *Viking Line* service between Stockholm and Helsinki. In 1993 she was chartered to *P&O European Ferries* to inaugurate a new service between Portsmouth and Bilbao. During the summer period she also operates, at weekends, a round trip between Portsmouth and Cherbourg. In 1994 she was purchased by the *Irish Continental Group* and re-registered in the Bahamas. *P&O* have since entered her into the British bareboat register. In 2002 her charter was extended for a further five years.

PRIDE OF CHERBOURG Built at Aalborg, Denmark as the VIKING VALIANT for Southampton (from 1976 Southampton/Portsmouth and 1984 Portsmouth only) - Cherbourg/Le Havre services. Extensively rebuilt at Bremerhaven in 1986, through the placing of the existing superstructure and rear part of hull on a new front part of hull and from that date generally operated Portsmouth - Le Havre only. In 1989 she was renamed the PRIDE OF LE HAVRE. In 1994 transferred to the Portsmouth - Cherbourg service and renamed the PRIDE OF CHERBOURG. To be withdrawn at the end of September 2002 (or possibly earlier); she will probably be renamed before withdrawal to allow the new PRIDE OF CHERBOURG (see below) to enter service.

PRIDE OF HAMPSHIRE Built at Aalborg, Denmark as the VIKING VENTURER. Details otherwise as the PRIDE OF CHERBOURG. She was renamed the PRIDE OF HAMPSHIRE in 1989. In 1995 she was transferred to the Portsmouth - Cherbourg service. To be withdrawn at the end of September 2002 (or possibly earlier).

PRIDE OF LE HAVRE Built at Bremerhaven, Germany as the OLAU HOLLANDIA for *TT-Line* of Germany, to operate for associated company *Olau Line* between Sheerness (Great Britain) and Vlissingen (Netherlands). In May 1994 the service ceased and she was chartered to *P&O European Ferries*, re-registered in the UK and renamed the PRIDE OF LE HAVRE. After a brief period on the Portsmouth - Cherbourg service she became a regular vessel on the Portsmouth - Le Havre service.

PRIDE OF PORTSMOUTH Built at Bremerhaven, Germany as the OLAU BRITANNIA for *TT-Line* of Germany, to operate for associated company *Olau Line*. In 1994 she was chartered to *P&O European Ferries*, re-registered in the UK and renamed the PRIDE OF PORTSMOUTH. After a brief period on the Portsmouth - Cherbourg service she became a regular vessel on the Portsmouth - Le Havre service from June 1994.

Acquired vessel being refurbished

7	PRIDE OF CHERBOURG	22365t	95	22k	181.6m	1650P	600C	130T	BA	UK

PRIDE OF CHERBOURG Built at Krimpen an der IJssel, Rotterdam as the ISLE OF INNISFREE for *Irish Ferries* to operate on the Holyhead - Dublin. In 1997 transferred to the Rosslare - Pembroke Dock service; for a short period, before modifications at Pembroke Dock were completed, she

operated between Rosslare and Fishguard. In spring 2001 she was replaced by the ISLE OF INISHMORE and laid up. In July 2002 she will be chartered to *P&O Portsmouth* for 5 years and renamed the PRIDE OF CHERBOURG. She will first be refurbished and is due replace the PRIDE OF CHERBOURG and PRIDE OF HAMPSHIRE in autumn 2002. She is likely to run along-side one or both of these vessels for a few weeks before a single ship operation starts in October.

P&O STENA LINE

THE COMPANY *P&O Stena Line* is a British private sector company, 60% owned by the *Peninsular and Oriental Steam Navigation Company* and 40% owned by *Stena Line AB* of Sweden. The new company took over the Dover and Newhaven services of *P&O European Ferries* and *Stena Line* in March 1998. Newhaven services ceased at the end of January 1999.

MANAGEMENT Joint Chairmen Lord Sterling *(P&O)* and Dan Sten Olsson *(Stena Line)*, **Managing Director** Russ Peters, **Passenger Marketing & Sales Director** John Govett, **Freight Director** Brian Cork.

ADDRESS Channel House, Channel View Road, Dover, Kent CT17 9TJ.

TELEPHONE Administration +44 (0)1304 863000, **Reservations *Passenger*** 08706 000600 (from UK only), ***Freight*** +44 (0)1304 863344.

FAX Administration & Reservations *Passenger* +44 (0)1304 863223, **Telex** 965104, ***Freight*** +44 (0)1304 863399, **Telex** 96316.

INTERNET *Passenger* Email customer.services@posl.com **Website** www.posl.com *(English)*

***Freight* Email** freightops.dover@posl.com **Website** www.poslfreight.co.uk *(English)*

ROUTE OPERATED *Passenger Sailings* Dover - Calais (1 hr 15 mins - 1 hr 30 mins; *(1,2,3,4,5,6,7)*; up to 35 per day), Dover - Zeebrugge (4 hrs 30 mins; *(1,2,3)*; 5 per day), ***Freight-only Sailings*** Dover *(dep: 08.25, 15.10)* - Calais *(dep: 14.00, 18.30)* (1 hr 15 mins; *(3)*; 2 per day).

1	EUROPEAN HIGHWAY	22986t	92	21k	179.7m	200P	-	120L	BA2	UK
2	EUROPEAN PATHWAY	22986t	92	21k	179.7m	200P	-	120L	BA2	UK
3	EUROPEAN SEAWAY	22986t	91	21k	179.7m	200P	-	120L	BA2	UK
4	P&OSL AQUITAINE	28833t	91	21k	163.6m	2000P	600C	100L	BA2	UK
5	P&OSL BURGUNDY	28138t	93	21k	179.7m	1420P	600C	120L	BA2	UK
6	P&OSL CALAIS	26433t	87	22k	169.6m	2290P	650C	100L	BA2	UK
7	P&OSL CANTERBURY	25122t	80	19k	163.5m	1800P	550C	85L	BA2	UK
8	P&OSL DOVER	26433t	87	22k	163.5m	2290P	650C	100L	BA2	UK
9	P&OSL KENT	20446t	80	21k	163.4m	1825P	460C	64L	BA2	UK
10	P&OSL PROVENCE	28559t	83	19k	154.9m	2036P	550C	85L	BA2	UK

EUROPEAN HIGHWAY, EUROPEAN PATHWAY, EUROPEAN SEAWAY Built at Bremerhaven, Germany for *P&O European Ferries* for the Dover - Zeebrugge freight service. In 1998 they were transferred to *P&O Stena Line*. In summer 1999 the EUROPEAN HIGHWAY operated full time between Dover and Calais. She returned to the Dover - Zeebrugge route in the autumn when the P&OSL AQUITAINE was transferred to the Dover - Calais service. In 2000 a regular twice daily freight only Dover-Calais service was established, using the EUROPEAN SEAWAY. In 2001 passengers (not foot or coach passengers) began to be conveyed on the Dover - Zeebrugge service.

P&OSL AQUITAINE Built at Temse, Belgium as the PRINS FILIP for *Regie voor Maritiem Transport (RMT)* of Belgium the Ostend - Dover service. Although completed in 1991, she did not enter service until May 1992. In 1994 the British port became Ramsgate. Withdrawn in 1997 and laid up for sale. In 1998 she was sold to *Stena RoRo* and renamed the STENA ROYAL. In November 1998 she was chartered to *P&O Stena Line* to operate as a freight only vessel on the Dover - Zeebrugge route. In spring 1999 it was decided to charter the vessel on a long term basis and she was repainted into *P&O Stena Line* colours and renamed the P&OSL AQUITAINE. In autumn 1999 she was modified to

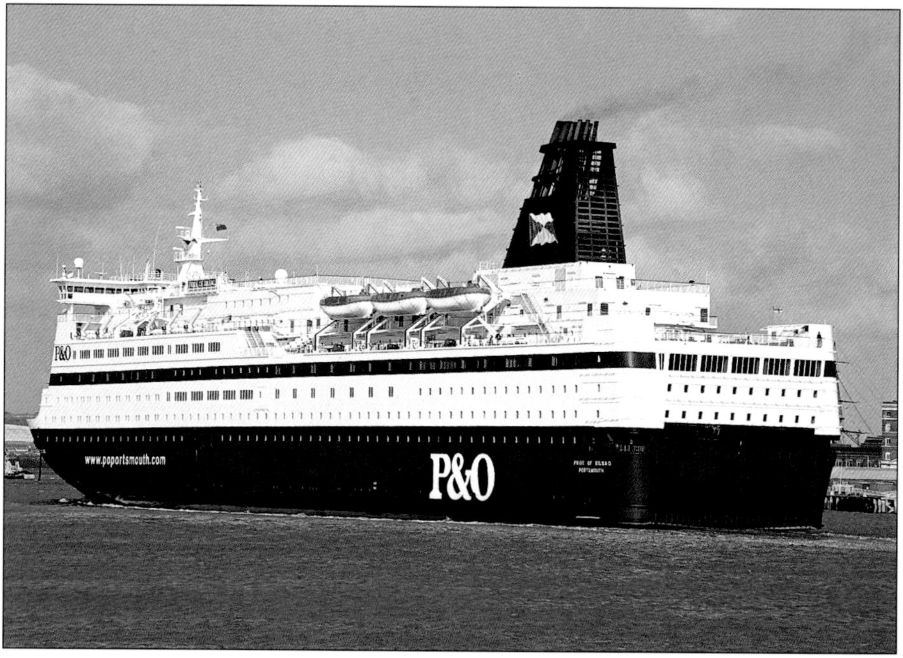

Pride of Bilbao *(John Bryant)*

P&OSL Burgundy *(Miles Cowsill)*

make her suitable to operate between Dover and Calais and was transferred to that route, becoming a passenger vessel again.

P&OSL BURGUNDY Built at Bremerhaven, Germany for *P&O European Ferries* for the Dover - Calais service. When construction started she was due to be a sister vessel to the EUROPEAN HIGHWAY, EUROPEAN PATHWAY and EUROPEAN SEAWAY (see Section 3) called the EUROPEAN CAUSEWAY and operate on the Zeebrugge freight route. However, it was decided that should be completed as a passenger/freight vessel (the design allowed for conversion) and she was launched as the PRIDE OF BURGUNDY. In 1998, transferred to *P&O Stena Line.* In 1998 renamed the P&OSL BURGUNDY.

P&OSL CALAIS Built at Bremerhaven, Germany for *European Ferries* as the PRIDE OF CALAIS for the Dover - Calais service. In 1998, transferred to *P&O Stena Line.* In 1999 renamed the P&OSL CALAIS.

P&OSL CANTERBURY Built at Malmö, Sweden as the SCANDINAVIA for *Rederi AB Nordö* of Sweden. After service in the Mediterranean for *UMEF*, she was, in 1981, sold to *SOMAT* of Bulgaria, renamed the TZAREVETZ and used on *Medlink* services between Bulgaria and the Middle East and later on other routes. In 1986 she was chartered to *Callitzis* of Greece for a service between Italy and Greece. In 1988 she was sold to *Sealink*, re-registered in the Bahamas and renamed the FIESTA. She was then chartered to *OT Africa Line.* During autumn 1989 she was rebuilt at Bremerhaven to convert her for passenger use and in March 1990 she was renamed the FANTASIA and placed her on the Dover - Calais service. Later in 1990 she was renamed the STENA FANTASIA. In 1998, transferred to *P&O Stena Line.* In 1999 she was renamed the P&OSL CANTERBURY.

P&OSL DOVER Built at Bremerhaven, Germany for *European Ferries* as the PRIDE OF DOVER for the Dover - Calais service. In 1998, transferred to *P&O Stena Line.* In 1999 renamed the P&OSL DOVER.

P&OSL KENT Built at Bremerhaven, Germany for *European Ferries (Townsend Thoresen)* as the SPIRIT OF FREE ENTERPRISE for the Dover - Calais service, also operating on the Dover - Zeebrugge service during the winter. She was renamed the PRIDE OF KENT in 1987. Sister vessel of the PRIDE OF BRUGES. During winter 1991/92 she was lengthened in Palermo, Italy to give her similar capacity to the PRIDE OF CALAIS and the PRIDE OF DOVER. Now operates Dover - Calais only. In 1998, transferred to *P&O Stena Line.* Later in 1998 renamed the P&OSL KENT.

P&OSL PROVENCE Built at Dunkerque, France as the STENA JUTLANDICA for *Stena Line* for the Gothenburg - Frederikshavn service. In 1996 she was transferred to the Dover - Calais route and renamed the STENA EMPEREUR. In 1998, transferred to *P&O Stena Line.* Later in 1998 renamed the P&OSL PROVENCE.

SEA CONTAINERS FERRIES

THE COMPANY *Sea Containers Ferries Ltd* is a British private sector company, part of the *Sea Containers Group.*

MANAGEMENT Senior Vice President, Passenger Transport David Benson.

ADDRESS Sea Containers House, 20 Upper Ground, London SE1 9PF.

TELEPHONE Administration +44 (0)20 7805 5000.

FAX Administration +44 (0)20 7805 5900.

INTERNET Email info@seacontainers.com **Website** www.seacontainers.com *(English)*

Ferry services in the UK are operated through three subsidiaries - *Hoverspeed Ltd, Sea Containers Ferries Scotland Ltd* (trading as *SeaCat*) and the *Isle of Man Steam Packet Company* (trading as *Steam Packet*). See also *Silja Line* in Section 6. Because of interchange of fast ferries between companies, they are shown in one section at the end. *IOMSP Co* and *Sea Containers Ferries Scotland* routes are now integrated and are also shown together.

HOVERSPEED

THE COMPANY *Hoverspeed Ltd* is a British private sector company. It was formed in October 1981 by the merger of *Seaspeed*, a wholly owned subsidiary of the *British Railways Board*, operating between Dover and Calais and Dover and Boulogne and *Hoverlloyd*, a subsidiary of *Broström AB* of Sweden, operating between Ramsgate (Pegwell Bay) and Calais. The Ramsgate - Calais service ceased after summer 1982. In early 1984 the company was sold by its joint owners to a management consortium. In 1986 the company was acquired by *Sea Containers*. It was retained by *Sea Containers* in 1990 following the sale of most of *Sealink British Ferries* to *Stena Line*.

MANAGEMENT Managing Director Geoffrey Ede, **PR Manager** Nick Stevens.

ADDRESS The International Hoverport, Marine Parade, DOVER, Kent CT17 9TG.

TELEPHONE Administration +44 (0)1304 865000, **Reservations** 08705 240241 (from UK only).

FAX Administration +44 (0)1304 865087, **Reservations** +44 (0)1304 240088.

INTERNET Email info@hoverspeed.co.uk **Website** www.hoverspeed.co.uk *(English)*

ROUTES OPERATED SeaCats Dover - Calais (45 mins; *(4,7,8)*; up to 16 per day), Dover - Ostend (2 hrs; *(3)*; up to 2 per day), Newhaven - Dieppe (2 hrs; *(11)*; up to 3 per day).

ISLE OF MAN STEAM PACKET COMPANY

THE COMPANY The *Isle of Man Steam Packet Company Limited*, trading as *Steam Packet Company*, is an Isle of Man registered company owned by *Sea Containers Ferries Ltd.*

MANAGEMENT Managing Director Hamish Ross, **Passenger Marketing Manager** Vacant.

ADDRESS Imperial Buildings, Douglas, Isle of Man IM1 2BY.

TELEPHONE Administration +44 (0)1624 645645, **Reservations *From UK*** 08705 523523, ***From elsewhere*** +44 (0)1624 661661.

FAX Administration +44 (0)1624 645609.

INTERNET Email spc@steam-packet.com **Website** www.steam-packet.com *(English)*

ROUTES OPERATED Conventional Ferries Douglas (Isle of Man) - Heysham (3 hrs 30 mins; *(1, 5 (during TT races only))*; up to 2 per day), Douglas - Liverpool (4 hrs; *(5)*; winter), **SeaCats** Listed with *Sea Containers Ferries Scotland* services below.

SEA CONTAINERS FERRIES SCOTLAND

THE COMPANY *Sea Containers Ferries Scotland Ltd* is a subsidiary of *Sea Containers Ferries Ltd.*

MANAGEMENT Managing Director Hamish Ross, **General Manager, Sales and Marketing, Belfast** Diane Poole, **Chief Operating Manager** John Burrows.

ADDRESS SeaCat Terminal, Troon Harbour, Troon, Ayrshire KA10 6DX.

TELEPHONE Administration +44 (0)1292 319103, **Reservations *From UK*** 08705 523523, ***From elsewhere*** +44 (0)28 9031 3543.

FAX Administration +44 (0)1292 319108.

INTERNET Email spc@steam-packet.com **Website** www.steampacket.com *(English)*

ROUTES OPERATED - SEA CONTAINERS' IRISH SEA FAST FERRIES SERVICES - IOMSP & SEA CONTAINERS FERRIES, SCOTLAND Douglas - Liverpool (2 hrs 30 mins; *(9,13)* up to 3 per day), Douglas - Belfast (2 hrs 45 mins; *(9)*; up to 3 per week), Douglas - Dublin (2 hrs 45 mins; *(9)*; up to 3 per week), Troon - Belfast (2 hrs 30 mins; *(10)*; 3 per day), Liverpool - Dublin; (3 hrs 45 mins; *(9,13)*; 1/2 per day), Heysham - Belfast (4 hrs; *(6)*; 1/2 per day).

1	BEN-MY-CHREE	12504t	98	19k	124.9m	500P	-	90T	A	IM

2•	CLAYMORE	1871t	78	14k	77.2m	300P	50C	8T	AS	UK
3»	DIAMANT	3454t	96	37k	81.1m	654P	140C	-	A	LX
4»	HOVERSPEED GREAT BRITAIN	3000t	90	37k	74.3m	577P	80C	-	BA	UK
5	LADY OF MANN	4482t	76	21k	104.5m	800P	130C	0T	S	IM
6»	RAPIDE	4112t	96	37k	81.1m	654P	140C	-	A	LX
7»	SEACAT DANMARK	3003t	91	37k	74.3m	432P	80C	-	BA	UK
8»	SEACAT FRANCE	3012t	90	35k	74.3m	350P	80C	-	BA	UY
9»	SEACAT ISLE OF MAN	3003t	91	37k	74.3m	500P	80C	-	BA	UK
10»	SEACAT SCOTLAND	3003t	91	37k	74.3m	450P	80C	-	BA	UK
11»	SUPERSEACAT ONE	4462t	97	38k	100.0m	782P	175C	-	A	LX
12»•	SUPERSEACAT TWO	4462t	97	38k	100.0m	782P	175C	-	A	LX
13»	SUPERSEACAT THREE	4697t	99	38k	100.0m	800P	175C	-	A	IT
14»•	THE PRINCESS ANNE	-	69	50k	56.4m	360P	55C	-	BA	UK
15»•	THE PRINCESS MARGARET	-	68	50k	56.4m	360P	55C	-	BA	UK

BEN-MY-CHREE Built at Krimpen an der IJssel, Rotterdam for the *IOMSP Co* and operates between Douglas and Heysham and Christmas period Douglas - Dublin sailings.

CLAYMORE Built at Leith, UK for *Caledonian MacBrayne* for the Oban - Castlebay/Lochboisdale service, also serving Coll and Tiree between October and May, replacing the IONA (see the PENTALINA B, *Pentland Ferries*). In 1989 she was transferred to the Kennacraig - Port Ellen/Port Askaig (Islay) route, again replacing the IONA. In summer she also operated a weekly service from Port Askaig (Islay) to Colonsay and Oban. She relieved on the Ardrossan - Brodick service during winter 1990. In autumn 1993 she was replaced by the ISLE OF ARRAN and became a spare vessel. Her summer duties in 1994, 1995 and 1996 included Saturday sailings from Ardrossan to Douglas (Isle of Man), returning on Sundays plus standby duties and charter to the *Isle of Man Steam Packet Company* to provide extra sailings between Heysham and Douglas during the TT Season. During the winter she was general relief vessel, spending several months on Islay sailings. In 1997 she was sold to *Sea Containers* to operate for *Sea Containers Ferries Scotland Ltd* (trading as the *Argyll and Antrim Steam Packet Company*) between Campbeltown (Scotland) and Ballycastle (Northern Ireland) (summer only). During the winter she has been chartered back to *Caledonian MacBrayne* to cover during the refit period. The Campbeltown - Ballycastle service did not resume in 2000 and during the summer she was chartered to *Strandfaraskip Landsins* of the Faroe Islands and used on the Tórshavn - Suderoy service. Currently laid up for sale.

DIAMANT InCat 81m catamaran built at Hobart, Tasmania, Australia. Ordered by *Del Bene SA* of Argentina. In 1996, before completion, purchased by the *Holyman Group* of Australia and named the HOLYMAN EXPRESS. In 1997 she was renamed the HOLYMAN DIAMANT, transferred to *Holyman Sally Ferries* and in March was introduced onto the Ramsgate - Ostend route. In March 1998 transferred to the Dover - Ostend route, operating for the *Hoverspeed - Holyman (UK)* joint venture, and renamed the DIAMANT. In 1999 this became a 100% *Hoverspeed* operation and in 2000 *Sea Containers* purchased her. During winter 1999/2000 she also operated between Dover and Calais at times. During summer 2001 she operated between Newhaven and Dieppe; in summer 2002 she will operate between Dover and Ostend and Dover and Calais.

HOVERSPEED GREAT BRITAIN InCat 74m catamaran built at Hobart, Tasmania. Launched as the CHRISTOPHER COLUMBUS but renamed before entering service. During delivery voyage from Australia, she won the Hales Trophy for the 'Blue Riband' of the Atlantic. She inaugurated a car and passenger service between Portsmouth and Cherbourg, operated by *Hoverspeed*. This service was suspended in early 1991 and later that year she was, after modification, switched to a new service between Dover (Eastern Docks) and Boulogne/Calais, replacing hovercraft. In 1992 operated on Channel routes, including services from Folkestone. During winter 1992/3 she was chartered to *Ferry Lineas* of Argentina, operating between Buenos Aires (Argentina) and Montevideo (Uruguay). In summer 1993 she was used to provide additional sailings on the Belfast – Stranraer route, transferring back to the channel later that year. Following the ending of the Folkestone - Boulogne service in autumn 2000, she was transferred to the Dover - Calais route. In summer 2001 she operated between Heysham and Belfast; in summer 2002 she will operate between Dover and Calais.

LADY OF MANN Built at Troon, UK for the *IOMSP Co.* Cars and small vans are side loaded but no ro-ro freight is conveyed. In 1994 replaced by the SEACAT ISLE OF MAN and laid up for sale. She was used in 1995 during the period of the 'TT' motor cycle races between 26th May to 12th June. Later in 1995 she was chartered to *Porto Santo Line* of Madeira for a service from Funchal to Porto Santo. In 1996 she operated throughout the summer, as no SeaCat was chartered. In 1997, she operated for the TT races and then inaugurated a new Liverpool - Dublin service in June, with a weekly Fleetwood - Douglas service until replaced by the SUPERSEACAT TWO in March 1998. In 1998 and 2000 she operated during the TT race period, plus a number of special cruises and was then chartered to *Acor Line* for service in the Azores. In 2001 the TT was cancelled, as were her extra sailings and cruises, but the charter went ahead. During winter 1998/99 she provided back-up to the fast ferries on the Liverpool - Dublin and Douglas - Liverpool routes. Between November 2000 and February 2001 she operated on the Liverpool – Douglas route and this was repeated between November 2001 and February 2002. However, she is unlikely to be chartered to *Acor Line* in summer 2002.

RAPIDE InCat 81m catamaran built at Hobart, Tasmania, Australia. Built for the *Holyman Group* as the CONDOR 12. In summer 1996 operated by *Condor Ferries* (at that time part owned by the *Holyman Group*). In 1997 she was renamed the HOLYMAN RAPIDE, transferred to *Holyman Sally Ferries* and in March was introduced onto the Ramsgate - Ostend route. In March 1998 transferred to the Dover - Ostend route, operating for the *Hoverspeed - Holyman (UK)* joint venture, and renamed the RAPIDE. In 1999 this became a 100% *Hoverspeed* operation and in 2000 *Sea Containers* purchased her. During winter 1999/2000 she also operated between Dover and Calais at times. In summer 2001, she operated between Liverpool and Dublin and Liverpool and Douglas; in summer 2002 she will operate between Heysham and Belfast.

SEACAT DANMARK InCat 74m catamaran built at Hobart, Tasmania, Australia. Christened in 1991 as the HOVERSPEED BELGIUM and renamed HOVERSPEED BOULOGNE before leaving the builders yard. She was the third SeaCat, introduced in 1992 to enable a three vessel service to be operated by *Hoverspeed* across the Channel, including a new SeaCat route between Folkestone and Boulogne (replacing the *Sealink Stena Line* ferry service which ceased at the end of 1991). With the HOVERSPEED FRANCE (now SEACAT ISLE OF MAN) and the HOVERSPEED GREAT BRITAIN she operated on all three Channel routes (Dover - Calais, Dover - Boulogne and Folkestone - Boulogne). In 1993 she was transferred to *SeaCat AB* and renamed the SEACATAMARAN DANMARK and inaugurated a new high-speed service between Gothenburg and Frederikshavn. For legal reasons it was not possible to call her the SEACAT DANMARK as intended but in 1995 these problems were resolved and she was renamed the SEACAT DANMARK. From January 1996 transferred to the new joint venture company *ColorSeaCat KS*, jointly with *Color Line* of Norway. During winter 1996/97 she operated on the Dover - Calais route. *ColorSeaCat* did not operate in 1997 and she again operated for *SeaCat AB*. In autumn 1997 she replaced the SEACAT SCOTLAND on the Stranraer - Belfast route. During summer 1998, she operated for the *IOMSP Co.* In 1999 operated for *Sea Containers Ferries Scotland* between Belfast and Heysham and Belfast and Douglas. In 2000 she was transferred to *SeaCat AB* to operate between Gothenburg, Frederikshavn and Langesund under the *Silja Line SeaCat* branding. In August 2000 moved to the Dover - Calais service.

SEACAT FRANCE Built at Hobart, Tasmania as the SEACAT TASMANIA for *Sea Containers* subsidiary *Tasmanian Ferry Services* of Australia to operate between George Town (Tasmania) and Port Welshpool (Victoria). In 1992 chartered to *Hoverspeed* to operate Dover - Calais and Folkestone - Boulogne services. Returned to Australia after the 1992 summer season but returned to Britain in summer 1993 to operate Dover - Calais and Folkestone - Boulogne services during the summer. She was repainted into *Hoverspeed* livery and renamed the SEACAT CALAIS. In 1994 chartered for five years (with a purchase option) to *Navegacion Atlantida* for *Ferry Linas Argentinas AS* of Uruguay service between Montevideo (Uruguay) - Buenos Aires (Argentina) service and renamed the ATLANTIC II. The purchase option was not taken up and in 1999 she was returned to *Sea Containers* and operated for Hoverspeed between Dover and Calais. In 2000 she was chartered to *SNAV Aliscafi* of Italy to operate between Ancona (Italy) and Split (Croatia) in a joint venture with *Sea Containers* and renamed the CROATIA JET. This operation was repeated in 2001. In 2002 renamed the SEACAT FRANCE and transferred to operate between Dover and Calais.

SEACAT ISLE OF MAN InCat 74m catamaran built at Hobart, Tasmania, Australia. Built as the

SuperSeaCat Three *(Andrew Cooke)*

Ben-my-Chree *(Miles Cowsill)*

HOVERSPEED FRANCE, the second SeaCat. She inaugurated Dover - Calais/Boulogne service in 1991. In 1992 she was chartered to *Sardinia Express* of Italy and renamed the SARDEGNA EXPRESS; she did not operate on the Channel that year. This charter was terminated at the end of 1992 and in 1993 she was renamed the SEACAT BOULOGNE and operated on the Dover - Calais and Folkestone - Boulogne services. In 1994 she was chartered to *IOMSP Co*, renamed the SEACAT ISLE OF MAN and replaced the LADY OF MANN on services between Douglas (Isle of Man) and Britain and Ireland. During winter 1994/5 operated for *SeaCat Scotland* between Stranraer and Belfast. She returned to *IOMSP Co* in June 1995. During spring 1995 she was chartered to *Condor Ferries*; she then was chartered again to *IOMSP Co* and returned to *Sea Containers* in the autumn. In 1996 she was chartered to *ColorSeaCat KS*, renamed the SEACAT NORGE and inaugurated a new service between Langesund (Norway) and Frederikshavn (Denmark). During winter 1996/97 she operated between Dover and Calais. In early 1997 she was again renamed the SEACAT ISLE OF MAN. During summer 1997 she operated for *IOMSP Co*, serving on Liverpool, Dublin and Belfast seasonal services to Douglas (May to September) plus a weekly Liverpool - Dublin service when the LADY OF MANN operated from Fleetwood. In late 1997 she was transferred to the *Hoverspeed* Dover - Calais route and operated on this route throughout 1998. In 1999 she operated between Douglas and Liverpool and Douglas and Dublin for *IOMSP Co*. In 2000 and 2001 she also operated between Douglas and Belfast and Douglas and Heysham, a service pattern which will be repeated in 2002, when she will also provide some additional sailings between Liverpool and Dublin.

SEACAT SCOTLAND InCat 74m catamaran built at Hobart, Tasmania, Australia, the fifth SeaCat to be constructed. In 1992 she inaugurated a new high-speed car and passenger service for *SeaCat Scotland* on the Stranraer - Belfast route. In autumn 1994 she was chartered to *Q-Ships* of Qatar for services between Doha (Qatar) and Bahrain and Dubai and renamed the Q-SHIP EXPRESS. In spring 1995 she returned to the Stranraer - Belfast service and resumed the name SEACAT SCOTLAND. In autumn 1997 chartered to *Navegacion Atlantida SA* of Uruguay for service between Colonia (Uruguay) and Buenos Aires (Argentina). She returned to the UK in spring 1998 and operated on to the Stranraer - Belfast route. In 1999 and 2000 she operated for *Sea Containers Ferries Scotland* between Stranraer and Belfast (service now ended) and Troon and Belfast. This was repeated in 2001 and will continue in 2002.

SUPERSEACAT ONE Fincantieri MDV1200 monohull vessel built at La Spézia, Italy. Built for *Sea Containers*. Between 1997 and 1999 operated for *SeaCat AB* on the Gothenburg - Frederikshavn route. In 2000 transferred to *Hoverspeed* to operate on the Newhaven - Dieppe service. In summer 2001 she operated between Dover and Ostend and Dover and Calais. In 2002 she will operate between Newhaven and Dieppe.

SUPERSEACAT TWO Fincantieri MDV1200 monohull vessel built at Riva Trigoso, Italy. Built for *Sea Containers*. In 1997 operated on the *Hoverspeed* Dover - Calais route. She was withdrawn from this route at the end of 1997 and in March 1998, she inaugurated a Liverpool - Dublin fast ferry service, operated by *IOMSP Co*. In summer 1999 she operated for *Hoverspeed* between Newhaven and Dieppe. In 2000 she returned to the Irish Sea, operating on the Belfast - Heysham service. In summer 2001 she operated between Dover and Calais and Dover and Oostende. In 2001 she was laid up for sale or charter.

SUPERSEACAT THREE Fincantieri MDV1200 monohull vessel built at La Spézia, Italy. In 1999 operated on the Liverpool - Dublin service, operated by *Sea Containers Ferries Scotland*, replacing the SUPERSEACAT TWO. In 2000 she also operated on the Liverpool - Douglas service. In summer 2001 she operated between Dover and Calais and Dover and Ostend; in summer 2002 she will operate from Liverpool to Dublin and Douglas.

THE PRINCESS ANNE, THE PRINCESS MARGARET British Hovercraft Corporation SRN4 type hovercraft built at Cowes, UK for *Seaspeed*. Built at to Mark I specification. In 1978/1979 respectively lengthened to Mark III specification. They underwent complete refurbishment at the beginning of 1999. Withdrawn 2000 and laid up at the Hovercraft Museum at Lee on Solent.

SEAFRANCE

THE COMPANY *SeaFrance SA* (previously *SNAT (Société Nouvelle Armement Transmanche)*) is a French state owned company. It is jointly owned by *Société Nationale des Chemins de fer Français (French Railways)* and *Compagnie Générale Maritime Français (French National Shipping Company)*. *SNAT* was established in 1990 to take over the services of *SNCF Armement Naval*, a wholly owned division of *SNCF*. At the same time a similarly constituted body called *Société Proprietaire Navires (SPN)* was established to take over ownership of the vessels; *Sealink British Ferries* (and later *Stena Line Ltd*) also had involvement in this company. Joint operation of services with *Stena Line* ceased at the end of 1995 and *SeaFrance SA* was formed. *Stena Line* involvement in *SPN* ended in 1999.

MANAGEMENT Président du Directoire Eudes Riblier, **Directeur Sealink Calais** M Jachet, **Managing Director (UK)** Robin Wilkins.

ADDRESS ***France*** 3 rue Ambroise Paré, 75475, Paris Cedex 10, France, ***UK*** Whitfield Court, Honeywood Close, Whitfield, Dover, Kent CT16 3PX.

TELEPHONE Administration ***France*** +33 1 55 31 58 92, ***UK*** +44 (0)1304 828300, **Reservations** ***France*** +33 3 21 46 80 79, ***UK (Passenger)*** 08705 711711 (from UK only), ***UK (Freight)*** +44 (0)1304 203030.

FAX Administration & Reservations ***France*** +33 1 48 74 62 37, ***UK*** +44 (0)1304 828384.

INTERNET Email sfadmin@seafrance.com **Website** www.seafrance.com *(English, French)*

ROUTE OPERATED Calais - Dover (1 hr 10 mins - 1 h 30 mins; *(1,2,3,4)*; 15 per day).

1	SEAFRANCE CEZANNE	25122t	80	19.5k	163.5m	1800P	600C	66L	BA2	FR
2	SEAFRANCE MANET	15093t	84	18k	130.0m	1800P	330C	43L	BA2	FR
3•	SEAFRANCE RENOIR	15612t	81	18k	130.0m	1600P	330C	43L	BA2	FR
4	SEAFRANCE RODIN	34000t	01	25k	185.0m	1900P	700C	133L	BA2	FR

SEAFRANCE CEZANNE Built at Malmö, Sweden as the ARIADNE for *Rederi AB Nordö* of Sweden. Renamed the SOCA before entering service on *UMEF* freight services (but with capacity for 175 drivers) in the Mediterranean. In 1981 she was sold to *SO Mejdunaroden Automobilen Transport (SOMAT)* of Bulgaria and renamed the TRAPEZITZA. She operated on *Medlink* services between Bulgaria and the Middle East. In 1988 she was acquired by *Sealink British Ferries*, re-registered in the Bahamas and in 1989 renamed the FANTASIA. Later in 1989 she was modified in Bremerhaven, renamed the CHANNEL SEAWAY and, in May, she inaugurated a new freight-only service between Dover (Eastern Docks) and Calais. During winter 1989/90 she was modified in Bremerhaven to convert her for passenger service. In spring 1990 she was renamed the FIESTA, transferred to *SNAT*, re-registered in France and replaced the CHAMPS ELYSEES (now the SEAFRANCE MANET) on the Dover - Calais service. In 1996 she was renamed the SEAFRANCE CEZANNE.

SEAFRANCE MANET Built at Nantes, France for *SNCF* as the CHAMPS ELYSEES to operate Calais - Dover and Boulogne - Dover services, later operating Calais - Dover only. In 1990 transferred to the Dieppe - Newhaven service. Chartered to *Stena Sealink Line* in June 1992 when they took over the operation of the service. She was renamed the STENA PARISIEN and carried a French crew. In 1997 the charter was terminated; she returned to *SeaFrance* and was renamed the SEAFRANCE MANET.

SEAFRANCE RENOIR Built at Le Havre, France for *SNCF* as the COTE D'AZUR for the Dover - Calais service. She also operated Boulogne - Dover in 1985. In 1996 she was renamed the SEAFRANCE RENOIR. Now a spare vessel and may be sold.

SEAFRANCE RODIN Built at Rauma, Finland for *SeaFrance*.

SMYRIL LINE

THE COMPANY *Smyril Line* is a Faroe Islands registered company.

MANAGEMENT Managing Director Óli Hammer, **Marketing Manager** Samuel J Arnoldson.

ADDRESS Jonas Bronksgöta 37, PO Box 370, FO-100 Tórshavn, Faroe Islands.

TELEPHONE Administration +298-345900, **Reservations** Faroe Islands +298-345900, ***UK*** +44 (0)1224 572615 (*P&O Scottish Ferries*).

FAX Administration & Reservations +298-343950, **Telex** 81296.

INTERNET Email office@smyril-line.fo **Website** www.smyril-line.com *(English, Danish, German, Faroese, Icelandic, Norwegian)*

ROUTES OPERATED Tórshavn (Faroes) - Hanstholm (Denmark) (31 hrs; *(1)*; 1 per week), Tórshavn - Lerwick (Shetland) (14 hrs; *(1)*; 1 per week) - Bergen (Norway) (via Lerwick) (24 hrs - 27 hrs 30 mins; *(1)*; 1 per week), Tórshavn - Seydisfjordur (Iceland) (15 hrs - 18 hrs; *(1)*; 1 per week) (15 May to 10 September only). Note Lerwick sailings ceased after the 1992 season but resumed in 1998. The service now operates all year round but is restricted to Tórshavn - Hanstholm during winter months.

1	NORRÖNA	11999t	73	19k	129.0m	1050P	300C	40L	BA2	FA

NORRÖNA Built at Rendsburg, Germany as the GUSTAV VASA for *Lion Ferry AB* of Sweden, a sister vessel of the NILS DACKE (see the QUIBERON, *Brittany Ferries*). In 1982 the Travemünde - Malmö service ceased and in 1983 she was sold to *Smyril Line* and renamed the NORRÖNA. She was rebuilt at Flensburg, Germany, to increase passenger capacity and in the summer took over services from the SMYRIL of *Strandfaraskip Landsins*. In 1993 Esbjerg replaced Hanstholm as the Danish port and calls at Lerwick (Shetland) ceased. Because the service only operated in the summer period, she has, since purchase, undertaken a number of charters and cruises during the winter months. During autumn 1994 she initially served on the short-lived service between Wismar (Germany) and Newcastle for *North Sea Baltic Ferries*. During the early part of 1996 she was chartered to *Stena Line* to operate between Stranraer and Belfast. In 1998 the Danish port became Hanstholm again and Lerwick sailings resumed. Since 1999/2000 a limited winter service has been operated and she now operates for *Smyril Line* all year round.

Under Construction

2	NORRÖNA	40000t	03	21k	163.3m	1482P	800C	134T	BA	FA

NORRÖNA Under construction in Lübeck, Germany for *Smyril Line*, to replace the existing NORRÖNA. Originally due to enter service in 2002, start of building was delayed by financing difficulties. Originally to have been built at Flensburg, Germany but delays led to change of shipyard.

STENA LINE

THE COMPANY *Stena Line Scandinavia AB* is a Swedish private sector company, wholly owned by *Stena AB*. Whilst British subsidiary *Stena Line Ltd* and Dutch subsidiary *Stena Line bv* still exist as legal entities, the company is operated on a route management basis, with each Route Director reporting directly to HQ in Gothenburg. Some central services are also undertaken by units in UK and Netherlands which report directly to Gothenburg.

MANAGEMENT Chief Executive Bo Severed (*Stena Line Scandinavia AB*, Sweden), **Route Director - Hoek van Holland - Harwich** Pim de Lange, **Route Director - Fishguard - Rosslare** Mary Gallagher, **Route Director - Holyhead - Dun Laoghaire/Dublin** Vic Goodwin, **Route Director - Stranraer - Belfast** Alan Gordon.

ADDRESS *UK* Charter House, Park Street, Ashford, Kent TN24 8EX, ***Netherlands*** PO Box 2, 3150 AA, Hoek van Holland, Netherlands.

TELEPHONE Administration *UK* +44 (0)1233 647022, ***Netherlands*** +31 (0)174 389333, **Reservations *UK*** 08075 707070 (from UK only), ***Netherlands*** +31 (0)174 315811.

SeaFrance Rodin *(FotoFlite)*

Stena Discovery *(Miles Cowsill)*

FAX Administration & Reservations ***UK*** +44 (0)1233 202349, ***Netherlands*** +31 (0)174 387045, **Telex** 31272.

INTERNET Email info@stenaline.com **Website** www.stenaline.com *(English, Swedish)*

ROUTES OPERATED Conventional Ferries Stranraer - Belfast (3 hrs 15 mins; *(2)*; 2 per day), Holyhead - Dublin (3 hrs 45 mins; *(6)*; 2 per day), Fishguard - Rosslare (3 hrs 30 mins; *(4)*; 2 per day), **Ro-pax Ferries** Harwich - Hoek van Holland (Netherlands) (7 hrs 30 mins; *(1,7)*; 2 per day) (car passengers only conveyed - no foot passengers). **Fast Ferries** Stranraer - Belfast (1 hr 45 mins; *(9)*; 5 per day), Holyhead - Dun Laoghaire (1 hr 39 mins; *(5)*; up to 4 per day), Fishguard - Rosslare (Summer Only) (1 hr 39 mins; *(8)*; up to 4 per day), Harwich - Hoek van Holland - (3 hrs 40 mins; *(3)*; 2 per day.

1	STENA BRITANNICA	33796t	00	22k	188.3m	380P	-	216T	BA	UK
2	STENA CALEDONIA	12619t	81	19.5k	129.6m	1000P	280C	56L	BA2	UK
3»	STENA DISCOVERY	19638t	97	40k	126.6m	1500P	375C	50L	A	NL
4	STENA EUROPE	24828t	81	19k	149.0m	2076P	456C	60T	BA2	UK
5»	STENA EXPLORER	19638t	96	40k	126.6m	1500P	375C	50L	A	UK
6	STENA FORWARDER	24000t	01	22.5k	186.5m	1000P	100C	154T	A2	IT
7	STENA HOLLANDICA	33796t	01	22k	188.3m	380P	-	216T	BA	NL
8»	STENA LYNX III	4113t	96	35k	81.1m	620P	181C	-	A	UK
9»	STENA VOYAGER	19638t	96	40k	126.6m	1500P	375C	50L	A	UK

STENA BRITANNICA Ro-pax ferry built at Cadiz Spain for *Stena RoRo* and chartered to *Stena Line bv* to operate between Hoek van Holland and Harwich.

STENA CALEDONIA Built at Belfast, UK as the ST DAVID for the Holyhead - Dun Laoghaire and Fishguard - Rosslare services. It was originally planned that she would replace the chartered STENA NORMANDICA (5607t, 1975) but it was subsequently decided that an additional large vessel was required for the Irish Sea routes. Until 1985 her normal use was, therefore, to substitute for other Irish Sea vessels as necessary (including the Stranraer - Larne route) and also to operate additional summer services on the Holyhead - Dun Laoghaire route. During the spring of 1983 she operated on the Dover - Calais service while the ST CHRISTOPHER (now the STENA ANTRIM) was being modified. From March 1985 she operated between Dover and Ostend, a service which ceased in December 1985 with the decision of *RMT* to link up with *Townsend Thoresen*. During the early part of 1986 she operated between Dover and Calais and then moved to the Stranraer - Larne route (later Stranraer – Belfast) where she became a regular vessel. In 1990 she was renamed the STENA CALEDONIA. In September 1996 she became mainly a freight-only vessel but passengers were carried on certain sailings and when the STENA VOYAGER was unavailable; cars and passengers are now conveyed on all sailings.

STENA DISCOVERY Finnyards HSS1500 ('High-speed Sea Service') built at Rauma, Finland for *Stena Line* to replace two vessels on the Harwich - Hoek van Holland service.

STENA EUROPE Built at Gothenburg, Sweden as the KRONPRINSESSAN VICTORIA for *Göteborg-Frederikshavn-Linjen* of Sweden (trading as *Sessan Linjen*) for their Gothenburg - Frederikshavn service. Shortly after delivery, the company was taken over by *Stena Line* and services were marketed as *Stena-Sessan Line* for a period. In 1982 she was converted to an overnight ferry by the conversion of one vehicle deck to two additional decks of cabins and she was switched to the Gothenburg - Kiel route (with, during the summer, daytime runs from Gothenburg to Frederikshavn and Kiel to Korsør (Denmark)). In 1989 she was transferred to the Oslo - Frederikshavn route and renamed the STENA SAGA. In 1994, transferred to *Stena Line bv*, renamed the STENA EUROPE and operated between Hoek van Holland and Harwich. She was withdrawn in June 1997, transferred to the *Lion Ferry* (a *Stena Line* subsidiary) Karlskrona - Gdynia service and renamed the LION EUROPE. In 1998 she was transferred back to *Stena Line* (remaining on the same route) and renamed the STENA EUROPE. In early 2002 the cabins installed in 1982 were removed and other modifications made and she was transferred to the Fishguard - Rosslare route.

STENA EXPLORER Finnyards HSS1500 built at Rauma, Finland for *Stena RoRo* and chartered to *Stena Line*. Operates on the Holyhead - Dun Laoghaire route.

STENA FORWARDER Built at Porto Viro Italy for *Visentini Group* of Italy and chartered to *Stena Line* on delivery to operate on the Holyhead - Dublin service.

STENA HOLLANDICA Ro-pax ferry built at Cadiz, Spain for *Stena RoRo* and chartered to *Stena Line bv* to operate between Hoek van Holland and Harwich.

STENA LYNX III InCat 81m catamaran built at Hobart, Tasmania, Australia. Chartered new by *Del Bene* of Argentina to *Stena Line* in June 1996 and named the STENA LYNX III. Initially used on the Dover - Calais service. From summer 1997 until autumn 1998 she operated between Newhaven and Dieppe. In March 1998 she was transferred to *P&O Stena Line* and renamed the ELITE. She was then renamed the P&O STENA ELITE (although only carrying the name ELITE on the bow). In late 1998 she was transferred back to *Stena Line* and renamed the STENA LYNX III. In 1999 she was placed on the Fishguard - Rosslare service, replacing the STENA LYNX (3231t, 1993). The charter ended in autumn 2000 but was immediately renewed (with winter lay up).

STENA VOYAGER Finnyards HSS1500 built at Rauma, Finland for *Stena RoRo* and chartered to *Stena Line*. Operates on the Stranraer - Belfast route.

Under Construction

10	NEWBUILDING 1	44000t	02	22k	210.8m	900P	-	250T	BA2	UK
11	NEWBUILDING 2	44000t	03	22k	210.8m	900P	-	250T	BA2	UK

NEWBUILDING 1, NEWBUILDING 2 Ro-pax vessels under construction at Ulsan, South Korea, for *Stena RoRo*. First to be chartered to *Stena Line* for use on Harwich-Hook of Holland route.

SUPERFAST FERRIES

THE COMPANY *SuperFast Ferries* is a Greek company, owned by *Attica Enterprises*.

MANAGEMENT Managing Director Alexander P Panagopulos, **Corporate Marketing Director** Yannis B Criticos.

ADDRESS *Greece* 157 Alkyonidon Avenue, Voula, GR-16673 Athens, Greece, ***UK*** Superfast Ferries, The Terminal Building, Port of Rosyth, Fife KY11 2XP, ***Belgium*** Superfast Ferries, Terminal A, Port of Zeebrugge, Doverlaan 7, Box 14, 8380 Zeebrugge, Belgium.

TELEPHONE Administration *Greece & Scotland* +30 (0)1 891 9500, ***Belgium*** +32 (0)50 252211, **Reservations *UK*** 0870 234 0870, ***Belgium*** +32 (0)50 252252.

FAX Administration *Greece & Scotland* +30 (0)10 8919509.

INTERNET Email criticos@superfast.com **Website** www.superfast.com *(English, German, Dutch, French)*

ROUTES OPERATED Rosyth (Scotland) - Zeebrugge) (17 hrs 30 mins; *(1,2)*; 1 per day). Service starts in May 2002.

1	SUPERFAST IX	29800t	01	29.2k	203.3m	626P	661C	140T	BA2	GR
2	SUPERFAST X	29800t	01	29.2k	203.3m	626P	661C	140T	BA2	GR

SUPERFAST IX, SUPERFAST X Built at Kiel, Germany for *Attica Enterprises* to operate for *Superfast Ferries*. SUPERFAST IX and SUPERFAST X operated between Rostock and Söderalje January - April 2002. Both will open the new Rosyth - Zeebrugge in May 2002.

SWANSEA CORK FERRIES

THE COMPANY *Swansea Cork Ferries* is a company established in 1987 to re-open the Swansea - Cork service abandoned by *B&I Line* in 1979. It was originally jointly owned by *West Glamorgan County Council, Cork Corporation, Cork County Council* and *Kerry County Council*. The service did not operate in 1989 but resumed in 1990. In 1993 the company was acquired by *Strintzis Lines* of Greece. In 1999 it was purchased from *Strintzis Lines* by a consortium of Irish businessmen.

MANAGEMENT Managing Director Thomas Hunter McGowan, **Sales Manager** Alec Maguire.

Stena Europe (Gordon Hislip)

Sardinia Vera (FotoFlite)

ADDRESS 52 South Mall, Cork, Republic of Ireland.

TELEPHONE Administration *Head Office* +353 (0)21 427 6000, ***Cork Ferry Port*** +353 (0)21 437 8036, **Reservations *IR*** +353 (0)21 427 1166, ***UK*** +44 (0)1792 456116.

FAX Administration *IR* +353 (0)21 427 5814, ***UK*** +44 (0)1792 644356, **Reservations *IR*** +353 (0)21 427 5061, ***UK*** +44 (0)1792 644356.

INTERNET Email scf@iol.ie **Website** www.swansea-cork.ie *(English)*

ROUTE OPERATED *March - November* Cork - Swansea (10 hrs; *(1)*; 1 per day or alternate days, according to season. Due to tidal restrictions at Swansea, the service operates to Pembroke Dock on a few days each year.

1	SUPERFERRY	14797t	72	21k	137.8m	1400P	350C	50L	BA2	GR

SUPERFERRY Built at Hashihama, Japan as the CASSIOPEIA for *Ocean Ferry KK* of Japan. In 1976 the company became *Ocean Tokyu Ferry KK* and she was renamed the IZU NO 3. She was used on the service between Tokyo (Honshu) - Tokushima (Shikoko) - Kokura (Kyshu). In 1991 she was sold to *Strintzis Lines* and briefly renamed the IONIAN EXPRESS. Following major rebuilding, she was renamed the SUPERFERRY and used on their services between Greece and the Greek islands. In 1993 time chartered to *Swansea Cork Ferries*. The charter continued following the sale of *SCF* by *Strintzis Lines*. In winter returned to *Strintzis Lines* in Greece for refit and also operated for them on Mediterranean routes. The charter was not renewed for 2001 and she remained in the Mediterranean, operating for *Strintzis Lines* under the *Blue Ferries* name (following the reorganisation of the company after its acquisition by *Attica Enterprises*). She was renamed the BLUE AEGEAN. In 2002 she was sold to *Swansea Cork Ferries* and renamed the SUPERFERRY.

TRANSMANCHE FERRIES

THE COMPANY *Transmanche Ferries* is a French company, controlled by the *Syndicat Mixte de L'Activité Transmanche*. The service is operated in co-operation with *Hoverspeed*.

ADDRESS Transmanche Ferries, Quai Gaston Lalitte, 76200, Dieppe, France.

TELEPHONE Administration +33 02 32 14 52 03, **Reservations** 0800 9171201 *(Hoverspeed)*, 0800 650100.

FAX Administration +33 02 32 14 5200.

INTERNET Website www.transmancheferries.com *(English, French)*

ROUTE OPERATED Newhaven - Dieppe (4 hrs; *(1,2)*; 4 per day). Service started spring 2001.

1	DIEPPE	17672t	81	19k	145.9m	250P	-	140T	BA	UK
2	SARDINIA VERA	11637t	75	18.5k	120.8m	700P	479C	58T	BA	IT

DIEPPE Built at Kalmar, Sweden as the SAGA STAR for *TT-Saga-Line* and, from 1982, used on freight services between Travemünde and Trelleborg/Malmö. In 1989 sold to *Cie Meridonale* of France, renamed the GIROLATA and used on *SNCM* (later *CMR*) services in the Mediterranean. In 1993 she was chartered back to *TT-Line*, resumed her original name and was used on the Travemünde - Trelleborg service. Following delivery of the ROBIN HOOD and the NILS DACKE in 1995, she was transferred to the Rostock - Trelleborg route. In July 1997 she was purchased by *TT-Line* and in 1998 passenger facilities were completely renovated to full ro-pax format; following the delivery of the TOM SAWYER she was transferred back to the Travemünde - Trelleborg route, operating additional freight sailings. Briefly transferred back to Rostock - Trelleborg when the charter of the TT-TRAVELLER ended. Withdrawn in 2002, sold to *Transmanche Ferries* and renamed the DIEPPE.

SARDINIA VERA Built at Bremerhaven, Germany for *Stena Line AB* of Sweden. Laid down as the STENA ATLANTICA but launched as the MARINE ATLANTICA. On delivery, chartered to *CN Marine* (from 1986 *Marine Atlantic*) of Canada for service between North Sydney (Nova Scotia) and Port-aux-Basques (Newfoundland). In 1986 she was sold to *Tourship Co AS* of Italy (parent company of *Corsica Ferries*) and renamed the CORSICA VERA. In 1987 renamed the SARDINIA VERA. Used on services between Italy and France and Corsica and Sardinia. In 2001 chartered to the *Transmanche Ferries*.

AR MŁODZIEŻY
DAR MŁODZIEŻY
GDYNIA

Dar Mlodziezy, **Primrose** and **Eurovoyager** *(Mike Louagie)*

section 2 domestic services

gb & ireland

ARGYLL AND BUTE COUNCIL

THE COMPANY *Argyll and Bute Council* is a British local government authority.

MANAGEMENT Director of Roads & Transportation Services Alistair Gow.

ADDRESS Manse Brae, Lochgilphead, Argyll PA31 8RD.

TELEPHONE Administration +44 (0)1546 604657.

FAX Administration +44 (0)1546 606443.

INTERNET Email alistair.gow@argyll-bute.gov.uk **Website** www.argyll-bute.gov.uk *(English)*

ROUTES OPERATED Seil - Luing (5 mins; *(1)*; frequent service), Port Askaig (Islay) - Feolin (Jura) (5 mins; *(2)*; approx hourly).

1	BELNAHUA	35t	72	8k	17.1m	40P	5C	1L	BA	UK
2	EILEAN DHIURA	86t	98	9k	25.6m	50P	13C	1L	BA	UK

BELNAHUA Built at Campbeltown, UK for *Argyll County Council* for the Seil - Luing service. In 1975, following local government reorganisation, transferred to *Strathclyde Regional Council*. In 1996, transferred to *Argyll and Bute Council*.

EILEAN DHIURA Built at Bromborough, Birkenhead, UK for *Argyll and Bute County Council* to replace the *Western Ferries (Argyll)* SOUND OF GIGHA on the Islay - Jura route. *Serco-Denholm Ltd* manage and operate this vessel on behalf of the *Argyll and Bute Council*.

ARRANMORE ISLAND FERRY SERVICES

THE COMPANY *Arranmore Island Ferry Services* is an Irish Republic company, supported by *Údarás na Gaeltachta (The Gaeltacht Authority)*, a semi-state owned body responsible for tourism and development in the Irish speaking areas of The Irish Republic. The operation is also known as *Maoin-Na-Farraige* (literally 'sea treasure' or 'sea wealth').

MANAGEMENT Managing Director Cornelius Bonner.

ADDRESS Bridge House, Leabgarrow, Arranmore, County Donegal, Republic of Ireland.

TELEPHONE Administration & Reservations +353 (0)75 20532.

FAX Administration & Reservations + 353 (0)75 20750.

ROUTE OPERATED Burtonport (County Donegal) - Leabgarrow (Arranmore Island) (20 mins; *(1,2,3)*; up to 8 per day (summer), 5 per day (winter)) (Note only one vessel is generally in use at any one time).

1	ÁRAINN MHÓR	64t	72	8k	23.8m	138P	6C	-	B	IR
2	COLL	69t	74	8k	25.3m	152P	6C	-	B	IR
3	RHUM	69t	73	8k	25.3m	164P	6C	-	B	IR

ÁRAINN MHÓR Built at Port Glasgow, UK as the KILBRANNAN for *Caledonian MacBrayne*. Used on a variety of routes until 1977, she was then transferred to the Scalpay (Harris) - Kyles Scalpay service. In 1990 she was replaced by the CANNA and, in turn, replaced the CANNA in her reserve/relief role. In 1992 sold to *Arranmore Island Ferry Services* and renamed the ÁRAINN

MHÓR. She was subsequently sold to *Údarás na Gaeltachta* and leased back to *Arranmore Island Ferry Services*.

COLL Built at Port Glasgow, UK for *Caledonian MacBrayne*. For several years she was employed mainly in a relief capacity. In 1986 she took over the Tobermory (Mull) - Kilchoan service from a passenger only vessel; the conveyance of vehicles was not inaugurated until 1991. In 1996 she was transferred to the Oban - Lismore route. In 1998 she was sold to *Arranmore Island Ferry Services*.

RHUM Built at Port Glasgow, UK for *Caledonian MacBrayne*. Until 1987, she was used primarily on the Claonaig - Lochranza (Arran) service. After that time she served on various routes. In 1994 she inaugurated a new service between Tarbert (Loch Fyne) and Portavadie. In 1997 operated between Kyles Scalpay and Scalpay until the opening of the new bridge on 16th December 1997. In 1998 she was sold to *Arranmore Island Ferry Services*.

BERE ISLAND FERRIES

THE COMPANY *Bere Island Ferries Ltd* is an Irish Republic private sector company.

MANAGEMENT Operator Colm Harrington.

ADDRESS Ferry Lodge, West End, Bere Island, County Cork, Republic of Ireland.

TELEPHONE Administration +353 (0)27 75009, **Reservations** Not applicable.

INTERNET Email biferry@indigo.ie **Website** www.bereisland.net *(English)*

ROUTE OPERATED Castletownbere (County Cork) - Bere Island (10 mins; *(3)*; up to 10 per day).

1•	F.B.D. DUNBRODY	139t	60	8k	39.6m	107P	18C	-	BA	IR
2	MISNEACH	30t	78	7k	18.9m	80P	4C	-	B	IR
3	MORVERN	64t	73	8k	23.8m	138P	6C	-	B	IR

F.B.D. DUNBRODY Built at Hamburg, Germany as the BERNE-FARGE for the service between Berne and Farge, across the River Weser in Germany. Subsequently she was sold to *Elbe Clearing* of Germany, renamed the ELBE CLEARING 12 and used as a floating platform for construction works in the Elbe. In 1979 she was sold to *Passage East Ferry Company* and renamed the F.B.D. DUNBRODY. Withdrawn in January 1998 and became a spare vessel. Later in 1998 she was sold to *Bere Island Ferries* and replaced the MISNEACH as main vessel. In 2000 badly damaged when she broke loose during gales and laid up. She is currently for sale, and will be used as a work platform or similar; she is no longer usable as a ferry.

MISNEACH Built at New Ross, Irish Republic for *Arranmore Island Ferry Services* of the Irish Republic and used on the Burtonport - Arranmore service. In 1992 sold to *Bere Island Ferries*. In 1993 inaugurated a car ferry service between Castletownbere and Bere Island. Became reserve vessel when F.B.D. DUNBRODY entered service but resumed full service when that vessel was withdrawn. Now reserve again following delivery of the MORVERN.

MORVERN Built at Port Glasgow, UK for *Caledonian MacBrayne*. After service on a number of routes she was, after 1979, the main vessel on the Fionnphort (Mull) - Iona service. In 1992 replaced by the LOCH BUIE and became a spare vessel. In 1995 sold to *Arranmore Island Ferry Services*. In 2001 sold to *Bere Island Ferries*.

Hebrides *(Miles Cowsill)*

Isle of Arran *(Miles Cowsill)*

CALEDONIAN MACBRAYNE

THE COMPANY *Caledonian MacBrayne Limited* is a British state owned company, the responsibility of the First Minister of Scotland. Until 1990 it was part of the state owned *Scottish Transport Group* (formed in 1969). *Caledonian MacBrayne Limited* as such was formed in 1973 by the merger of the *Caledonian Steam Packet Company Ltd* (which had been formed in 1889) and *David MacBrayne Ltd* (whose origins go back to 1851). The company has more vessels sailing under the British flag than any other.

MANAGEMENT Managing Director Lawrie Sinclair, **Marketing Manager** Mike Blair.

ADDRESS The Ferry Terminal, Gourock PA19 1QP.

TELEPHONE Administration +44 (0)1475 650100, **Vehicle Reservations** 08705 650000 (from UK only).

FAX Administration +44 (0)1475 637607, **Vehicle Reservations** +44 (0)1475 635235.

INTERNET Email mike.blair@calmac.co.uk **Website** www.calmac.co.uk *(English)*

ROUTES OPERATED ***All year vehicle ferries (frequencies are for summer)*** Ardrossan - Brodick (Arran) (55 mins; *(2)*; up to 6 per day), Largs - Cumbrae Slip (Cumbrae) (10 mins; *(14,21)*; every 30 or 15 mins), Wemyss Bay - Rothesay (Bute) (35 mins; *(12,13,26,28)*; up to 22 per day), Colintraive - Rhubodach (Bute) (5 mins; *(17)*; frequent service), Tarbert (Loch Fyne) - Portavadie (20 mins; *(9)*; up to 11 per day), Gourock - Dunoon (20 mins; *(12,13,28)*; hourly service with extras at peaks), Kennacraig - Port Ellen (Islay) (2 hrs 15 mins; *(6)*; 1 or 2 per day), Kennacraig - Port Askaig (Islay) (2 hrs; *(6)*; 1 or 2 per day), Tayinloan - Gigha (20 mins; *(20)*; hourly with some gaps), Oban - Lismore (50 mins; *(5)*; up to 4 per day), Oban - Colonsay (2 hrs 10 mins; *(4,11)*; 3 per week), Oban - Craignure (Mull) (40 mins; *(11)*; two hourly), Oban - Coll (2 hrs 45 mins (direct), 4 hrs 50 mins (via Tiree); *(4)*; up to 5 per week), Oban - Tiree (3 hrs 30 mins (direct), 4 hrs 15 mins (via Coll); *(4 (summer),25 (winter))*; up to 5 per week), Oban - Castlebay (Barra) (5 hrs (direct); *(4 (summer),25 (winter))*; 4 per week), Oban - Lochboisdale (South Uist) (5 hrs (direct), 7 hrs (via Barra); *(4 (summer),25 (winter))*; up to 5 per week), Bernaray - Leverburgh (Harris) (1 hr 10 mins; *(15)*; 3-4 per day), Lochaline - Fishnish (Mull) (15 mins; *(18)*; up to 16 per day), Mallaig - Armadale (Skye) (30 mins; *(25 (summer),24 (winter))*; up to 7 per day (2 in winter)), Sconser (Skye) - Raasay (15 mins; *(22)*; up to 10 per day), Uig (Skye) - Tarbert (Harris) (1 hr 45 mins; *(7)*; 1 or 2 per day), Uig (Skye) - Lochmaddy (North Uist) (1 hr 45 mins; *(7)*; 1 or 2 per day), Ullapool - Stornoway (Lewis) (2 hrs 40 mins; *(8, 10)*; up to 3 per day).

All year passenger and restricted vehicle ferries (frequencies are for summer) Fionnphort (Mull) - Iona (5 mins; *(16)*; frequent), Ballycastle (Northern Ireland) - Rathlin Island (40 mins; *(8)*; 2 per day), Mallaig - Eigg - Muck - Rum - Canna - Mallaig (round trip 7 hrs (all islands); *(24)*; at least 1 sailing per day - most islands visited daily). **Note** although these services are operated by vehicle ferries, special permission is required to take a vehicle and tourist vehicles are not normally conveyed.

Summer only vehicle ferries Claonaig - Lochranza (Arran) (30 mins; *(23)*; up to 10 per day), Kennacraig - Port Askaig - Colonsay - Oban (3 hrs 35 mins; *(6)*; 1 per week), Tobermory (Mull) - Kilchoan (35 mins; *(19)*; up to 11 per day), ***Winter only vehicle ferries*** Tarbert (Loch Fyne) - Lochranza (Arran) (1 hr; *(varies)*; 1 per day).

1	BRUERNISH	69t	73	8k	22.5m	121P	6C	-	B	UK
2	CALEDONIAN ISLES	5221t	93	15k	93.5m	1000P	120C	10L	BA	UK
3	CANNA	69t	73	8k	22.5m	140P	6C	-	B	UK
4	CLANSMAN	5400t	98	16.5k	99.0m	638P	90C	6L	BA	UK
5	EIGG	69t	75	8k	22.5m	75P	6C	-	B	UK
6	HEBRIDEAN ISLES	3040t	85	15k	85.1m	494P	68C	10L	BAS	UK
7	HEBRIDES	5299t	00	16.5k	99.0m	612P	110C	6L	BA	UK
8	ISLE OF ARRAN	3269t	84	15k	85.0m	446P	68C	8L	BA	UK
9	ISLE OF CUMBRAE	201t	77	8.5k	32.0m	139P	18C	-	BA	UK

SECTION 2 – DOMESTIC SERVICES

10	ISLE OF LEWIS	6753t	95	18k	101.2m	680P	123C	10L	BA	UK
11	ISLE OF MULL	4719t	88	15k	90.1m	962P	80C	20L	BA	UK
12	JUNO	854t	74	12k	69.0m	381P	40C	-	AS	UK
13	JUPITER	848t	74	12k	69.0m	381P	40C	-	AS	UK
14	LOCH ALAINN	396t	98	10k	41.0m	150P	24C	-	BA	UK
15	LOCH BHRUSDA	246t	96	8k	30.0m	150P	18C	-	BA	UK
16	LOCH BUIE	295t	92	9k	30.2m	250P	9C	-	BA	UK
17	LOCH DUNVEGAN	549t	91	9k	54.2m	200P	36C	-	BA	UK
18	LOCH FYNE	549t	91	9k	54.2m	200P	36C	-	BA	UK
19	LOCH LINNHE	206t	86	9k	30.2m	199P	12C	-	BA	UK
20	LOCH RANZA	206t	86	9k	30.2m	199P	12C	-	BA	UK
21	LOCH RIDDON	206t	86	9k	30.2m	199P	12C	-	BA	UK
22	LOCH STRIVEN	206t	86	9k	30.2m	199P	12C	-	BA	UK
23	LOCH TARBERT	211t	92	9k	30.2m	149P	18C	-	BA	UK
24	LOCHNEVIS	941t	00	9k	49.1m	190P	14C	-	A	UK
25	LORD OF THE ISLES	3504t	89	16k	84.6m	506P	56C	16L	BAS	UK
26	PIONEER	1071t	74	16k	67.4m	218P	33C	-	AS	UK
27	RAASAY	69t	76	8k	22.5m	75P	6C	-	B	UK
28	SATURN	851t	78	12k	69.0m	381P	40C	-	AS	UK

BRUERNISH Built at Port Glasgow, UK. Until 1980 she served on a variety of routes. In 1980 she inaugurated ro-ro working between Tayinloan and the island of Gigha and served this route until June 1992 when she was replaced by the LOCH RANZA and became a relief vessel. In summer 1994 she operated as secondary vessel on the Tobermory (Mull) - Kilchoan service for one season only. In December 1996 she started a vehicle ferry service between Ballycastle (on the North West coast of Northern Ireland) and Rathlin Island under charter; the route became a *Caledonian MacBrayne* operation in April 1997 - see the CANNA. In 1997 she operated on the Tarbert - Portavadie service and in 1998 on the Oban - Lismore service. Since 1999 she has been a spare vessel.

CALEDONIAN ISLES Built at Lowestoft, UK for the Ardrossan - Brodick (Arran) service.

CANNA Built at Port Glasgow, UK. She was the regular vessel on the Lochaline - Fishnish (Mull) service. In 1986 she was replaced by the ISLE OF CUMBRAE and until 1990 she served in a relief capacity in the north, often assisting on the Iona service. In 1990 she replaced the KILBRANNAN (see the ÁRAINN MHÓR, *Arranmore Island Ferry Services*) on the Kyles Scalpay (Harris) - Scalpay service (replaced by a bridge in autumn 1997). In spring 1997 she was transferred to the Ballycastle - Rathlin Island route.

CLANSMAN Built at Appledore, UK to replace the LORD OF THE ISLES on the Oban - Coll and Tiree and Oban - Castlebay and Lochboisdale service in the summer. She also serves as winter relief vessel on the Stornoway, Tarbert, Lochmaddy, Mull, Islay and Brodick routes.

EIGG Built at Port Glasgow, UK. Since 1976 she was employed mainly on the Oban - Lismore service. In 1996 she was transferred to the Tobermory (Mull) - Kilchoan route, very occasionally making special sailings to the Small Isles (Canna, Eigg, Muck and Rum) for special cargoes. In 1999 her wheelhouse was raised to make it easier to see over taller lorries and she returned to the Oban - Lismore route.

HEBRIDEAN ISLES Built at Selby UK for the Uig - Tarbert/Lochmaddy service. She was used initially on the Ullapool - Stornoway and Oban - Craignure/Colonsay services pending installation of link-span facilities at Uig, Tarbert and Lochmaddy. She took up her regular role in May 1986. Since May 1996 she no longer operated direct services between Tarbert and Lochmaddy, this role being taken on by the new Harris - North Uist services of the LOCH BHRUSDA. In 2001 replaced by the HEBRIDES and transferred to the Islay service.

HEBRIDES Built at Port Glasgow, UK for the Uig - Tarbert and Uig - Lochmaddy services.

ISLE OF ARRAN Built at Port Glasgow, UK for the Ardrossan - Brodick service. In 1993 transferred to the Kennacraig - Port Ellen/Port Askaig service, also undertaking the weekly Port Askaig -

Isle of Mull *(Miles Cowsill)*

Colonsay - Oban summer service. Until 1997/98 she also relieved on the Brodick, Coll/Tiree, Castlebay/Lochboisdale, Craignure and Tarbert/Lochmaddy routes in winter. In 2001 replaced by the HEBRIDEAN ISLES and is now reserve for the larger vessels. She also operates between Ullapool and Stornoway, as back-up to the ISLE OF LEWIS.

ISLE OF CUMBRAE Built at Troon, UK for the Largs - Cumbrae Slip (Cumbrae) service. In 1986 she was replaced by the LOCH LINNHE and the LOCH STRIVEN and transferred to the Lochaline - Fishnish (Mull) service. She used to spend most of the winter as secondary vessel on the Kyle of Lochalsh - Kyleakin service; however this ceased following the opening of the Skye Bridge in 1995. In 1997 she was transferred to the Colintraive - Rhubodach service. In summer 1999 she was transferred to the Tarbert - Portavadie service.

ISLE OF LEWIS Built at Port Glasgow, UK for the Ullapool - Stornoway service.

ISLE OF MULL Built at Port Glasgow, UK for the Oban - Craignure (Mull) service. She also operates the Oban - Colonsay service and until 1997/98 was the usual winter relief vessel on the Ullapool - Stornoway service. She has also deputised on the Oban - Castlebay/Lochboisdale and Oban - Coll/Tiree routes.

JUNO, JUPITER, SATURN Built at Port Glasgow, UK for the Gourock - Dunoon, Gourock - Kilcreggan and Wemyss Bay - Rothesay services. The JUPITER has been upgraded to Class III standard for the Ardrossan - Brodick service. Before 1986, the JUNO and JUPITER operated mainly on the Gourock - Dunoon and Gourock - Kilcreggan (now withdrawn) services and the SATURN on the Wemyss Bay - Rothesay service. Since 1986 they have usually rotated on a three weekly basis on the three services; until 2000 this, in summer, included Clyde cruising but this was not repeated in 2001.

LOCH ALAINN Built at Buckie, UK for the Lochaline - Fishnish service. Launched as the LOCH ALINE but renamed the LOCH ALAINN before entering service. After a brief period on the service she was built for, she was transferred to the Colintraive - Rhubodach route. In summer 1998 she was transferred to the Largs - Cumbrae Slip service.

LOCH BHRUSDA Built at Bromborough, Birkenhead, UK to inaugurate a new Otternish (North Uist) - Berneray - Leverburgh (Harris) service. In 2001 the service became Berneray - Leverburgh. In 2003 to be moved to the Eriskay - Barra service currently operated by *Comhairle Nan Eilean Siar* vessels. Note 'Bhrusda' is pronounced "Vroosda".

LOCH BUIE Built at St Monans, UK for the Fionnphort (Mull) - Iona service to replace the MORVERN (see *Arranmore Island Ferry Services*) and obviate the need for a relief vessel in the summer. Due to height restrictions, loading arrangements for vehicles taller than private cars are bow only. Only islanders' cars and service vehicles (eg mail vans, police) are carried; no tourist vehicles are conveyed.

LOCH DUNVEGAN Built at Port Glasgow, UK for the Kyle of Lochalsh - Kyleakin service. On the opening of the Skye Bridge in October 1995 she was withdrawn from service and put up for sale. In autumn 1997, returned to service on the Lochaline - Fishnish route. In 1998 she was due to be transferred to the Colintraive - Rhubodach route but this was delayed due to problems in providing terminal facilities. She operated on the Clyde and between Mallaig and Armadale during the early summer and spent the rest of the summer laid up. In 1999 she was transferred to the Colintraive - Rhubodach route.

LOCH FYNE Built at Port Glasgow UK for the Kyle of Lochalsh - Kyleakin service (see the LOCH DUNVEGAN). In autumn 1997, she also served on the Lochaline - Fishnish route and was transferred to this route as regular vessel in 1998.

LOCH LINNHE Built at Hessle, UK. Until 1997 she was used mainly on the Largs - Cumbrae Slip (Cumbrae) service and until winter 1994/95 she was usually used on the Lochaline - Fishnish service during the winter. Since then she had relieved on various routes in winter. In summer 1998 she operated mainly on the Tarbert - Portavadie route. In 1999 she was transferred to the summer only Tobermory - Kilchoan service.

LOCH RANZA Built at Hessle, UK for the Claonaig - Lochranza (Arran) seasonal service and used a relief vessel in the winter. In 1992 she was replaced by the LOCH TARBERT and transferred to the

Tayinloan - Gigha service.

LOCH RIDDON Built at Hessle, UK. Until 1997 she was used almost exclusively on the Colintraive - Rhubodach service. In 1997, she was transferred to the Largs - Cumbrae Slip service.

LOCH STRIVEN Built at Hessle, UK. Used mainly on the Largs - Cumbrae Slip service until 1997. In winter 1995/6 and 1996/67 she was used on the Tarbert - Portavadie and Claonaig - Lochranza routes. In 1997 she took over the Sconser - Raasay service.

LOCH TARBERT Built at St Monans, UK for the Claonaig - Lochranza service. She has been the regular winter vessel on the Largs - Cumbrae Slip route since winter 1994/5 and is also the winter relief vessel for the Otternish - Leverburgh route.

LOCHNEVIS Built at Troon, UK to replace the LOCHMOR on the Mallaig - Small Isles service and the winter Mallaig - Armadale service. Although a vehicle ferry, cars are not normally carried to the Small Isles; the ro-ro facility is used for the carriage of agricultural machinery and livestock and it is possible to convey a vehicle on the ferry from which goods can be unloaded directly onto local transport rather than transhipping at Mallaig. Ramps are being provided at each island and, when complete, the practice of tendering at Eigg, Muck and Rum will cease, the LAIG BAY being disposed of.

LORD OF THE ISLES Built at Port Glasgow, UK to replace the CLAYMORE on the Oban - Castlebay and Lochboisdale services and also the COLUMBA (1420t, 1964) on the Oban - Coll and Tiree service. She took over Mallaig - Armadale and Mallaig - Outer Isles service in July 1998 but returns to her previous routes during the winter period.

PIONEER Built at Leith, UK to operate on the West Loch Tarbert - Port Ellen service (see the PENTALINA B, *Pentland Ferries*). When the IONA was at last able to operate this service in 1978 (following the move to Kennacraig) the PIONEER was transferred to the Mallaig - Armadale service, operating as a relief vessel in the winter on Upper Clyde and Small Isles routes. In 1989 she was replaced at Mallaig by the IONA and became the company's spare vessel, replacing the GLEN SANNOX (1269t, 1957). Since summer 1995 she has undertaken Wemyss Bay - Rothesay and Rothesay - Largs - Brodick sailings. She serves as a Clyde and Small Isles relief vessel in the winter replacing the JUNO, JUPITER, SATURN and LOCHNEVIS for annual overhaul. In 1998 she opened the Mallaig - Armadale/Outer Isles service and temporarily operated between Oban and Craignure before returning to the Clyde in July. In summer 2000 she operated on the Wemyss Bay - Rothesay route. Her role as reserve for the larger vessels has ceased following the delivery of the HEBRIDES but she continued to operate on the Wemyss Bay - Rothesay route in 2001 and this was repeated in 2002.

RAASAY Built at Port Glasgow, UK for and used primarily on the Sconser (Skye) - Raasay service. In 1997 she was replaced by the LOCH STRIVEN and became a spare/relief vessel.

SATURN Built at Troon, UK. As the JUNO and JUPITER. In earlier days operated mainly on the Wemyss Bay - Rothesay service.

Caledonian MacBrayne also operates the LAIG BAY, a 10.5m motor vessel built in 2000 and carrying up to 35 passengers. She tenders to the LOCHNEVIS at Eigg. She will be withdrawn and sold when a ramp is built on the island.

SECTION 2 – DOMESTIC SERVICES

Under construction

29	NEWBUILDING 1	-	03	14k	60m	250P	40C	-	BA	UK
30	NEWBUILDING 2	-	03	11k	50m	200P	32C	-	BA	UK

NEWBUILDING 1 Under construction at Appledore, UK. To replace the LORD OF THE ISLES on the Mallaig - Armadale route during the summer. She will also operate on the Clyde during the winter. The LORD OF THE ISLES will move to Oban to provide additional capacity on routes from there.

NEWBUILDING 2 Under construction at Bromborough, Birkenhead, UK. To replace the LOCH BHRUSDA on the Otternish - Berneray - Leverburgh service. The LOCH BHRUSDA will be moved to the Eriskay - Barra route, replacing the *Comhairle Nan Eilean Siar* vessels currently used.

COMHAIRLE NAN EILEAN SIAR

THE COMPANY *Comhairle Nan Eilean Siar* (formerly the *Western Isles Council*) is a British municipal authority.

MANAGEMENT Director of Technical Services Murdo A Murray.

ADDRESS Balvanich, Isle of Benbecula, HS7 5LA.

TELEPHONE Administration +44 (0)1870 602425.

FAX Administration +44 (0)1870 602988.

INTERNET Email calum-mcleod@cne-siar.gov.uk **Website** www.cne-siar.gov.uk *(English)*

ROUTES OPERATED Car Ferry Ceann a Gharaidh (Eriskay) - Aird Mhor (Barra) (50 mins; *(1,2)*; up to 4 per day), **Note** *Comhairle Nan Eilean Siar* vessels will be replaced by *Caledonian MacBrayne's* LOCH BHRUSDA in 2003.

1	EILEAN BHEARNARAIGH	67t	83	7k	18.6m	35P	4C	-	B	UK
2	EILEAN NA H-OIGE	69t	80	7k	18.6m	35P	4C	-	B	UK

EILEAN BHEARNARAIGH Built at Glasgow, UK for *Western Isles Islands Council* for their Otternish (North Uist) - Berneray service. From 1996 until 1999 she was operated by *Caledonian MacBrayne* in conjunction with the LOCH BHRUSDA on the service between Otternish and Berneray and during the winter she was laid up. Following the opening of a causeway between North Uist and Berneray in early 1999, the ferry service ceased and she became reserve vessel for the Eriskay route. This route ceased in July 2001 following the opening of a causeway and she was laid up. In 2002 she started operating between Eriskay and Barra.

EILEAN NA H-OIGE Built at Stornoway, UK for *Western Isles Islands Council* (from 1st April 1996 the *Western Isles Council* and from 1st January 1998 *Comhairle Nan Eilean Siar*) for their Ludaig - Eriskay service. From 2000 operated from temporary slipway at the Eriskay causeway. This route ceased in July 2001 following the opening of a causeway and she was laid up. In 2002 she started operating between Eriskay and Barra.

CROMARTY - NIGG FERRY

THE COMPANY The Cromarty - Nigg Ferry is operated under contract to *The Highland Council*. Until 2001 it was operated by *Seaboard Marine (Nigg) Ltd*, British private company. It was put out to tender in later 2001. It will resume in spring 2002 but at the time of going to press it in not known who has been selected to operate the service. The vessel shown is that operated by *Seaboard Marine (Nigg) Ltd* until 2001.

ROUTE OPERATED *Summer only* Cromarty - Nigg (Ross-shire) (10 mins; *(1)*; operates at peak times only).

1	CROMARTY ROSE	28t	87	8k	14.0m	50P	2C	-	B	UK

CROMARTY ROSE Built at Ardrossan, UK for *Seaboard Marine (Nigg) Ltd.*

CROSS RIVER FERRIES

THE COMPANY *Cross River Ferries Ltd* is an Irish Republic company, jointly owned by *Marine Transport Services Ltd* of Cobh and *Arklow Shipping Ltd* of Arklow, County Wicklow.

MANAGEMENT Operations Manager Eoin O'Sullivan.

ADDRESS Westlands House, Rushbrooke, Cobh, County Cork, Republic of Ireland.

TELEPHONE Administration +353 (0)21 481 1223, **Reservations** Not applicable.

FAX Administration +353 (0)21 481 2645, **Reservations** Not applicable.

ROUTE OPERATED Carrigaloe (near Cobh, on Great Island) - Glenbrook (Co Cork) (4 mins; *(1,2)*;

frequent service 07.00 - 00.15 (one or two vessels used according to demand)).

1	CARRIGALOE	‡225t	70	8k	49.1m	200P	27C	-	BA	IR
2	GLENBROOK	‡225t	71	8k	49.1m	200P	27C	-	BA	IR

CARRIGALOE, GLENBROOK Built at Newport (Gwent) UK as the KYLEAKIN and the LOCHALSH for *Caledonian Steam Packet Company* (later *Caledonian MacBrayne*) for the Kyle of Lochalsh - Kyleakin service. In 1991 replaced by the LOCH DUNVEGAN and the LOCH FYNE and sold to *Marine Transport Services Ltd* who renamed them the CARRIGALOE and the GLENBROOK respectively. They entered service in March 1993.

GLENELG - KYLERHEA FERRY

THE COMPANY The *Glenelg - Kylerhea Ferry* is privately operated.

MANAGEMENT Ferry Master R MacLeod.

ADDRESS Corriehallie, Inverinate, Kyle IV40 8HD.

TELEPHONE Administration & Reservations +44 (0)1599 511302.

FAX Administration & Reservations +44 (0)1599 511477.

INTERNET Email roddy@skyeferry.co.uk **Website** www.skyeferry.co.uk *(English)*

ROUTE OPERATED ***Easter - October only*** Glenelg - Kylerhea (Skye) (10 mins; *(1)*; frequent service).

1	GLENACHULISH	44t	69	9k	20.0m	12P	6C	-	BSt	UK

GLENACHULISH Built at Troon, UK for the *Ballachulish Ferry Company* for the service between North Ballachulish and South Ballachulish, across the mouth of Loch Leven. In 1975 the ferry was replaced by a bridge and she was sold to *Highland Regional Council* and used on a relief basis on the North Kessock - South Kessock and Kylesku - Kylestrome routes. In 1984 she was sold to the operator of the Glenelg - Kylerhea service. She is the last turntable ferry in operation.

THE HIGHLAND COUNCIL

THE COMPANY *The Highland Council* (previously *Highland Regional Council*) is a British local government authority.

MANAGEMENT Area Road & Transport Manager James C Tolmie, **Ferry Manager** J McAuslane.

ADDRESS ***Area Office*** Lochybridge Depot, Carr's Corner Industrial Estate, Fort William PH33 6TQ, ***Ferry Office*** Ferry Cottage, Ardgour, Fort William.

TELEPHONE Administration ***Area Office*** +44 (0)1397 703701, ***Corran*** +44 (0)1855 841243, ***Camusnagaul*** +44 (0)1397 772483, **Reservations** Not applicable.

FAX Administration ***Area Office*** +44 (0)1397 705735, ***Corran*** +44 (0)1855 841243, **Reservations** Not applicable.

ROUTES OPERATED Conventional Ferries Corran - Ardgour (5 mins; *(2,3)*; half hourly), **Passenger Only Ferry** Fort William - Camusnagaul (10 mins; *(1)*; Frequent).

1p	CAILIN AN AISEAG	-	80	7.5k	9.8m	26P	0C	0L	-	UK
2	CORRAN	351t	01	10k	42.0m	150P	30C	2L	BA	UK
3	MAID OF GLENCOUL	‡166t	75	8k	32.0m	116P	16C	1L	BA	UK

CAILIN AN AISEAG Built at Buckie, UK for *Highland Regional Council* and used on the Fort William - Camusnagaul service.

CORRAN Built at Hull, UK for *The Highland Council* to replace the MAID OF GLENCOUL as main vessel.

MAID OF GLENCOUL Built at Ardrossan, UK for *Highland Regional Council* for the service between

John Burns *(Matthew Punter)*

Red Jet 2 *(Andrew Cooke)*

Kylesku and Kylestrome. In 1984 the ferry service was replaced by a bridge and she was transferred to the Corran - Ardgour service. In April 1996, ownership transferred to *The Highland Council*. In 2001 became the reserve vessel.

ISLES OF SCILLY STEAMSHIP COMPANY

THE COMPANY *Isles of Scilly Steamship Company* is a British private sector company.

MANAGEMENT Group Operations Manager R Johns, **Marketing Manager** J Hoelen.

ADDRESS *Scilly* PO Box 10, Hugh Town, St Mary's, Isles of Scilly TR21 0LJ, ***Penzance*** Steamship House, Quay Street, Penzance, Cornwall, TR18 4BD.

TELEPHONE Administration & Reservations *Scilly* +44 (0)1720 422357, ***Penzance*** +44 (0)1736 334220.

FAX Administration & Reservations *Scilly* +44 (0)1720 422192, ***Penzance*** +44 (0)1736 351223.

INTERNET Email sales@islesofscilly-travel.co.uk **Website** www.islesofscilly-travel.co.uk *(English)*

ROUTES OPERATED *Passenger service* Penzance - St Mary's (Isles of Scilly) (2 hrs 40 mins; *(1,3)*; 1 per day), ***Freight services*** St Mary's - Tresco/St Martin's/St Agnes/Bryher; *(2)*; irregular).

1	GRY MARITHA	590t	81	10.5k	57.2m	12P	5C	1L	C	UK
2	LYONESSE LADY	50t	91	9k	-	12P	1C	0L	A	UK
3	SCILLONIAN III	1256t	77	15.5k	67.7m	600P	-	-	C	UK

GRY MARITHA Built at Kolvereid, Norway for *Gjofor* of Norway. In design she is a coaster rather than a ferry. In 1990 sold to *Isles of Scilly Steamship Company*. She operates a freight and passenger service all year (conveying all residents' cars and other vehicles to and from the islands - tourist cars are not conveyed). During the winter she provides the only sea passenger service to the islands, the SCILLONIAN III being laid up.

LYONESSE LADY Built at Fort William UK, for inter-island ferry work. Does not normally convey passengers.

SCILLONIAN III Built at Appledore, UK for the Penzance - St Mary's service. She operates from Easter to late autumn and is laid up in the winter. Last major conventional passenger/cargo ferry built for UK waters and probably Western Europe. Extensively refurbished during winter 1998/99. Note the SCILLONIAN III can carry cars in her hold as cargo; however, since the purchase of the GRY MARITHA most cars conveyed to and from the island have been carried on this vessel and she has functioned as a passenger vessel.

KERRERA FERRY

THE COMPANY The *Kerrera Ferry* is privately operated.

MANAGEMENT Ferry Master Duncan MacEachen.

ADDRESS The Ferry, Isle of Kerrera, By Oban PA34 4SX.

TELEPHONE Administration +44 (0)1631 563665.

ROUTE OPERATED Gallanach (Argyll) - Kerrera (5 mins; *(1)*; on demand 10.30 - 12.30 and 14.00 - 18.00, Easter - October, other times by arrangement).

1	GYLEN LADY	9t	99	8k	10.0m	12P	1C	-	B	UK

GYLEN LADY Built at Corpach, UK to inaugurate a vehicle ferry service to the Isle of Kerrera, replacing open passenger boat.

SECTION 2 - DOMESTIC SERVICES

MURPHY'S FERRY SERVICE

THE COMPANY *Murphy's Ferry Service* is privately operated.

MANAGEMENT Operator Patrick Murphy.

ADDRESS Lawrence Cove, Bere Island, Co Cork, Republic of Ireland.

TELEPHONE Administration +353 (0)27 75014 **Mobile** +353 (0)87 2386095.

FAX Administration +353 (0)27 75014.

INTERNET Email murpferr@eircom.net **Website** www.murphysferry.com *(English)*

ROUTE OPERATED Castletownbere (Pontoon - 3 miles to east of town centre) - Bere Island (Lawrence Cove, near Rerrin) (20 mins ; *(1)*; up to 8 per day).

1	IKOM K	55t	99	10k	16.0m	60P	4C	1L	B	IR

IKOM K Built at Arklow, Irish Republic for *Murphy's Ferry Service*.

NORTHLINK ORKNEY AND SHETLAND FERRIES

THE COMPANY *NorthLink Orkney and Shetland Ferries* is a Scottish company jointly owned by *Caledonian MacBrayne* and *The Royal Bank of Scotland*. It is due to take over service from Scotland to Orkney and Shetland from *P&O Scottish Ferries* in October 2002.

MANAGEMENT Chief Executive John Horton, **Marketing Manager** Gareth Crichton.

ADDRESS The New Harbour Building, Ferry Road, Stromness, Orkney KW16 3BH.

TELEPHONE Administration +44 (0)1856 851144.

FAX Administration +44 (0)1856 851155.

INTERNET Email info@northlinkferries.co.uk **Website** www.northlinkferries.co.uk *(English)*

ROUTES OPERATED ***From October 2002*** Scrabster - Stromness (Orkney) (1 hr 30 min; *(1)*; up to 3 per day), Aberdeen - Lerwick (Shetland) (direct) (12 hrs; *(2,3)*; 4 per week), Aberdeen - Kirkwall, Hatston New Harbour (Orkney) (5 hrs) - Lerwick (14 hrs; *(2,3)*; 3 per week.

Under Construction

1	HAMNAVOE	8600t	02	19k	110.0m	600P	95C	20L	BA	UK
2	HJALTLAND	12000t	02	24k	125.0m	600P	150C	30L	BA	UK
3	HROSSEY	12000t	02	24k	125.0m	600P	150C	30L	BA	UK

HAMNAVOE Under construction in Rauma, Finland for *NorthLink Orkney and Shetland Ferries* to operate on the Scrabster - Stromness route when services start in 2002.

HJALTLAND, HROSSEY Under construction in Rauma, Finland for *NorthLink Orkney and Shetland Ferries* to operate on the Aberdeen - Stromness - Lerwick route when services start in 2002.

ORKNEY FERRIES

THE COMPANY *Orkney Ferries Ltd* (previously the *Orkney Islands Shipping Company*) is a British company, owned by *The Orkney Islands Council*.

MANAGEMENT Operations Director N H Mills, **Ferry Services Manager** A Learmonth.

ADDRESS Shore Street, Kirkwall, Orkney KW15 1LG.

TELEPHONE Administration +44 (0)1856 872044, **Reservations** +44 (0)1856 872044.

FAX Administration & Reservations +44 (0)1856 872921, **Telex** 75475.

INTERNET Email info@orkneyferries.co.uk **Website** www.orkneyferries.co.uk *(English)*

ROUTES OPERATED Kirkwall (Mainland) to Eday (1 hr, 15 mins), Westray (1 hr 25 mins), Sanday (1 hr 25 mins), Stronsay (1 hr 35 mins), Papa Westray (1 hr 50 mins), North Ronaldsay (2 hrs 30 mins) ('North Isles service') (timings are direct from Kirkwall - sailings via other islands take longer; *(1,2,9)*; 1 per day except Papa Westray which is twice weekly and North Ronaldsay which is weekly), Pierowall (Westray) - Papa Westray (25 mins; *(4)*; up to six per day (passenger only)), Kirkwall - Shapinsay (25 mins; *(7)*; 6 per day), Houton (Mainland) to Lyness (Hoy) (35 mins; *(6)*; 5 per day), and Flotta (35 mins; *(6)*; 4 per day) ('South Isles service') (timings are direct from Houton - sailings via other islands take longer), Tingwall (Mainland) to Rousay (20 mins; *(3)*; 6 per day), Egilsay (30 mins; *(3)*; 5 per day) and Wyre (20 mins; *(3)*; 5 per day) (timings are direct from Tingwall - sailings via other islands take longer), Stromness (Mainland) to Moaness (Hoy) (25 mins; *(5)*; 2/3 per day) and Graemsay (25 mins; *(5)*; 2/3 per day) (passenger/cargo service - cars not normally conveyed).

1	EARL SIGURD	771t	90	12k	45.4m	190P	26C	-	BA	UK
2	EARL THORFINN	771t	90	12k	45.4m	190P	26C	-	BA	UK
3	EYNHALLOW	79t	87	9.5k	26.2m	95P	8C	-	BA	UK
4p	GOLDEN MARIANA	33t	73	9.5k	16.2m	40P	0C	-	-	UK
5	GRAEMSAY	82t	96	10k	17.1m	73P	1C	-	C	UK
6	HOY HEAD	358t	94	9.8k	39.6m	125P	18C	-	BA	UK
7	SHAPINSAY	199t	89	9.5k	30.2m	91P	12C	-	BA	UK
8	THORSVOE	400t	91	10.5k	35.1m	96P	16C	-	BA	UK
9	VARAGEN	950t	89	12k	50.0m	144P	33C	5L	BA	UK

EARL SIGURD, EARL THORFINN Built at Bromborough, Birkenhead, UK to inaugurate ro-ro working on the 'North Isles' service (see above).

EYNHALLOW Built at Bristol, UK to inaugurate ro-ro services from Tingwall (Mainland) to Rousay, Egilsay and Wyre. In 1991 she was lengthened by 5 metres, to increase car capacity.

GOLDEN MARIANA Built at Bideford, UK. Passenger only vessel. Generally operates feeder service between Pierowall (Westray) and Papa Westray.

GRAEMSAY Built at Troon UK to operate between Stromness (Mainland), Moaness (Hoy) and Graemsay. Designed to offer an all year round service to these islands, primarily for passengers and cargo.

HOY HEAD Built at Bideford, UK to replace the THORSVOE on the 'South Isles' service (see above).

SHAPINSAY Built at Hull, UK for the service from Kirkwall (Mainland) to Shapinsay.

THORSVOE Built at Campbeltown, UK for the 'South Isles' service (see above). In 1994 replaced by new HOY HEAD and became the main reserve vessel for the fleet.

VARAGEN Built at Selby, UK for *Orkney Ferries*, a private company established to start a new route between Gills Bay (Caithness, Scotland) and Burwick (South Ronaldsay, Orkney). However, due to problems with the terminals it was not possible to maintain regular services. In 1991, the company was taken over by *OISC* and the VARAGEN became part of their fleet, sharing 'North Isles' services with the EARL SIGURD and the EARL THORFINN and replacing the freight vessel ISLANDER (494t, 1969).

P&O SCOTTISH FERRIES

THE COMPANY *P&O Scottish Ferries* is British private sector company, a subsidiary of the *Peninsular and Oriental Steam Navigation Company.* The name was changed from *P&O Ferries* to *P&O Scottish Ferries* in 1989. The service will cease in October 2002, when *NorthLink Orkney and Shetland Ferries* take over.

MANAGEMENT Managing Director Terry Cairns.

ADDRESS PO Box 5, Jamieson's Quay, Aberdeen AB11 5NP.

TELEPHONE Administration +44 (0)1224 589111, **Reservations** +44 (0)1224 572615.

FAX Administration & Reservations +44 (0)1224 574411.

INTERNET Email passenger@poscottishferries.co.uk **Website** www.posf.co.uk *(English)*

ROUTES OPERATED ***Until end of September 2002*** Scrabster - Stromness (Orkney) (1 hr 45 mins; *(2)*; up to 3 per day)), Aberdeen - Lerwick (Shetland) (direct) (14 hrs; *(1,3)*; up to 4 per week), Aberdeen - Stromness (8 hrs (day), 14 hrs (night)) - Lerwick (8 hrs; *(3)*; 1 per week.

1	ST CLAIR	8696t	71	19k	118.0m	600P	160C	30L	A	UK
2	ST OLA	4833t	71	16k	85.9m	500P	140C	12L	BA	UK
3	ST SUNNIVA	6350t	71	16k	104.6m	400P	199C	28L	A	UK

ST CLAIR Built at Bremerhaven, Germany as the TRAVEMÜNDE for *Gedser-Travemünde Ruten* for their service between Gedser (Denmark) and Travemünde (Germany). In 1981 she was sold to *Prekookeanska Plovidba* of Yugoslavia, renamed the NJEGOS and used on their services between Yugoslavia, Greece and Italy. In 1984 chartered to *Sally Line* for use on their Ramsgate - Dunkerque service. In 1985 she was taken on a two year charter by *Brittany Ferries*, renamed the TREGASTEL and moved to the Plymouth - Roscoff service. In 1987 she was purchased and re-registered in France. In 1989 she was replaced by the QUIBERON and transferred to *Truckline Ferries* for their Poole - Cherbourg service. In 1991 she was renamed the TREG and sold to *P&O Scottish Ferries.* Following a major refit she was, in 1992, renamed the ST CLAIR and in March 1992 introduced onto the Aberdeen - Lerwick service, replacing the previous ST CLAIR (4468t, 1965). In addition to operating between Aberdeen and Lerwick, in 1993 she inaugurated a weekly peak season Lerwick - Bergen (Norway) service; this service last operated in 1997.

ST OLA Built at Papenburg Germany as the SVEA SCARLETT for *Stockholms Rederi AB Svea* of Sweden and used on the *SL (Skandinavisk Linjetrafik)* service between Copenhagen (Tuborg Havn) and Landskrona (Sweden). In 1980 she was sold to *Scandinavian Ferry Lines* of Sweden and *Dampskibsselskabet Øresund A/S* of Denmark (jointly owned). Initially she continued to serve Landskrona but later that year the Swedish terminal became Malmö. In 1981 she operated on the Helsingborg - Helsingør service for a short while, after which she was withdrawn and laid up. In 1982 she was sold to *Eckerö Linjen* of Finland, renamed the ECKERÖ and used on services between Grisslehamn (Sweden) and Eckerö (Åland Islands). In 1991 she was sold to *P&O Scottish Ferries* and renamed the ST OLA. In March 1992 she replaced the previous ST OLA (1345t, 1974) on the Scrabster - Stromness service.

ST SUNNIVA Built at Helsingør, Denmark as the DJURSLAND for *Jydsk Færgefart* of Denmark for their service between Grenaa (Jutland) and Hundested (Sealand). In 1974 she was replaced by a larger vessel called DJURSLAND II (4371t, 1974) and switched to the company's other route, between Juelsminde (Jutland) and Kalundborg (Sealand), being renamed the LASSE II. In 1979 she was sold to *P&O Ferries*, renamed the N F PANTHER ('N F' standing for *'Normandy Ferries'*) and became the third vessel on the Dover - Boulogne service. Sold to *European Ferries* in 1985 and in summer 1986 replaced (with sister vessel NF TIGER (4045t, 1972)) by the FREE ENTERPRISE IV (5049t, 1969) and FREE ENTERPRISE V (5044t, 1970). In 1987 sold to *P&O Scottish Ferries*, renamed the ST SUNNIVA, converted to an overnight ferry and introduced onto the Aberdeen - Lerwick service, supplementing ST CLAIR and also providing a weekly Aberdeen - Stromness - Lerwick and return service (twice weekly in high summer).

PASSAGE EAST FERRY

THE COMPANY *Passage East Ferry Company Ltd* is an Irish Republic private sector company.

MANAGEMENT Managing Director Derek Donnelly. **Operations Manager** Conor Gilligan.

ADDRESS Barrack Street, Passage East, Co Waterford, Republic of Ireland.

TELEPHONE Administration +353 (0)51 382480, **Reservations** Not applicable.

FAX Administration +353 (0)51 382598, **Reservations** Not applicable.

INTERNET Email passageferry@eircom.net **Website** www.passageferry.com *(English)*

ROUTE OPERATED Passage East (County Waterford) - Ballyhack (County Wexford) (7 mins; *(1)*; frequent service).

1	EDMUND D	300t	68	9k	45.1m	143P	30C	-	BA	IR

EDMUND D Built at Dartmouth UK as the SHANNON HEATHER for *Shannon Ferry Ltd* and used on their service between Killimer (County Clare) and Tarbert (County Kerry). Withdrawn from regular service in 1996 and, in 1997, sold to *Passage East Ferry* and renamed the EDMUND D. She entered service in January 1998.

PENTLAND FERRIES

THE COMPANY *Pentland Ferries* is a UK private sector company.

Managing Director Andrew Banks, **Marketing Manager** Linda Knott.

ADDRESS Pier Road, St Margaret's Hope, South Ronaldsay, Orkney KW172SW.

TELEPHONE Administration & Reservations +44 (0)1856 831226.

FAX Administration & Reservations +44 (0)1856 831614.

INTERNET Email sales@pentlandferries.co.uk **Website** www.pentlandferries.com *(English)*

ROUTE OPERATED ***Summer only*** Gills Bay (Scotland) - St Margaret's Hope (South Ronaldsay, Orkney) (1 hr; *(1)*; 3 per day).

1	PENTALINA B	1908t	70	16k	74.3m	250P	46C	7L	BAS	UK

PENTALINA B Built at Troon, UK as the IONA for *David MacBrayne*. She was built to operate the Islay service. However, shortly after the order was placed, plans to build a new pier at Redhouse, near the mouth of West Loch Tarbert, were abandoned, so she was not able to operate on this route until *Caledonian MacBrayne* acquired the *Western Ferries'* pier in deeper water at Kennacraig in 1978. She operated on the Gourock - Dunoon service in 1970 and 1971, between Mallaig and Kyle of Lochalsh and Stornoway in 1972 and between Oban and Craignure in 1973. From 1974 until 1978 she operated mainly on the Oban to Castlebay/Lochboisdale service and in addition the winter Oban - Coll/Tiree route. From 1978 until 1989 she operated mainly on the Islay service. In 1989 she was replaced by the CLAYMORE and then replaced the PIONEER as the summer Mallaig - Armadale vessel. Full ro-ro working was introduced on the route in 1994 and she also operated a twice weekly sailing between Mallaig, Lochboisdale and Castlebay and, in 1997, a weekly Mallaig - Coll and Tiree sailing. She was withdrawn in October 1997 and sold to *Pentland Ferries*. In 1998 she was renamed the PENTALINA B. In spring 1998 she was chartered back to *Caledonian MacBrayne* to operate between Oban and Craignure following the breakdown of the ISLE OF MULL. *Pentland Ferries* services started in summer 2001.

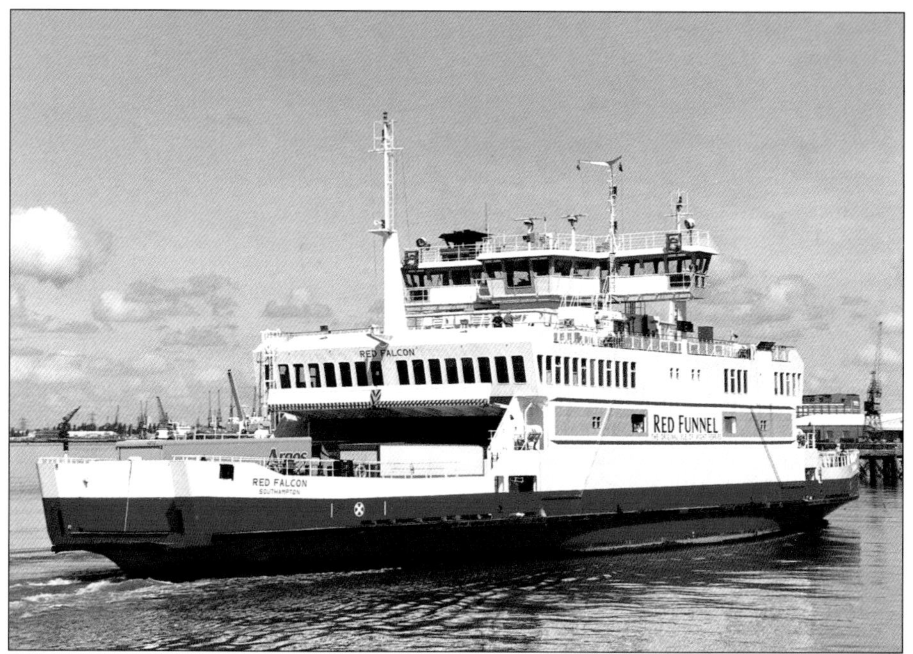

Red Falcon *(Andrew Cooke)*

RED FUNNEL FERRIES

THE COMPANY *Red Funnel Ferries* is the trading name of the *Southampton Isle of Wight and South of England Royal Mail Steam Packet Public Limited Company*, a British private sector company. The company was acquired by *JP Morgan International Capital Corporation* in 2000.

MANAGEMENT Managing Director A M Whyte, **Marketing Director** Ms O H Glass.

ADDRESS 12 Bugle Street, Southampton SO14 2JY.

TELEPHONE Administration +44 (0)23 8033 3042, **Reservations** +44 (0)23 8033 4010.

FAX Administration & Reservations +44 (0)23 8063 9438.

INTERNET Email admin@redfunnel.co.uk **Website** www.redfunnel.co.uk *(English)*

ROUTES OPERATED Conventional Ferries Southampton - East Cowes (55 mins; *(1,2,6)*; hourly). **Fast Passenger Ferries** Southampton - Cowes (20 mins; *(3,4,5)*; every half hour).

1	RED EAGLE	3028t	96	13k	83.6m	895P	140C	16L	BA	UK
2	RED FALCON	2881t	94	13k	83.6m	895P	140C	16L	BA	UK
3»p	RED JET 1	168t	91	34k	31.5m	138P	0C	0L	-	UK
4»p	RED JET 2	168t	91	34k	31.5m	138P	0C	0L	-	UK
5»p	RED JET 3	213t	98	34k	32.9m	190P	0C	0L	-	UK
6	RED OSPREY	2881t	94	13k	83.6m	895P	140C	16L	BA	UK
7»p•	SHEARWATER 5	62t	80	32k	21.9m	67P	0C	0L	-	UK
8»p•	SHEARWATER 6	62t	82	32k	21.9m	67P	0C	0L	-	UK

RED EAGLE, RED FALCON, RED OSPREY Built at Port Glasgow, UK for the Southampton - East

Columba (Colin Smith)

Cowes service.

RED JET 1, RED JET 2, RED JET 3 FBM Marine catamarans built at Cowes, UK for the Southampton - Cowes service.

SHEARWATER 5 Rodriquez RHS40 hydrofoil built at Messina, Italy for the Southampton - Cowes service. Now laid up.

SHEARWATER 6 Rodriquez RHS40 hydrofoil built at Messina, Italy for the Southampton - Cowes service. In 1998 withdrawn and laid up.

SHANNON FERRY LTD

THE COMPANY *Shannon Ferry Ltd* is an Irish Republic private company owned by six families on both sides of the Shannon Estuary.

MANAGEMENT Managing Director J J Meehan.

ADDRESS Ferry Terminal, Killimer, County Clare, Republic of Ireland.

TELEPHONE Administration +353 (0)65 9053124, **Reservations** Not applicable.

FAX Administration +353 (0)65 9053125, **Reservations** Not applicable.

INTERNET Email enquiries@shannonferries.com **Website** www.shannonferries.com *(English, German, French, Italian)*

ROUTE OPERATED Killimer (County Clare) - Tarbert (County Kerry) (20 mins; *(1,2)*; hourly (half hourly during June, July, August and September). The company is also planning to establish a new service been Headford and Oughterard in Country Galway, across Lake Corrib. The vessel would be cable operated and accommodate up to 24 cars. It is unlikely to start before 2003/4.

1	SHANNON BREEZE	611t	00	10k	80.8m	350P	60C	-	BA	IR
2	SHANNON DOLPHIN	501t	95	10k	71.9m	350P	52C	-	BA	IR
3•	SHANNON WILLOW	360t	78	10k	47.9m	300P	44C	-	BA	IR

SHANNON BREEZE, SHANNON DOLPHIN Built at Appledore, UK for *Shannon Ferry Ltd.*

SHANNON WILLOW Built at Bowling, Dumbarton, UK for *Shannon Ferry Ltd.* In 2000 replaced by the SHANNON BREEZE and laid up for sale.

SHETLAND ISLANDS COUNCIL

THE COMPANY *Shetland Islands Council* is a British Local Government authority.

MANAGEMENT Director of Marine Operations Capt G H Sutherland, FNI, MRIN, **Divisional Manager - Ferry Operations** Capt Michael J Hogan MNI, **Marine Superintendents** Capt William MacTear MNI and Capt William Clark AMNI.

ADDRESS Port Administration Building, Sella Ness, Mossbank, Shetland ZE2 9QR.

TELEPHONE Administration +44 (0)1806 244216, 244262, 244252, **Reservations** +44 (0)1957 722259, **Voice Banks** +44 (0)1426 980317 (Bressay), +44 (0)1426 983633 (Fair Isle, Foula), +44 (0)1426 980209 (Unst/Fetlar), +44 (0)1426 983633 (Whalsay), +44(0)1426 980735 (Yell).

FAX Administration & Reservations +44 (0)1806 242237, **Telex** 75142 Sulvoe G.

INTERNET Emails marine.ferries@shetland.gov.uk Mike.Hoga@sic.shetland.gov.uk

Lara.Jamieson@sic.shetland.gov.uk Bill.Mactearn@sic.shetland.gov.uk Bill.Clark@sic.shetland.gov.uk

Website www.shetland.gov.uk/ferryinfo/ferry.htm *(English)*

ROUTES OPERATED Toft (Mainland) - Ulsta (Yell) (20 mins; *(1,5)*; up to 26 per day), Gutcher (Yell) - Belmont (Unst) (10 mins; *(3)*; 30 per day), Gutcher (Yell) - Oddsta (Fetlar) (25 mins; *(4)*; 6 per

SECTION 2 – DOMESTIC SERVICES

day), Lerwick (Mainland) - Maryfield (Bressay) (5 mins; *(10)*; 19 per day), Laxo (Mainland) - Symbister (Whalsay) (30 mins; *(8,12)*; 17 per day), Vidlin (Mainland) - Symbister (Whalsay) (30-45 mins; *(8,11)*; operates when weather conditions preclude using Laxo), Lerwick (Mainland) - Out Skerries (3 hrs; *(2)*; 2 per week), Vidlin (Mainland) - Out Skerries (1 hr 30 mins; *(2)*; 7 per week), Grutness (Mainland) - Fair Isle (3 hrs; *(6)*; 2 per week), West Burrafirth (Mainland) - Papa Stour (40 mins; *(9)*; 7 per week), Foula - Walls (Mainland) (3 hrs; *(12)*; 2 per week).

1	BIGGA	274t	91	11k	33.5m	96P	21C	4L	BA	UK
2	FILLA	130t	83	9k	24.4m	12P	6C	1L	A	UK
3	FIVLA	230t	85	11k	29.9m	95P	15C	4L	BA	UK
4	FYLGA	147t	75	8.5k	25.3m	93P	10C	2L	BA	UK
5	GEIRA	226t	88	10.8k	29.9m	95P	15C	4L	BA	UK
6	GOOD SHEPHERD IV	76t	86	10k	18.3m	12P	1C	0L	C	UK
7	GRIMA	147t	74	8.5k	25.3m	93P	10C	2L	BA	UK
8	HENDRA	225t	82	11k	33.8m	100P	18C	4L	BA	UK
9	KOADA	35t	69	8k	14.6m	12P	1C	0L	C	UK
10	LEIRNA	420t	92	9k	35.1m	100P	20C	4L	BA	UK
11	LINGA	400t	01	11k	35.8m	100P	16C	2L	BA	UK
12	NEW ADVANCE	25t	96	8.7k	9.8m	12P	1C	-	C	UK
13	THORA	147t	75	8.5k	25.3m	93P	10C	2L	BA	UK

BIGGA Built at St Monans, UK. Used on the Toft (Mainland) - Ulsta (Yell) service.

FILLA Built at Flekkefjord, Norway. Used on the Lerwick (Mainland) - Out Skerries and Vidlin (Mainland) - Out Skerries services. At other times she operates freight and charter services around the Shetland Archipelago. She resembles a miniature oil rig supply vessel. Passenger capacity was originally 20 from 1 April to 31 October inclusive but is now 12 all year. She will shortly be replaced by a larger vessel and she will be transferred to the West Burrafirth - Papa Stour route, replacing the KOADA. A new pier and linkspan will be built on the island.

FIVLA Built at Troon, UK. Used on the Gutcher (Yell) - Belmont (Unst) service.

FYLGA Built at Tórshavn, UK. Used on the Gutcher (Yell) - Oddsta (Fetlar) service.

GEIRA Built at Hessle, UK. Used on the Toft (Mainland) - Ulsta (Yell) service.

GOOD SHEPHERD IV Built at St Monans, UK. Used on the service between Grutness (Mainland) and Fair Isle. Vehicles conveyed by special arrangement and generally consist of agricultural vehicles. She is pulled up on marine slip on Fair Isle at the conclusion of each voyage.

GRIMA Built at Bideford, UK. Used on the Lerwick (Mainland) - Maryfield (Bressay) service until 1992 when she was replaced by the LEIRNA and became a spare vessel.

HENDRA Built at Bromborough, Birkenhead, UK. Used on the Laxo (Mainland) - Symbister (Whalsay) service.

KOADA Built at Bideford, UK. Built as an inshore trawler and bought by the shareholders on Fair Isle to operate to Shetland and named the GOOD SHEPHERD III. In 1986 the service was taken over by *Shetland Islands Council* and she was replaced by GOOD SHEPHERD IV. She was however acquired by the *Shetland Islands Council* and renamed the KOADA. She now operates between West Burrafirth (Mainland) and Papa Stour (operation to Foula having ceased following the delivery of the NEW ADVANCE). Car carrying capacity used occasionally. She is due to be replaced by the FILLA.

LEIRNA Built at Port Glasgow, UK. Used on the Lerwick - Maryfield (Bressay) service.

LINGA Diesel electric ro-ro passenger vessel built at Gdansk, Poland for the Symbister - Laxo service. She has replaced the THORA.

NEW ADVANCE Built at Penryn, UK for the Foula service. Although built at Penryn, she was completed at Stromness in Orkney. She has a Cygnus Marine GM38 hull and is based on the island where she can be lifted out of the water. Vehicle capacity is to take new vehicles to the island - not for tourist vehicles. Mainland ports used are Walls and Scalloway.

THORA Built at Tórshavn, Faroe Islands. Sister vessel to the FYLGA and the GRIMA. After a period as a spare vessel, in 1998 she took over the Laxo - Symbister service from the withdrawn KJELLA. Withdrawn in 2001. Now a spare vessel.

Planned orders

14	NEWBUILDING 1	-	04	12k	61m	145P	30C	4L	BA	UK
15	NEWBUILDING 2	-	04	12k	61m	145P	30C	4L	BA	UK

NEWBUILDING 1, NEWBUILDING 2 Diesel electric ro-ro passenger ferries to be ordered to replace the B1GGA and GEIRA on Yell Sound. These vessels will be used as spares and the THORA and GRIMA will be sold. This programme will be preceded with the construction of new terminals at Toft and Ulsta on Yell Sound.

STRANGFORD LOUGH FERRY SERVICE

THE COMPANY The *Strangford Lough Ferry Service* is operated by the *DRD (Department for Regional Development)*, a Northern Ireland Government Department (formerly operated by *DOE (Northern Ireland)*).

MANAGEMENT Ferry Manager D Pedlow.

ADDRESS Strangford Lough Ferry Service, Strangford, Co Down BT30 7NE.

TELEPHONE Administration +44 (0)28 4488 1637, **Reservations** Not applicable.

FAX Administration +44 (0)28 4488 1249, **Reservations** Not applicable.

ROUTE OPERATED Strangford - Portaferry (County Down) (10 mins; *(2,3)*; half hourly).

1•	PORTAFERRY	151t	62	9k	30.8m	200P	18C	-	BA	UK
2	PORTAFERRY II	312t	01	12k	38.2m	260P	28C	-	BA	UK
3	STRANGFORD FERRY	186t	69	10k	32.9m	263P	20C	-	BA	UK

PORTAFERRY Built at Pembroke, UK as the CLEDDAU KING for *Pembrokeshire County Council* (from 1974 *Dyfed County Council*) for their service between Hobbs Point (Pembroke Dock) and Neyland. Following the opening of a new bridge, the service ceased and, in 1976, she was sold to *DOE (Northern Ireland)* and renamed the PORTAFERRY. Now laid up for sale.

PORTAFERRY II Built at Bromborough, Birkenhead, UK for *DRD (Northern Ireland)* to replace the PORTAFERRY.

STRANGFORD FERRY Built at Cork, Irish Republic for *Down County Council*. Subsequently transferred to the *DOE (Northern Ireland)* and then the *DRD (Northern Ireland)*. Following delivery of the PORTAFERRY II, she became reserve ferry.

C TOMS & SON LTD

THE COMPANY *C Toms & Son Ltd* is a British private sector company.

MANAGEMENT Managing Director Mr Alan Toms.

ADDRESS East Street, Polruan, Fowey, Cornwall PL23 1PB.

TELEPHONE Administration +44 (0)1726 870232.

FAX Administration +44 (0)1726 870318.

ROUTE OPERATED Fowey - Bodinnick (Cornwall) (5 mins; *(1,2)*; frequent).

1	JENACK	60t	00	4.5k	36.0m	50P	15C	-	BA	UK
2	NO 4	-	75	-	15.8m	48P	8C	-	BA	-

JENACK Built at Fowey, UK by *C Toms & Sons Ltd*. Self propelled and steered.

NO 4 Built at Fowey, UK by *C Toms & Son Ltd*. Float propelled by motor launch.

VALENTIA ISLAND FERRIES

THE COMPANY *Valentia Island Ferries Ltd* is an Irish Republic private sector company.

MANAGEMENT Manager Richard Foran.

ADDRESS Valentia Island, County Kerry, Republic of Ireland.

TELEPHONE Administration +353 (0)66 76141, **Reservations** Not applicable.

FAX Administration +353 (0)66 76377, **Reservations** Not applicable.

INTERNET Email reforan@indigo.ie **Website** www.kerrygems.ie/valentiaferry/ *(English)*

ROUTE OPERATED Reenard (Co Kerry) - Knightstown (Valentia Island) (5 minutes; *(1)*; frequent service, 1st April - 30th September).

1	GOD MET ONS III	95t	63	-	43.0m	95P	18C	-	BA	IR

GOD MET ONS III Built at Millingen, Netherlands for *FMHE Res* of the Netherlands for a service across the River Maas between Cuijk and Middelaar. In 1987 a new bridge was opened and the service ceased. She was latterly used on contract work in the Elbe and then laid up. In 1996 acquired by *Valentia Island Ferries* and inaugurated a car ferry service to the island. Note: this island never had a car ferry service before. A bridge was opened at the south end of the island in 1970; before that a passenger/cargo service operated between Reenard Point and Knightstown.

WESTERN FERRIES

THE COMPANY *Western Ferries (Clyde) Ltd* is a British private sector company.

MANAGEMENT Managing Director Kenneth C Cadenhead.

ADDRESSES Hunter's Quay, Dunoon PA23 8HJ.

TELEPHONE Administration +44 (0)1369 704452, **Reservations** Not applicable.

FAX Administration +44 (0)1369 706020, **Reservations** Not applicable.

INTERNET Email enquiries@western-ferries.co.uk **Website** www.westernferriesclyde.co.uk *(English)*

ROUTE OPERATED McInroy's Point (Gourock) - Hunter's Quay (Dunoon) (20 mins; *(1,2,3,4,5)*; half hourly).

1	SOUND OF SANDA	403t	64	10k	48.4m	220P	37C	4/5L	BA	UK
2	SOUND OF SCALPAY	403t	61	10k	48.4m	220P	37C	4/5L	BA	UK
3	SOUND OF SCARBA	489t	01	11k	49.9m	220P	40C	4/5L	BA	UK
4	SOUND OF SHUNA	244t	62	10k	41.8m	200P	25C	4/5L	BA	UK
5	SOUND OF SLEAT	466t	61	10k	39.9m	296P	30C	4/5L	BA	UK

SOUND OF SANDA Built at Walsum, Germany as the G24 for *Amsterdam City Council* and operated from Centraal Station to the other side of the River IJ. In 1996 purchased by *Western Ferries* and renamed the SOUND OF SANDA.

SOUND OF SCALPAY Built at Arnhem, Netherlands as the G23 for *Amsterdam City Council*. In 1995 sold to *Western Ferries* and renamed the SOUND OF SCALPAY.

SOUND OF SCARBA Built at Port Glasgow, UK for *Western Ferries*.

SOUND OF SHUNA Built at Åmål, Sweden as the ÖLANDSSUND IV for *Rederi AB Ölandssund* of Sweden for service between Revsudden on the mainland and Stora Rör on the island of Öland. Following the opening of a new bridge near Kalmar, about 4 miles to the South, the ferry service ceased. In 1973 she was sold to *Western Ferries*, renamed the SOUND OF SHUNA and, with the SOUND OF SCARBA (175t, 1960), inaugurated the McInroy's Point - Hunter's Quay service. Now a reserve vessel.

SOUND OF SLEAT Built at Hardinxveld, Netherlands as the DE HOORN for the service between

Maassluis and Rozenburg, across the 'Nieuwe Waterweg' (New Waterway) in The Netherlands. In 1988 she was purchased by *Western Ferries* and renamed the SOUND OF SLEAT.

WIGHTLINK

THE COMPANY *Wightlink* is a British private sector company, owned by the management. The routes and vessels were previously part of *Sealink* but were excluded from the purchase of most of the *Sealink* operations by *Stena Line AB* in 1990. They remained in *Sea Containers* ownership until purchased by *CINVen* Ltd, a venture capital company. The company was the subject of a management buy-out in 2001.

MANAGEMENT Chairman Michael Aiken, **Head of Marketing** Janet Saville.

ADDRESS PO Box 59, Portsmouth PO1 2XB.

TELEPHONE Administration +44 (0)23 9281 2011, **Reservations** 08705 827744 (from UK only), +44 (0)23 9281 2011 (from overseas).

FAX Administration & Reservations +44 (0)23 9285 5257, **Telex** 86440 WIGHTLG.

INTERNET Email info@wightlink.co.uk **Website** www.wightlink.co.uk *(English)*

ROUTES OPERATED Conventional Ferries Lymington - Yarmouth (Isle of Wight) (approx 30 mins; *(1,2,3)*; half hourly), Portsmouth - Fishbourne (Isle of Wight) (approx 35 mins; *(8,9,10,11,12)*; half hourly or hourly depending on time of day). **Fast Passenger Ferries** Portsmouth - Ryde (Isle of Wight) (passenger only) (approx 15 mins; *(4,5,6,7)*; half hourly/hourly).

1	CAEDMON	‡763t	73	9.5k	57.9m	512P	58C	6L	BA	UK
2	CENRED	‡761t	73	9.5k	57.9m	512P	58C	6L	BA	UK
3	CENWULF	‡761t	73	9.5k	57.9m	512P	58C	6L	BA	UK
4»p	FASTCAT RYDE	478t	96	34k	40.0m	361P	0C	0L	-	UK
5»p	FASTCAT SHANKLIN	478t	96	34k	40.0m	361P	0C	0L	-	UK
6»p	OUR LADY PAMELA	312t	86	28.5k	29.5m	410P	0C	0L	-	UK
7»p	OUR LADY PATRICIA	312t	86	28.5k	29.5m	410P	0C	0L	-	UK
8	ST CATHERINE	2038t	83	12.5k	77.0m	771P	142C	12L	BA	UK
9	ST CECILIA	2968t	86	12.5k	77.0m	771P	142C	12L	BA	UK
10	ST CLARE	3500t	01	13k	86.0m	800P	180C	-	BA	UK
11	ST FAITH	3009t	90	12.5k	77.0m	771P	142C	12L	BA	UK
12	ST HELEN	2983t	83	12.5k	77.0m	771P	142C	12L	BA	UK

CAEDMON Built at Dundee, UK for *Sealink* for the Portsmouth - Fishbourne service. In 1983 transferred to the Lymington - Yarmouth service.

CENRED, CENWULF Built at Dundee, UK for *Sealink* for the Lymington - Yarmouth service.

FASTCAT RYDE Kværner Fjellstrand Flyingcat 40m built at Singapore as the WATER JET 1 for *Waterjet Netherlands Antilles* and operated in the Philippines. In 1999 withdrawn from service and renamed the SUPERCAT 17. In summer 2000 sold to *Wightlink* and renamed the FASTCAT RYDE. After modifications, entered service on the Portsmouth - Ryde route in autumn 2000.

FASTCAT SHANKLIN Kværner Fjellstrand Flyingcat 40m built at Singapore as the WATER JET 2 for *Waterjet Netherlands Antilles* and operated in the Philippines. In 1999 withdrawn from service and renamed the SUPERCAT 18. In summer 2000 sold to *Wightlink* and renamed the FASTCAT SHANKLIN. After modifications, entered service on the Portsmouth - Ryde route in autumn 2000.

OUR LADY PAMELA, OUR LADY PATRICIA InCat 30 m catamarans built at Hobart, Tasmania, Australia for *Sealink* for the Portsmouth - Ryde service. Now spare vessels.

ST CATHERINE, ST HELEN Built at Leith, UK for *Sealink* for the Portsmouth - Fishbourne service.

ST CECILIA, ST FAITH Built at Selby, UK for *Sealink* for the Portsmouth - Fishbourne service.

ST CLARE Built at Gdansk, Poland for *Wightlink* for the Portsmouth - Fishbourne service. She is a double ended ferry with a central bridge.

St Faith *(Chris Randall)*

St Clare *(Andrew Cooke)*

WOOLWICH FREE FERRY

THE COMPANY The *Woolwich Free Ferry* is operated by the *London Borough of Greenwich*, a British municipal authority.

MANAGEMENT Ferry Manager Capt P Deeks.

ADDRESS New Ferry Approach, Woolwich, London SE18 6DX.

TELEPHONE Administration +44 (0)20 8921 5786, +44 (0)20 8921 5967, **FAX Administration** +44 (0)20 8316 6096, **Reservations** Not applicable.

INTERNET Email peter.deeks@greenwich.gov.uk **Website** www.londontransport.co.uk/river/r_info08.htm *(English)*

ROUTE OPERATED Woolwich - North Woolwich (free ferry) (5 mins; *(1,2,3)*; every 9 mins (weekdays - two ferries in operation), every 16 mins (weekends - one ferry in operation)). Note one ferry always in reserve/under maintenance.

1	ERNEST BEVIN	738t	63	8k	56.7m	310P	32C	6L	BA	UK
2	JAMES NEWMAN	738t	63	8k	56.7m	310P	32C	6L	BA	UK
3	JOHN BURNS	738t	63	8k	56.7m	310P	32C	6L	BA	UK

ERNEST BEVIN, JAMES NEWMAN, JOHN BURNS Built at Dundee, UK for the *London County Council* who operated the service in 1963. In 1965 ownership was transferred to the *Greater London Council*. Following the abolition of the *GLC* in April 1986, ownership was transferred to the *Department of Transport* and in 2001 to *Transport for London*. The *London Borough of Greenwich* operate the service on their behalf. An alternative loading is 6m x 18m articulated lorries cars and 14 cars; lorries of this length are too long for the nearby northbound Blackwall Tunnel.

Bramble Bush Bay *(Matthew Punter)*

SECTION 2 – DOMESTIC SERVICES

Portsmouth Harbour
fastCAT
fastCAT

Wightlinks' three fastcats at Portsmouth *(Chris Randall)*

section 3 freight only services

gb & ireland

ARGOGOOD

THE COMPANY *ArgoGood Ferry Service* GmbH is a joint venture between *Argo Reederei Richard Adler & Söhne*, Bremen and *John Good & Sons (Shipping) Ltd*, Hull.

MANAGEMENT Managing Director John A Good, **Marketing Manager** Alan Platt.

ADDRESS ***Germany*** Argo Reederei RA&S, 2800 Bremen 1, Am Wall 187/189, Germany, ***UK*** John Good & Sons (Shipping) Ltd, 71 High Street, Hull HU1 1QT.

TELEPHONE Administration & Reservations ***Germany*** +49 (0)421 363070, ***UK*** +44 (0)1482 325781.

FAX Administration & Reservations ***Germany*** +49 (0)421 321575, ***UK*** +44 (0)1482 320266.

INTERNET Email argogood@johngood.co.uk **Website** www.johngood.co.uk *(English)*

ROUTE OPERATED Hull *(dep: 21.00 Mon)* - Cuxhaven *(arr: 18.00 Tue, dep: 23.00 Tue)* - Hanko *(arr: 21.00 Thu, dep: 03.00 Fri)* - Helsinki *(arr: 08.00 Fri, dep: 14.00 Fri)* - Cuxhaven *(arr: 16.00 Sun, dep: 18.00 Sun)* - Hull *(arr: 15.00 Mon)* (*(1)*; 1 per week).

1	BORDEN	10100t	77	17.5k	142.3m	12P	-	105T	A	FI

BORDEN Built at Fredrikstad, Norway as the BORE SKY for *Bore Line* of Finland and used on services between Finland, Northern Europe and Britain; subsequently sold and chartered back. In 1991 *Bore Line* began to pull out of regular shipping services, the charter ceased and she was renamed the BLUE SKY. In 1992 she was chartered to *Transfennica* and renamed the BORDEN. She was used on a service between Finland and Harwich (Navyard). She was later moved to other Transfennica routes. In summer 2001 she was chartered to *SeaWind Line* to provide extra capacity on their Stockholm - Turku service. In 2002 chartered to *ArgoGood*. She is now owned by *Rederi AB Engship*.

CCTL

THE COMPANY *CCTL* is a division of *Seawheel Ltd*, a UK company, part of the *Simon Group plc*.

MANAGEMENT Managing Director Les Rogers, **Marketing Manager** John Posey, **RO-RO Manager** Robin Anson.

ADDRESS ***Seawheel HO*** Western House, Hadleigh Road, Ipswich, Suffolk IP2 0HB, ***Local Office*** Seawheel Limited, CCTL Division, Humber Sea Terminal, Clough Lane, North Killingholme, North Lincolnshire, DN40 3JP.

TELEPHONE ***Seawheel HO*** **Administration and Reservations** +44 (0)1473 222000, ***Local Office*** +44 (0)1469 540 689.

FAX ***Seawheel HO*** **Administration & Reservations** +44 (0)1473 230083, ***Local Office*** +44 (0)1469 540 687.

INTERNET Email jposey@seawheel.com **Website** www.seawheel.com *(English)*

ROUTE OPERATED Killingholme *(dep: 20.30 Mon, 20.30 Wed, 08.00 Fri, 23.00 Sat)* - Hamburg (Germany) *(dep: 19.00 Mon, 19.00 Wed, 11.00 Fri, 22.00 Sat)* (30 - 33 hrs; *(1,2)*; 4 per week).

1	PASEWALK	10243t	83	14k	140.1m	12P	-	80T	A	LB

2	TYCHY	15652t	88	15k	148.5m	4P	-	86T	A	MA

PASEWALK Built at Wismar, East Germany as the AUERSBERG for *DSR RORO* of Germany (DDR) and used on various services. Following the unification of Germany, she was in 1993 transferred to subsidiary *Euroseabridge*. She was then placed on services between Germany and Lithuania and Denmark and Lithuania. In 1999 she was chartered *CCTL* and placed on a new service between Hull and Hamburg. Service switched to Killingholme in November 2000.

TYCHY Built at Gdynia, Poland as the TYCHY for *Polish Ocean Lines* and used on service from Poland to the Mediterranean. In 1992 chartered to *CMA* of France and renamed the VILLE DE LAITEKE; she was used on Mediterranean services. In 1993 she returned to *POL* and resumed the named TYCHY. In 2001 chartered to *CCTL*.

COBELFRET FERRIES

THE COMPANY *Cobelfret Ferries nv* is a Belgian private sector company, a subsidiary of *Cobelfret nv* of Antwerp.

MANAGEMENT Operations Manager (Belgium) Marc Vandersteen, **UK *Purfleet and Dagenham services*** Cobelfret Ferries UK Ltd - **General Manager, Line & Agency Division** Phil Tomkins, ***Immingham Services*** Cobelfret Ferries UK Ltd - **General Manager** Peter Kirman.

ADDRESS *Belgium* B-8380 Zeebrugge, Belgium, ***UK Purfleet*** Purfleet Thames Terminal, London Road, Purfleet, Essex RM19 1RP, ***UK Immingham*** Cobelfret Ferries UK Ltd, Manby Road, Immingham, South Humberside DN40 3EG.

TELEPHONE Administration & Reservations *Belgium* +32 (0)50 502243, ***UK (Purfleet)*** +44 (0)1708 891199, ***(Immingham)*** +44 (0)1469 573115.

FAX Administration & Reservations *Belgium* +32 (0)50 502219, ***UK (Purfleet)*** +44 (0)1708 890853, ***(Immingham)*** +44 (0)1469 573739.

INTERNET Email *Zeebrugge* pur.cobzee@cobelfretferries.be ***Purfleet*** phil.tomkins@cobelfretfrerries.co.uk **Website:** www.cobelfret.com *(English)*

ROUTES OPERATED Zeebrugge (*dep: 04.00 Tue-Fri, 10.00 Mon-Fri, 16.00 Mon-Fri, 22.00 Mon-Fri)* - Purfleet *(dep: 06.00 Tue-Fri, 12.00 Mon-Fri, 18.00 Mon-Fri, 23.00 Mon-Fri (Note: weekend service run subject to demand and are liable to vary) (9 hrs; (2,7,8,11,20); 4 per day)*, Zeebrugge *(dep: 06.00 Sun, Tue-Fri, 18.00 Mon-Fri)* - Dagenham *(dep: 10.00 Mon-Sat, 22.00 Mon-Fri)* (contract service for Ford Motor Company) *(11 hrs; (6,17,18); 2 per day)*, Rotterdam (*dep: 17.00 Sat, 20.00 Mon-Fri)* - Purfleet *(dep: 16.00 Sat, 19.00 Mon-Fri)* (14 hrs; *(5,19)*; 1 per day (Note: if the service is carrying imported Ford cars, the ship will, after discharge at Purfleet, continue to Dagenham to unload there), Zeebrugge *(dep: 17.00 Sat, 19.00 Mon-Fri)* - Immingham (*17.00 Sat, 19.00 Mon-Fri* (plus unadvertised extra sailings)) *(14 hrs; (3,10,12 (Sunday sailings as required))*; 1/2 per day), Rotterdam (Europoort) *(dep: 17.30)* - Immingham *(dep: 17.30)* (14 hrs; *(1,9)*; 1 per day), Zeebrugge *(dep: 06.00 Sun, 09.00 Mon, 12.00 Tue, 18.00 Wed, 18.00 Thu, 22.00 Fri)* - Gothenburg *(dep: 16.00 Sun, 00.01 Tue, 00.01 Wed, 04.00 Thu, 13.00 Fri, 13.00 Sat)* (33-38 hrs; *(13,15,16)*; 6 per week) (this service is operated by Wagenborg of the Netherlands for the Stora-Enso paper and board group, for the conveyance of their products. *Cobelfret Ferries* act as handling agents at Zeebrugge and market the surplus capacity on the vessels, which is available for general ro-ro traffic. Although this route is strictly outside the scope of this book it is included for the sake of completeness). Correct at 1 April 2002; ships are quite frequently moved between routes so the above may have changed by the time this book is published.

1	AMANDINE	14715t	78	14.5k	172.9m	12P	-	133T	A	UK
2	CELANDINE	23986t	00	18k	162.5m	12P	630C	157T	A	UK
3	CLEMENTINE	23986t	97	17.8k	162.5m	24P	630C	157T	A	LX
5	CYMBELINE	11866t	92	14.5k	147.4m	8P	350C	100T	A2	LX
6	EGLANTINE	10035t	89	14.5k	147.4m	8P	350C	100T	A2	LX
7	EVA ODEN	16950t	79	15k	170.3m	12P	180C	160T	A	SW

Anglian Way *(Mike Louagie)*

Roseanne *(Mike Louagie)*

8	HOBURGEN	9082t	86	15k	121.5m	12P	-	100T	A	BA
9	LOUISE RUSS	18400t	00	23.5k	174.0m	12P	-	171T	A	GI
10	LOVERVAL	10931t	78	17k	161.4m	12P	-	102T	A2	LX
11	LYRA	1 2817t	78	15k	172.0m	12P	-	127T	A	NA
12	MELUSINE	23987t	99	18k	162.5m	12P	630C	157T	A	LX
13	SCHIEBORG	21005t	00	17k	183.4m	12P	-	180T	A	NL
14	SEA CRUSADER	23986t	96	17.8k	162.5m	24P	630C	157T	A	UK
15	SLINGEBORG	21005t	00	17k	183.4m	12P	-	180T	A	NL
16	SPAARNEBORG	21005t	00	17k	183.4m	12P	-	180T	A	NL
17	SYMPHORINE	10030t	88	14.5k	147.4m	8P	350C	100T	A2	LX
18	UNDINE	11854t	91	14.5k	147.4m	8P	350C	100T	A2	LX
19	VALENTINE	23987t	99	18k	162.5m	12P	630C	157T	A	UK
20	VICTORINE	23987t	00	18k	162.5m	12P	630C	157T	A	UK

AMANDINE Built at Kiel, Germany as the MERZARIO PERSIA for *Merzario Line* of Italy and used on services between Italy and the Middle East. In 1986 she was chartered to *Grimaldi* of Italy and renamed the PERSIA, continuing on Middle East services. In 1988 she was sold to *Eimskip* of Iceland and renamed the BRUARFOSS. She was used on their service between Reykjavik, Immingham, Hamburg and Rotterdam. In 1996, the ro-ro service was replaced by a container only service and she was withdrawn. She was renamed the VEGA and was placed a number of short term charters including *Suardiaz* of Spain and *Fred. Olsen Lines*. In 1998, she was sold to *Cobelfret* and renamed the AMANDINE. Used mainly on the Rotterdam - Immingham service until 2002 when she briefly operated on the Rotterdam - Purfleet route.

CELANDINE, MELUSINE, VALENTINE, VICTORINE Built at Sakaide, Japan for *Cobelfret*. Similar to the CLEMENTINE. The CELANDINE was originally to be called the CATHERINE and the VICTORINE the CELANDINE. The names were changed before delivery. Three are generally used on the Zeebrugge - Purfleet service and one on the Zeebrugge - Immingham service; currently this is the MELUSINE but this could be changed. The VALENTINE moved to the Rotterdam-Purfleet service in 2002.

CLEMENTINE Built at Sakaide, Japan for *Cobelfret*. Currently used on the Zeebrugge - Immingham service.

CYMBELINE, EGLANTINE, SYMPHORINE, UNDINE Built at Dalian, China for *Cobelfret*. Used on the Dagenham - Zeebrugge route and other services.

EVA ODEN Built at Landskrona, Sweden as the EVA ODEN for *AB Norsjöfrakt* (later *Bylock & Norsjöfrakt*) of Sweden and chartered to *Oden Line* of Sweden for North Sea services, in particular associated with the export of Volvo cars and trucks from Gothenburg. In 1980 *Oden Line* was taken over by *Tor Lloyd AB*, a joint venture between *Tor Line* and *Broströms AB* and the charter transferred to them, moving to *Tor Line* in 1981 when *DFDS* took over. In 1987 she was enlarged and on re-entry into service in early 1988 was renamed the TOR BELGIA and became regular vessel on the Gothenburg - Ghent (Belgium) service. In 1998 renamed the EVA ODEN and in 1999 the charter was terminated. In 2000 she was chartered to *Cobelfret Ferries*. Current used on the Zeebrugge - Purfleet service but has also operated on the Zeebrugge - Immingham service.

HOBURGEN Launched at Galatz, Romania as the BALDER RA for *K/S A/S Balder RO/RO No 2* of Norway. On completion acquired by *Navrom* of Romania, renamed the BAZIAS 5 and used on Mediterranean services; subsequently transferred to *Romline* of Romania. In 1995 she was chartered to *Grimaldi* of Italy and renamed the PERSEUS; she was later chartered to *Sudcargos* of France. In 1996 she was chartered to *Dart Line* and renamed the DART 5. In 1999 she was arrested in respect of a claim against Romline and laid up in Zeebrugge. In 2000 she was sold at auction to *Rederi AB Gotland* of Sweden. She was placed on the charter market. In 2001 she was chartered to *Cobelfret Ferries* and placed on the Purfleet - Rotterdam service, initially on a short term basis and, after a short break, on a longer term basis. Now used on the Zeebrugge-Purfleet service.

LOUISE RUSS Launched at Hamburg, Germany as the LOUISE RUSS for *Ernst Russ* of Germany. On completion, renamed the PORTO EXPRESS and chartered to *ROROExpress* to operate between

Southampton, Oporto and Tangiers. The service ceased in autumn 2001 and she was returned to her owners and resumed the name LOUISE RUSS. In 2002 chartered to *Cobelfret Ferries* and placed on the Rotterdam - Immingham service.

LOVERVAL Built at Lödöse, Sweden as the VALLMO for the *Johansson Group* of Sweden and undertook a variety of charters. In 1982 she was sold to *Cobelfret* and renamed the MATINA. In 1984 renamed the LOVERVAL. In recent years has been chartered out for periods. Currently used on the Zeebrugge - Purfleet and Zeebrugge - Immingham service.

LYRA Built at Kiel, Germany as the MERZARIO ARABIA for *Merzario Line* of Italy and used on services between Italy and the Middle East. In 1986 she was chartered to *Ignazio Messina* of Italy and renamed the JOLLY OCRA, continuing on Middle East services. In 1987, she was chartered to *Lloyd Triestino Line* of Italy and renamed the DUINO. In 1988 she was sold to *Eimskip* of Iceland, renamed the LAXFOSS and used on their services from Iceland to the UK, Netherlands and Germany. In 1996, the ro-ro service was replaced by a container only service and she was withdrawn. She was chartered to *Nordana Line* of Denmark and renamed the SILKEBORG. In 1997 she was renamed the LYRA and briefly chartered to *Dart Line* and used on their Dartford - Zeebrugge service. Later in 1997 she was chartered to *Exxtor Ferries* to operate between Immingham and Rotterdam. When the service was taken over by *Cobelfret* later in the year, the charter was transferred to them and she currently to operating between Zeebrugge and Purfleet.

SEA CRUSADER Built at Sakaide, Japan as the CELESTINE. In 1996 chartered to the *British MOD* and renamed the SEA CRUSADER. May return to *Cobelfret* when six new ro-ros currently under construction for *Andrew Weir Shipping* for use by the *MOD* are delivered in 2002 and 2003.

SCHIEBORG, SLINGEBORG, SPAARNEBORG Built at Lübeck, Germany for *Wagenborg* of the Netherlands and time chartered to *Stora-Enso* to operate between Zeebrugge and Gothenburg.

COMMODORE FERRIES

THE COMPANY *Commodore Ferries (CI) Ltd* is a Guernsey private sector company.

MANAGEMENT & **ADDRESS** See Section 1.

TELEPHONE Administration & Reservations +44 (0)1481 728620.

FAX Administration & Reservations +44 (0)1481 728521.

INTERNET Email jvidamour@comferries.com

ROUTE OPERATED Portsmouth *(dep: 09.30*, 20.00)* - Guernsey *(dep: 04.00, 17.30*)* (6 hrs 30 min) - Jersey *(dep: 08.00, 21.30*)* (10 hrs 30 min; *(1)*; 2 per day) (*operated by ro-pax ferry COMMODORE CLIPPER - see Section 1), Guernsey *(dep: 07.00 Sat)* - Jersey *(dep: 11.00 Sat)* - St Malo *(arr: 14.00 Sat, dep: 17.00 Sat)* - Jersey *(arr: 06.00 Sun)* - Guernsey *(arr: 03.00 Mon)*; *(1)*; 1 per week).

1	COMMODORE GOODWILL	11166t	96	18.3k	126.4m	12P	-	92T	A	BA

COMMODORE GOODWILL Built at Vlissingen, Netherlands for *Commodore Ferries.*

DART LINE

THE COMPANY *Dart Line Ltd* is a British private sector company owned by *Bidcorp plc*. It took over the Dartford - Vlissingen service from *Sally Ferries* in 1996.

MANAGEMENT Managing Director Stephen Hepplewhite, **UK Sales Director** Nick Pank, **Continental Sales Director** Helmut Walgræve.

ADDRESS Crossways Business Park, Thames Europort, Dartford, Kent DA2 6QB.

TELEPHONE Administration & **Reservations** +44 (0)1322 281122.

FAX Administration & Reservations +44 (0)1322 281133.

INTERNET Email sales@dartline.co.uk **Website** www.dartline.co.uk *(English)*

ROUTES OPERATED Dartford *(dep: 08.30 Tue-Fri, 20.30 Daily)* - Zeebrugge *(dep: 09.30 Tue-Fri, 21.00 Mon, 21.30 Sun, Tue-Sat)* (8 hrs 30 mins; *(5,6)*; 2 per day), Dartford *(dep: 06.45 Tue-Fri, 20.45 Daily)* - Vlissingen *(dep: 11.45 Tue-Fri, 22.00 Daily)* (9 hrs 30 mins; *(1,2,3,4)*; 2 per day), Dartford *(dep:06.45 Sat, 10.15 Tue-Fri, 23.45 Mon, 23.59 Tue - Sat)* - Dunkerque *(dep: 11.00 Tue-Fri, 15.00 Sat, 21.30 Mon-Fri)* (6 hrs 45 mins; *(1,2,3, 4)*; 2 per day).

1	BAZIAS 1	9071t	84	15k	121.5m	12P	-	90T	A	RO
2	DART 2	9082t	84	15k	121.5m	12P	-	90T	A	BA
3	DART 3	9088t	85	15k	121.5m	12P	-	90T	A	BA
4	DART 4	9088t	85	16.5k	121.5m	12P	-	90T	A	BA
5	DART 8	22748t	80	18k	178.5m	12P	-	155T	A	BA
6	DART 9	22748t	80	18k	178.5m	12P	-	155T	A	BD
7	DART 10	22748t	80	18k	178.5m	12P	-	155T	A	BA

BAZIAS 1 Built at Galatz, Romania as the BALDER FJORD for *K/S A/S Balder RO/RO No 2* of Norway. In 1986 acquired by *Navrom* of Romania and renamed the BAZIAS 1. In 1990 transferred to *Romline* of Romania and subsequently sold to *Octogon Shipping* of Romania. In 1996 chartered to *Ignazio Messina* of Italy and later renamed the JOLLY ARANCIONE. In late 1997 chartered to *Dart Line* and renamed the DART 1. In late 1999 charter ended, and she was briefly chartered to *Merchant Ferries*, although she was taken back on short term charter by *Dart Line* in February 2000. In 2001 renamed the BAZIAS 1 and in April chartered to *Cobelfret Ferries* to operate between Rotterdam and Purfleet. In autumn she transferred to the Zeebrugge -Purfleet service. In March 2002 chartered to *Dart Line* to operate on the Dartford and Dunkerque Vlissingen service). She will probably be renamed the DART 1 in due course.

DART 2 Built at Galatz, Romania as the BALDER HAV for *K/S A/S Balder RO/RO No 2* of Norway. In 1985 acquired by *Navrom* of Romania, renamed the BAZIAS 2 and used on Mediterranean services. In 1995 chartered to *Dart Line* and renamed the DART 2. Operations began in 1996. Later in 1996 she was sold to *Jacobs Holdings*. Now operates on the Dartford - Dartford - Dunkerque/Vlissingen routes (alternating between the two routes on a daily basis).

DART 3 Built at Galatz, Romania as the BALDER STEN for *K/S A/S Balder RO/RO No 2* of Norway (part of the *Parley Augustsson* group). In 1995 acquired by *Navrom* of Romania and renamed the BAZIAS 3. In 1991 chartered to *Sally Ferries* for the Ramsgate - Ostend freight service and subsequently purchased by a joint *Sally Ferries/Romline* company. In 1993 renamed the SALLY EUROROUTE and re-registered in The Bahamas. In October 1996 she was chartered to *Belfast Freight Ferries* and renamed the MERLE. In 1997 *Sally Ferries'* interests in her were purchased by *Jacobs Holdings*. In January 2000 she joined *Dart Line* and was placed on the Vlissingen service, being renamed the DART 3. In autumn 2000 she was chartered to *NorseMerchant Ferries* and placed again on the Heysham - Belfast service. In autumn 2001 returned to *Dart Line* to operate with the DART 2 on the Dartford - Dunkerque/Vlissingen routes (alternating between the two routes on a daily basis).

DART 4 Built at Galatz, Romania as the BALDER BRE for *K/S A/S Balder RO/RO No 2* of Norway. Later in 1985 acquired by *Navrom* of Romania and renamed the BAZIAS 4. In 1991 chartered to *Sally Ferries* for the Ramsgate - Ostend freight service and subsequently purchased by *Rosal SA*, a joint *Sally Ferries/Romline* company. In 1993 renamed the SALLY EUROLINK and re-registered in The Bahamas. In 1997 *Sally Ferries'* interests in her were purchased by *Jacobs Holdings*. She was later transferred to *Dart Line* and renamed the DART 4. In 1998 she was chartered to *Belfast Freight Ferries*. She returned to *Dart Line* in February 1999. She now operates on the Dartford - Dunkerque/Vlissingen route.

DART 8 Built at Sakaide, Japan as the XI FENG KOU, a deep sea ro-ro/container ship for *China Ocean Shipping Company* of the People's Republic of China for service between the USA, Australia and New Zealand. In 1999, purchased by *Jacobs Holdings*. After delivery, she was converted in Nantong, China to short sea ro-ro specification, including the fitting of a stern ramp (replacing the quarter ramp) and luxury accommodation for 12 drivers and entered service in August 1999 on the Dartford - Zeebrugge service.

DART 9 Built at Sakaide, Japan as the GU BEI KOU. As the DART 8. She entered service in September

1999 on the Dartford - Zeebrugge service.

DART 10 Built at Sakaide, Japan as the ZHANG JIA KOU. As the DART 8. Rebuilt as the DART 10. On completion of rebuilding, chartered to *Sudcargos* of France and renamed the MONT VENTOUX and operated between France and North Africa. In December 2000 the charter ended. In January 2001 she briefly ran on the Dartford - Zeebrugge route in place of the DART 8. After two brief charters to the *British MOD* she was refitted and renamed the DART 10. She then entered long tem charter with the *British MOD*. May return to *Dart Line* when six new ro-ros currently under construction for *Andrew Weir Shipping* for use by the *MOD* are delivered in 2002 and 2003.

DFDS TOR LINE

THE COMPANY *DFDS Tor Line* is primarily a ro-ro operator on the North Sea and Baltic Sea. The Parent company *DFDS A/S* was formed in 1866 and is today quoted on the Copenhagen Stock Exchange. The *DFDS Tor Line* group consists of companies in Denmark, Sweden, Norway, the United Kingdom, the Netherlands, Belgium, Germany and Lithuania. 1,200 people are employed at sea and ashore and ro-ro, lo-lo and ro-pax vessels are operated to 18 destinations.

MANAGEMENT Managing Director Ole Frie, **Managing Director UK** Ebbe K Pedersen.

ADDRESS *Denmark (Head Office)* Sankt Annæ Plads 30, DK-1295 Copenhagen K, Denmark, ***UK*** Nordic House, Western Access Road, Immingham Dock, Immingham, South Humberside DN40 2LZ.

TELEPHONE Administration & Reservations *Denmark (Head Office)* +45 33 42 33 00, ***UK*** +44 (0)1469 575231.

FAX Administration & Reservations *Denmark* +45 33 42 33 01, ***UK*** +44 (0)1469 552690.

INTERNET Email info@dfdstorline.com **Website** www.dfdstorline.com *(English)*

ROUTES OPERATED Esbjerg *(dep: 19.00 Mon, 21.00 Tue, 03.00 Thu, 19.00 Fri, 21.00 Sat)* - Immingham *(dep: 15.00 Mon, 22.00 Tue, 23.59 Wed, 16.00 Fri, 23.00 Sat)* (21 hrs; *(7,13)*; 5 per week, Cuxhaven *(dep: 19.00 Mon, 01.00 Thu, 08.00 Sat)* - Immingham *(dep: 10.00 Sun, 21.30 Tue, 03.00 Fri)* (22 hrs; *(6)*; 3 per week), Esbjerg *(dep: 20.00 Tue, 22.00 Thu, 23.59 Sat)* - Harwich *(dep: 23.59 Sun, 20.00 Wed, 21.00 Fri)* (20 hrs; *(9)*; 3 per week (complemented by sailings from passenger vessel DANA ANGLIA giving 6/7 per week), Gothenburg *(dep: 19.00 Tue, 19.00 Thu, 18.00 Sat)* - Harwich *(dep: 19.00 Tue, 19.00 Thu, 16.00 Sat)* (36 hrs; *(1,3)*; 3 per week), Gothenburg *(dep: 21.00 Sun-Fri, 18.00 Sat)* - Immingham *(dep: 04.00 Sun-Fri, 10.00 Sat)* - (26 hrs; *(5,17,18)*; 7 per week), Rotterdam *(dep: 19.00 Mon, 18.00 Tue-Sat)* - Immingham *(dep: 18.15 Mon, Fri, 17.00 Tue-Thu, Sat)* (14 hrs 30 mins); *(10,12)*; 7 per week), Gothenburg *(dep: 03.00 Sun, Tue-Sat)* - Brevik (Norway) *(dep: 16.00 Mon, 11.00 Fri, 16.00 Sat)* - Ghent (Belgium) *(dep: 03.00 Sun, Tue-Sat (Brevik served Wed*, Fri and Sun)* (Gothenburg 42 hrs, Brevik 35 hrs; *(2,4,8,16)*; 6 per week) (*calls at Gothenburg before Brevik), Brevik *(dep: 03.00 Mon, 20.00 Thu)* - Kristiansand *(dep: 11.00 Mon, 02.30 Thu)* - Immingham *(dep: 20.30 Tue, 14.00 Sat)* (approx 27-29 hours Norwegian Port - Immingham; *(11)*; 2 per week) (Note Tue ex Immingham operates Immingham - Kristiansand - Brevik - Immingham, Sat ex Immingham operates Immingham - Brevik - Kristiansand - Immingham), Fredericia *(dep:. 02.30 Sat (via Copenhagen), 22.00 Tue (direct))* – Klaìpeda (Lithuania) *(dep:. 21.30 Sun (via Copenhagen), 12.30 Thu (direct)) (15)*; 2 per week), Copenhagen *(dep:. 15.00 Sat (direct), 21.00 Mon (via Fredericia)* – Klaìpeda (Lithuania) *(21.30 Sun (direct), 12.30 Thu (via Fredericia)* (*(15)*; 2 per week).

Space is also used for freight on *DFDS Seaways'* passenger vessels between Cuxhaven - Harwich (3 per week), Gothenburg - Kristiansand/Newcastle (2-3 per week) and IJmuiden - Newcastle (daily).

Note Non-UK routes shown above are strictly outside the scope of this book but are shown for the sale of completeness.

1	STENA GOTHICA	14406t	75	16k	188.7m	12P	-	148T	A	SW
2	TOR ANGLIA	17492t	77	15k	171.9m	12P	-	184T	A	SW
3	TOR BALTICA	14374t	78	18k	163.6m	12P	-	150T	A	UK
4	TOR BELGIA	21491t	78	18k	193.2m	12P	200C	184T	AS	SW

5	TOR BRITANNIA	24200t	00	21.1k	197.5m	12P	-	206T	A	DK
6	TOR CIMBRIA	12189t	86	17k	145.0m	12P	-	154T	A	DK
7	TOR DANIA	21850t	78	18k	193.3m	12P	200C	184T	AS	DK
8	TOR FLANDRIA	33652t	82	19k	193.6m	12P	300C	212T	A	SW
9	TOR FUTURA	18469t	96	20k	183.1m	12P	-	170T	AS	DK
10	TOR GOTHIA	12259t	71	17k	163.6m	12P	-	116T	A	UK
11	TOR HOLLANDIA	12254t	73	15.5k	163.6m	12P	-	122T	A	UK
12	TOR HUMBRIA	20165t	78	18.5k	183.1m	12P	-	158T	A	SW
13	TOR MAXIMA	17068t	78	17k	176.2m	12P	-	206T	A	NO
14	TOR MINERVA	21213t	78	18k	183.1m	12P	-	158T	A	DK
15	TOR NERINGA	12494t	75	19k	167.6m	12P	-	126T	A	LT
16	TOR SCANDIA	33652t	82	19k	193.6m	12P	300C	212T	A	SW
17	TOR SELANDIA	24196t	98	21.1k	197.5m	12P	-	206T	A	SW
18	TOR SUECIA	24200t	99	21.1k	197.5m	12P	-	206T	A	SW

STENA GOTHICA Built at Sandefjord, Norway as the MELBOURNE TRADER for *Australian National Line* for services in Australia. She was of the same design as *Tor Line's* TOR GOTHIA class. In 1987 sold to *Forest Shipping*. In 1988 she was chartered to *Elbe-Humber RoLine* and renamed the RAILRO 2. Later in 1988 she was sold to *Stena Line*, renamed the STENA PROJECT and was chartered by them to *CoTuNav* of Tunisia and renamed the MONAWAR L. In 1990, following the start of a joint *Stena Line/DFDS Tor Line* service between Gothenburg and Harwich (operated by *DFDS Tor Line*) she was renamed the STENA GOTHICA, lengthened by 31m and chartered to *DFDS Tor Line*, operating on a combined Gothenburg - Immingham/Harwich service. In 1999 the Immingham and Harwich services were separated. She initially operated between Gothenburg and Immingham but was then transferred to the Gothenburg - Harwich service.

TOR ANGLIA Built at Kiel, Germany as the MERZARIO GALLIA and chartered to *Merzario Line* of Italy for services between Italy and Saudi Arabia. In 1981 she was chartered to *Wilhelmsen*, renamed the TANA and used between USA and West Africa. In 1983 she was chartered to *Salenia AB* of Sweden and renamed the NORDIC WASA. In 1987 she had a brief period on charter to *Atlantic Marine* as the AFRICAN GATEWAY and in 1988 she was sold to *Tor Line* and renamed the TOR ANGLIA. In 1989 an additional deck was added. In recent years she operated on the Gothenburg - Ghent service but in late 1998 she was switched to the Immingham - Rotterdam service. In 2001 transferred back to the Gothenburg - Ghent service.

TOR BALTICA Built at Ulsan, South Korea as the ELK for *Stena Rederi* of Sweden and chartered to *P&O Ferrymasters* for use on services from Middlesbrough to Gothenburg and Helsingborg. Purchased by *P&O* in 1981 and lengthened in 1986; she was managed by *P&O North Sea Ferries Ltd.* In 2001 she was sold to *DFDS Tor Line*, who took over management of the vessel. *P&O Ferrymasters'* services ceased in May 2001. She was renamed the TOR BALTICA and transferred to the *DFDS Tor Line* Gothenburg - Harwich route.

TOR BELGIA Built at Dunkerque, France as the VILLE DU HAVRE for *Société Française de Transports Maritimes* of France. Between 1979 and 1981 she was chartered to *Foss Line*, renamed the FOSS HAVRE and operated between Europe and the Middle East. In 1987 she was renamed the KAMINA. In 1990 she was chartered to *Maersk Line* of Denmark, renamed the MAERSK KENT and used on *Kent Line* services between Dartford and Zeebrugge. In 1992 she was chartered to and later purchased by *Tor Line*, placed on the Gothenburg - Immingham route and renamed the TOR BRITANNIA. In 1994 she was lengthened by 23.7m. In 1999 she was renamed the TOR BELGIA and was later transferred to the Gothenburg - Ghent route.

TOR BRITANNIA Built at Ancona, Italy for *DFDS Tor Line*. Operates Gothenburg - Immingham route.

TOR CIMBRIA Built at Frederikshavn, Denmark. Launched as the MERCANDIAN EXPRESS II and immediately bare-boat chartered to *DFDS* for their North Sea freight services, being renamed the DANA CIMBRIA. Purchased by *DFDS* in 1989. Until 1996, generally used on Immingham and North Shields - Esbjerg services; between 1996 and 1998 she operated between Immingham and Esbjerg. In 1998 transferred to the Immingham - Cuxhaven service. In 2001 renamed the TOR CIMBRIA.

Transfinlandia *(Mike Louagie)*

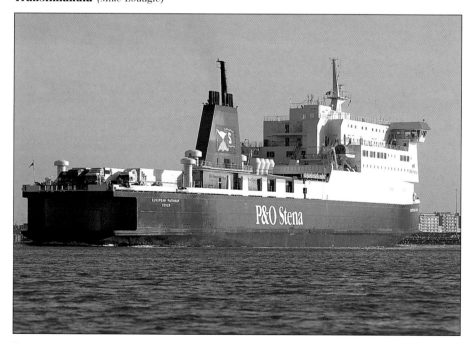

European Pathway *(Mike Louagie)*

TOR DANIA Built at Dunkerque, France as the VILLE DE DUNKERQUE for *Société Française de Transports Maritimes* of France. Between 1979 and 1981 she was chartered to *Foss Line*, renamed the FOSS DUNKERQUE and operated between Europe and the Middle East. In 1986 she was chartered to *Grimaldi* of Italy and renamed the G AND C EXPRESS. In 1988 she was briefly chartered to *Elbe-Humber RoLine* and renamed the RAILRO. She was then chartered to *DFDS* where she was renamed the DANIA HAFNIA. The following year she was chartered to *Maersk Line* of Denmark, renamed the MAERSK ESSEX and used on *Kent Line* services between Dartford and Zeebrugge. In 1992 she was chartered to and later purchased by *DFDS* and renamed the TOR DANIA. In 1993 she was renamed the BRIT DANIA but later in the year reverted to her original name. She was generally used on the Harwich - Esbjerg service, working in consort with the passenger ferry DANIA ANGLIA (see *DFDS Seaways*). In 1994 she was lengthened by 23.7m. and chartered to *Tor Line* and placed on the Gothenburg - Immingham route. In 2000 she was transferred to the Gothenburg - Ghent route and in 2001 to the Esbjerg - Immingham route.

TOR FLANDRIA Built at Malmö, Sweden as the FINNCLIPPER for the *Johansson Group* of Sweden and chartered out. In 1983 she was sold to *Zenit Shipping* and renamed the ZENIT CLIPPER. She was chartered to *Foss Line* and used on services between Northern Europe and the Middle East. In 1986 she was sold to *Crowley American Transport* of the USA and chartered to the US Military. She was renamed the AMERICAN FALCON and used for military transport purposes across the world. In 1998 sold to *Stena Rederi* and was renamed the STENA PARTNER. She was then chartered to *Tor Line* and renamed the TOR FLANDRIAIA; part of her charter conditions are that she be purchased at the end of the five year charter period; however, she was purchased in 2001. She is used on the Gothenburg - Brevik - Ghent route.

TOR FUTURA Built at Donada, Italy as the DANA FUTURA for *DFDS*. Operates mainly between Esbjerg and Harwich, but has also operated between Esbjerg and Immingham. In 2001 she was renamed the TOR FUTURA.

TOR GOTHIA Built at Sandefjord, Norway for *Tor Line*. Lengthened in 1977. She was usually used on the Immingham - Rotterdam service. In 1999 transferred to the Norway - UK service and in 2000 to the Norway - UK/Netherlands service. In 2001 she was moved to the Rotterdam - Immingham route.

TOR HOLLANDIA Built at Sandefjord, Norway as the TOR DANIA for charter to *Tor Line*. In 1975 she was chartered to *Salenrederierna* for service in the Middle East and renamed the BANDAR ABBAS EXPRESS. In 1977 she was lengthened and, in 1978, returned to *Tor Line* and resumed the name TOR DANIA. Purchased by *Tor Line* in 1986. In 1992 she was renamed the TOR DAN and in 1993 the TOR HOLLANDIA. She was usually used on the Immingham - Rotterdam service. In 1999 transferred to the Norway - UK/Netherlands services (Netherlands services ceased in 2001). In 2002 moved to the Norway - Immingham route.

TOR HUMBRIA Built at Oskarshamn, Sweden as the EMIRATES EXPRESS for *A/S Skarhamns Oljetransport* of Norway and chartered to *Mideastcargo* for services between Europe and the Middle East. In 1981 chartered to *OT West Africa Line* for services between Europe and West Africa and renamed the ABUJA EXPRESS. In 1983 chartered to *Foss Line*, renamed the FOSSEAGLE and returned to Middle East service. In 1985 she was renamed the FINNEAGLE, chartered briefly to *Finncarriers* and then to *Fred. Olsen Lines*. In 1987 they purchased her and renamed her the BORAC. In 1999 purchased by *DFDS Tor Line* and renamed the TOR HUMBRIA. In 2000 she was chartered to *Costa Container Lines spa* of Italy, operating between Savano and Catania. This service ended in early 2001 and she was then chartered to *CoTuNav* of Tunisia. Returned in April 2001. She now operates on the Rotterdam - Immingham service.

TOR MAXIMA Built at Osaka, Japan as the DANA MAXIMA for *DFDS* for their North Sea services. Until 1996, generally used on the Esbjerg - Grimsby and North Shields services. Now mainly operates between Esbjerg and Immingham. In summer 1995 she was lengthened to increase trailer capacity. In December 2000 she was renamed the TOR MAXIMA. In December 2001 sold to *Per Sand* of Norway and chartered back for 3 years.

TOR MINERVA Built at Oskarshamn, Sweden as the BANDAR ABBAS EXPRESS for *A/S Skarhamns Oljetransport* of Norway and chartered out. In 1980 renamed the SAUDI EXPRESS. During the early eighties she undertook a number of charters including *Mideastcargo* for services between Europe and the Middle East, *Atlanticargo* for services from Europe to USA and Mexico and *OT West Africa Line* from Europe to West Africa. In 1983 she was chartered to *Ignazio Messina* of Italy, renamed the JOLLY AVORIO and used on services from Italy to the Middle East. In 1986 this charter ended and she briefly reverted to the name the SAUDI EXPRESS before being chartered again to *OT West Africa Line* and renamed the KARAWA. In 1987 she was sold to *Fred. Olsen Lines* who renamed her the BORACAY; she operated between Norway and Northern Europe. In 1998 she was sold to *DFDS*, renamed the DANA MINERVA and placed on the Esbjerg - Immingham route. In 2001 she was renamed the TOR MINERVA; she operates mainly on the Esbjerg - Harwich route.

TOR NERINGA Built at Florø, Norway as the BALDUIN for *Fred. Olsen Lines*. In 1999 purchased by *DFDS Tor Line* and renamed the TOR NORVEGIA. Initially used on Norway - UK/Netherlands services; in 2001 moved to the Fredericia - Copenhagen - Klaìpeda (Lithuania) service. In 2001 December 2001 sold to *Lisco Baltic Service* of Lithuania, renamed the TOR NERINGA and chartered back to *DFDS Tor Line*.

TOR SCANDIA Built at Malmö, Sweden as the KUWAIT EXPRESS for the *Johansson Group* of Sweden and chartered to *NYK Line* of Japan for services between Japan and the Arabian Gulf. In 1983 she was sold to *Zenit Shipping* and renamed the ZENIT EXPRESS. She was chartered to *Foss Line* and used on services between Northern Europe and the Middle East. In 1984 she was sold to *Crowley American Transport* of the USA and chartered to the US Military. She was reamed the AMERICAN CONDOR and used for military transport purposes across the world. In 1998 sold to *Stena Rederi* and was renamed the STENA PORTER. She was sold to *Tor Line* and renamed the TOR SCANDIA. She is used on the Gothenburg - Brevik - Ghent route.

TOR SELANDIA, TOR SUECIA Built at Ancona, Italy for *DFDS Tor Line*. They operate on the Gothenburg - Immingham route.

Under Construction

19	NEWBUILDING 1	30800t	03	22k	199.8m	12P	-	270T	AS	DK
20	NEWBUILDING 2	30800t	03	22k	199.8m	12P	-	270T	AS	DK
21	NEWBUILDING 3	30800t	04	22k	199.8m	12P	-	270T	AS	DK
22	NEWBUILDING 4	30800t	04	22k	199.8m	12P	-	270T	AS	DK
23	NEWBUILDING 5	30800t	04	22k	199.8m	12P	-	270T	AS	DK

NEWBUILDING 1, NEWBUILDING 2, NEWBUILDING 3, NEWBUILDING 4, NEWBUILDING 5 Under construction at Flensburg, Germany. The first three will operate on the Gothenburg - Immingham route. The last two will operate between Esbjerg and Immingham.

FARMERS' FERRY

THE COMPANY *Farmers' Ferry Ltd* is a British private sector company. No other information is available.

ROUTE OPERATED Dunkerque - Dover (3 hrs; *(1)*; not known). Services operate primarily for the carriage of livestock. Some other trailer traffic is carried on some crossings. Services suspended in 2001 but may resume in 2002.

1	CAP AFRIQUE	‡1583t	78	13.5k	108.6m	12P	-	50T	A	KE

CAP AFRIQUE Built at Niigata, Japan as the CATHERINE SCHIAFFINO for *Schiaffino Line* of France and chartered out, generally operating on services in the Mediterranean. In 1983 she was transferred to the company's own service between Dover and Oostende; in 1984 the British terminal moved to Ramsgate. In 1989 she was renamed the SAINT CHARLES and in 1990 she was chartered to *Sally Ferries*, who took over the service. She was later sold to *Delom* of France and in 1991 she was renamed the CAP AFRIQUE. She undertook a number of charters and was also used on *Delom's* own services between France and Tunisia. In 1996 she was moved to Dunkerque and began a number of charters conveying livestock from Dover. In 1997 she returned to Mediterranean service but was back with *Farmers' Ferry* in autumn 1998. Laid up in spring 2001 when service was suspended; however, services may resume in 2002.

FERRYWAYS

THE COMPANY *Ferryways nv* is a Belgian company.

MANAGEMENT Managing Director J Dewilde, **Marketing Manager** Martin Gouwy.

ADDRESS *Ostend* Esplanadestraat 10, B-8400 Ostend, Belgium. ***Ipswich*** Waratah House, West Bank Terminal, Wherstead Road, Ipswich IP2 8NB.

TELEPHONE Administration & Reservations *Ostend* +32 (0)59 34 22 20, ***Ipswich*** +44 (0)1473 696200.

FAX Administration & Reservations *Ostend* +32 (0)59 34 22 29, ***Ipswich*** +44 (0)1473 696201.

INTERNET Email *Ostend* info@ferryways.com ***Ipswich*** info@ferryways.co.uk

Website www.ferryways.co.uk *(English)*

ROUTE OPERATED Ostend *(dep: 11.00 Mon, 10.30 Tue-Fri, 11.30 Sat, 22.00 Mon-Fri, 21.00 Sun)* - Ipswich *(dep: 09.30 Mon-Fri, 11.00 Sat, 22.00 Mon-Fri, 21.30 Sun)* (7 hrs; *(1,2)*; 2 per day), Ostend *(dep: 02.00 Sun, Tue-Sat)* - Killingholme *(dep: 01.00 Sun, Tue-Sat)* (14/19 hrs; *(3,4)*; 1 per day).

1	ANGLIAN WAY	7635t	78	15k	141.3m	12P	55C	84T	A	PA
2	FLANDERS WAY	7628t	77	16k	141.3m	12P	55C	84T	A	PA
3	TANGO	9983t	84	15.5k	138.5m	12P	-	69T	A	RO
4	VILJA	9698t	78	16k	152.3m	12P	-	95T	A	NO

ANGLIAN WAY Built at Bremerhaven, Germany as the THOMAS WEHR for *Wehr Transport* of Germany as THOMAS WEHR but on delivery chartered to *Wacro Line* and renamed the WACRO EXPRESS. In 1978 charter ended and she was renamed the THOMAS WEHR. Over the next few years she was chartered to several operators. In 1982 she was chartered to *Tor Lloyd* (later *Tor Line*) for North Sea service and renamed the TOR NEERLANDIA. In 1985 the charter was transferred to *DFDS* and she was renamed the DANA GERMANIA. This charter terminated in 1985 and she resumed her original name. In early 1986 she was chartered to *North Sea Ferries* for their Hull - Zeebrugge service. This charter ended in summer 1987. Subsequent charters included *Cobelfret* and *Elbe-Humber RoLine* and a twelve month period with *North Sea Ferries* again - this time on the Hull - Rotterdam and Teesport - Zeebrugge routes. In 1993 she was renamed the MANA, then the SANTA MARIA and finally chartered to *TT-Line* and renamed the FULDATAL. 1994 she was chartered to *Horn Line* for service between Europe and the Caribbean and renamed the HORNLINK. Later that year she was chartered to *P&O European Ferries* for the Portsmouth - Le Havre freight service and resumed the name THOMAS WEHR. In late 1995 transferred to the Felixstowe - Zeebrugge freight service. In autumn 1999 the charter was ended. In 2000 she was chartered to *Ferryways*. In 2001 she was purchased by *Ferryways* and renamed the ANGLIAN WAY.

FLANDERS WAY Built at Bremerhaven, Germany as the GABRIELE WEHR for *Wehr Transport* of Germany and chartered to several operators. In 1982, chartered to *Tor Lloyd* (later *Tor Line*) for North Sea service and renamed the TOR ANGLIA. This charter terminated in 1985 when she resumed her original name and, in early 1986, she was chartered to *North Sea Ferries* for their Hull - Zeebrugge service. This charter ended in summer 1987 when the lengthened NORLAND and NORSTAR entered service. Subsequent charters included *Kent Line* and *Brittany Ferries*. In 1989 she was chartered to *P&O European Ferries* for the Portsmouth - Le Havre freight service. Her charter was terminated following the transfer of the EUROPEAN TRADER to the route in late 1992 but in 1993 it was renewed, following the transfer of the EUROPEAN CLEARWAY (now the EUROPEAN PATHFINDER) to *Pandoro*. In 1996, she was transferred to the Felixstowe - Zeebrugge service. In autumn 1999 the charter was ended. In 2000 she was chartered to *Ferryways*. In 2001 she was purchased by *Ferryways* and renamed the FLANDERS WAY.

TANGO Built at Wismar, East Germany. Launched as the RITZBERG for *DDR RoRo* of East Germany, but delivered to *NavRom* of Romania and renamed the TUTOVA; she was used for charter to many operators. In 1996 sold to *Octogon Shipping* of Romania and renamed the OCTOGON 3. In November she was chartered to *East Coast Ferries* and placed on their Hull - Dunkerque service. This service ceased in January 1999. Later in 1999 she was renamed the TANGO; she was engaged in a number of short term charters. In 2002 she entered service with *Ferryways* on their Zeebrugge - Killingholme service.

VILJA Built at Krimpen an der IJssel, Rotterdam, Netherlands as the ANZERE for *Keller Shipping* and chartered to *Nautilus Line* for services between Europe and West Africa. In 1991 she was sold to *AS Tiderø* of Norway and renamed the TIDERO STAR. She was initially chartered to *Fred. Olsen Lines* and later to *Arimure Line* for service in the Far East. In 1994 chartered to *Fred. Olsen Lines* again. In early 1996 she was briefly chartered to *North Sea Ferries* for their Hull - Rotterdam service and then chartered to *Pandoro* and placed on the Liverpool - Dublin service. In 1997, chartered to *P&O Ferrymasters* operating between Middlesbrough and Gothenburg. Later in 1997 she was chartered again to *P&O North Sea Ferries* and placed on the Middlesbrough - Rotterdam service. The charter ended in 1999. After that she undertook a number of short term charters including *Lineas Suardiaz* and NATO. In early 2002 she was renamed the VILJA and entered service with *Ferryways* on their Zeebrugge - Killingholme service.

FINNLINES

THE COMPANY *Finnlines PLC* is a Finnish private sector company. Services to the UK are marketed by *Finanglia Ferries*, a joint operation between *Finnlines* and *Andrew Weir Shipping*, (owners of the *United Baltic Corporation*), a British private sector company. From 1 January 2001, *Finncarriers* was merged into the parent company, trading as *Finnlines Cargo Service*.

MANAGEMENT *Finnlines* President Asser Ahleskog, **Vice-President** Simo Airas.

ADDRESS *Finnlines* PO Box 197, Salmisaarenkatu 1, FIN-00181 Helsinki, Finland, ***Finanglia Ferries*** 8 Heron Quay, London E14 4JB.

TELEPHONE Administration & Reservations *Finnlines* +358 (0)10 34350, ***Finanglia Ferries*** +44 (0)20 7519 7300.

FAX Administration *Finnlines* +358 (0)10 3435200, ***Finanglia Ferries*** +44 (0)20 7536 0255.

INTERNET Email *Finnlines* info@finnlines.fi ***Finanglia Ferries*** london@finnlines.co.uk

Websites www.finnlines.fi *(English, Finnish)* www.finanglia.co.uk *(English)*

ROUTES OPERATED Helsinki (Finland) *(dep: 21.00 Tue, 18.00 Sun)* - Hamina (Finland) *(dep: 15.00 Tue, 22.00 Thu)* - Felixstowe *(arr: 08.00 Tue, Fri, dep: 14.00 Tue, 23.00 Fri)* - Amsterdam *(arr: 08.00 Wed, dep: 15.00 Thu)* - Antwerp *(arr: 08.00 Sat, dep: 14.00 Sat)* - Helsinki *(arr: 12.00 Sun, 07.00 Tue, dep: 18.00 Sun, 21.00 Tue)* - Hamina *(arr: 06.00 Mon, Wed)*; *(3,4,16,24)*; 1/2 per week), Hamina *(dep: 23.00 Thu)* - Helsinki *(arr: 07.00 Fri, dep: 15.00 Fri)* - Hull *(arr: 07.00 Mon, dep: 18.00 Mon)* - Hamina *(arr: 12.00 Thu)* (3 days; *(10)*; 1 per week), Rauma *(dep: 20.00 Wed)* - Hull *(arr: 07.00 Sat, dep: 20.00 Sat)* - Helsinki *(arr: 08.00 Tue, dep: 15.00 Tue)* - Rauma *(arr: 07.00 Wed)*, (3/4 days; *(14)*; 1 per week) (3 days; *(15)*; 1 per week), Kemi *(dep: 18.00 Mon, Thu)* - Oulu *(arr: 06.00 Tue, Fri dep: 18.00 Tue, Fri)* - Felixstowe *(arr: 06.00 Wed, 08.00 Sat, dep: 14.00 Wed, 18.00 Sat)* - Antwerp *(arr: 07.00 Sun, 06.00 Tue, dep: 14.00 Sun, 18.00 Tue)* - Copenhagen *(arr: 06.00 Fri, dep: 22.00 Fri)* - Helsinki *(arr: 08.00 Sun, 11.00 Sun)* - Kemi *(arr: 08.00 Mon, Thu) (26,27,28)*; 2 per week (3 ships operate 2 round trips every 3 weeks), Gdynia (Poland) *(arr:/dep: Friday)* - Hull *(arr: Mon, dep: Tues)*(3 days; *(23)*; 1 per week).

In view of the fact that ships are liable to be transferred between routes, the following is a list of all *Finnlines Cargo* ro-ro vessels, including those which currently do not serve the UK. Ro-pax vessels (none of which normally serve the UK) are listed in Section 6.

1	ANTARES	5989t	88	20.3k	157.6m	18P	-	154T	A	NO
2	ASTREA	7380t	91	15k	129.1m	0P	-	60T	A	FI
3	AURORA	20391t	82	18.5k	155.0m	12P	-	160T	A	NO
4	BALTIC EIDER	20865t	89	19k	157.7m	0P	-	160T	A	IM
5	FINNBEAVER	5972t	91	17k	114.4m	0P	-	76T	A	FI
6	FINNBIRCH	15396t	78	17k	155.9m	0P	-	155T	A	SW
7	FINNFOREST	15525t	78	17k	155.9m	0P	-	155T	A	SW

8	FINNHAWK	11530t	01	20k	162.2m	12P	-	140T	A	UK
9	FINNKRAFT	11530t	00	20k	162.2m	12P	-	140T	A	UK
10	FINNMASTER	11530t	00	20k	162.2m	12P	-	140T	A	UK
11	FINNMERCHANT	21195t	82	17k	154.9m	12P	-	160T	A	FI
12	FINNMILL	11400t	02	20k	184.8m	12P	-	230T	A	IR
13	FINNOAK	7953t	91	16.5k	139.5m	0P	-	94T	A	FI
14	FINNPULP	11400t	02	20k	184.8m	12P	-	230T	A	IR
15	FINNREEL	11530t	00	20k	162.2m	12P	-	140T	A	UK
16	FINNRIVER	20172t	79	16.5k	165.1m	0P	-	134T	Q	SW
17	FINNROSE	20169t	78	19k	165.1m	0P	-	134T	Q	SW
18	FINNSEAL	7395t	91	16.4k	123.3m	0P	-	88T	A	FI
19	MIRANDA	10471t	99	20.3k	153.5m	12P	-	120T	A2	FI
20	NORCLIFF	8407t	94	14.5k	125.2m	0P	-	78T	A	NO
21	OIHONNA	20203t	84	14k	155.0m	0P	-	160T	A	FI
22	POLARIS	7944t	88	14.7k	122.0m	0P	500C	38T	A	GY
23	TRADEN	8188t	77	14.5k	129.2m	10P	-	92T	A	FI
24	TRANSBALTICA	21224t	90	19k	157.7m	0P	-	163T	A	CY
25	TRANSFINLANDIA	19524t	81	18.5k	157.8m	12P	-	172T	A	GY
26	UNITED CARRIER	12251t	98	20k	155.5m	12P	-	124T	A2	FI
27	UNITED EXPRESS	12251t	97	20k	154.5m	12P	-	124T	A2	FI
28	UNITED TRADER	12251t	98	20k	154.5m	12P	-	124T	A2	FI

ANTARES Built at Gdansk, Poland as the FINNFORREST for *Neste* of Finland and chartered to *Finncarriers*. In 1988 renamed the ANTARES. Used on the Uusi/Kaupunki - Travemünde service.

ASTREA Built at Tomrefjord, Norway for *Finncarriers*. Operates between Finland and Spain via Antwerp.

AURORA Built at Rauma, Finland as the ARCTURUS for *EFFOA* of Finland and chartered to *Finncarriers*. In 1991 renamed the AURORA. Used on the Helsinki/Hamina - Felixstowe/Amsterdam/Antwerp service.

BALTIC EIDER Built at Ulsan, South Korea for *United Baltic Corporation*. Used on the Helsinki/Hamina - Felixstowe/Amsterdam/Antwerp service.

FINNBEAVER Built at Hjörungavaag, Norway as the ANN-MARI for *Bore Line* of Finland and chartered to *Transfennica*. In 1998 she was chartered to *Finncarriers* and renamed the FINNBEAVER.

FINNBIRCH Laid down at Ulsan, South Korea as the STENA PROSPER and completed as the ATLANTIC PROSPER for *Stena Rederi* and chartered to *ACL* of Great Britain for service between Britain and Canada. In 1981 chartered to *Merzario Line* of Italy for services between Italy and Saudi Arabia and renamed, initially, the STENA IONIA and then the MERZARIO IONIA. In 1982 she reverted to the name STENA IONIA and was chartered to *OT West Africa Line* for services between Europe and Nigeria. In 1985 she was renamed the STENA GOTHICA and used on *Stena Portlink* services. In 1988 she was chartered to *Bore Line* of Finland and renamed the BORE GOTHICA. In 1992 chartered to *Finncarriers*. In 1996 renamed the FINNBIRCH. In 1997 she began operating a service between Hull and Zeebrugge on charter to *P&O North Sea Ferries* in the course of her normal two week circuit from Finland. This ceased in 1999. In 2000 transferred to the Helsinki - Århus service.

FINNFOREST Laid down at Ulsan, South Korea as the STENA PROJECT and completed as ATLANTIC PROJECT for *Stena Rederi* and chartered to *ACL* (see above). In 1981 chartered to *Merzario Line* of Italy for services between Italy and Saudi Arabia and renamed the MERZARIO HISPANIA. In 1983 returned to *Stena Line* and renamed the STENA HISPANIA. In 1984 chartered to *Kotka Line* of Finland, renamed the KOTKA VIOLET and used on their services between Finland, UK and West Africa. This charter ended in 1985 and she was again named the STENA HISPANIA. In 1986 she was renamed the STENA BRITANNICA and used on *Stena Portlink* (later *Stena Tor Line*) service between Sweden and Britain. In 1988 she was chartered to *Bore Line* of Finland, renamed the BORE

BRITANNICA and used on services between Finland and Britain. In 1992 chartered to *Finncarriers.* In 1997 renamed the FINNFOREST. In 1997 she began operating a service between Hull and Zeebrugge on charter to *P&O North Sea Ferries* in the course of her normal two week circuit from Finland. This ceased in 1999. In 2000 transferred to the Helsinki - Århus service.

FINNHAWK Built at Nanjing, China for *Finnlines.* Currently operating on the Kemi/Oulu - Lübeck route.

FINNKRAFT Built at Nanjing, China for *Forest Terminals* and chartered to *Finncarriers.*

FINNMASTER Built at Nanjing, China for *Forest Terminals* and chartered to *Finncarriers.* Operates on the Hamina - Helsinki - Hull service.

FINNMERCHANT Built at Rauma, Finland for *Finnlines.* Operates on the Helsinki/Kotka/Turku/Rauma - Lübeck service.

FINNMILL Built at Nanjing, China for *Forest Terminals* and chartered to *Finnlines.* Not known at the time of going to press.

FINNOAK Built at Rissa, Norway as the AHTELA for *Holming Shipping* of Finland and chartered to *Transfennica.* In 1997 renamed the FINNOAK and chartered to *Finncarriers.* Used on the *Polfin Line* service between Helsinki/Kotka and Gdynia/Szczecin (joint with *Euroafrica Shipping* of Poland).

FINNPULP Built at Nanjing, China for *Forest Terminals* and chartered to *Finnlines.* Currently used on the Helsinki - Kotka - Rauma - Lübeck service.

FINNREEL Launched as the FINNMAID but renamed before delivery. Built at Nanjing, China for *Forest Terminals* and chartered to *Finncarriers.* Currently operating on the Helsinki - Rauma - Hull service.

FINNRIVER Built at Ichihara, Japan as the VASALAND for *Broström AB* of Sweden and chartered to *EFFOA* of Finland for services between Scandinavia and Mediterranean ports. In 1983 chartered to *Swedish Orient Line* for similar services and renamed the HESPERUS. In 1986 chartered to *Finncarriers* and renamed the CELIA. In 1996 the charter was extended for a further five years and she was renamed the FINNROVER.

FINNROSE Built at Ichihara, Japan as the TIMMERLAND for *Broström AB* of Sweden and chartered to *EFFOA* of Finland for services between Scandinavia and Mediterranean ports. In 1984 chartered to *Swedish Orient Line* for similar services and renamed the HEKTOS. In 1986 chartered to *Finncarriers* and renamed the CORTIA. In 1996 the charter was extended for a further five years and she was renamed the FINNROSE.

FINNSEAL Built at Hjörungavaag, Norway as the BORE NORDIA for *Bore Line* of Finland. In 1997 chartered to *Finncarriers* and renamed the FINNSEAL. Currently operating on the Helsinki - Copenhagen/Oslo/Helsingborg service.

MIRANDA Built at Hamburg, Germany for *Godby Shipping A/S* of Finland. Initially chartered to *Transfennica.* In 2000 she was chartered to *Finnlines.* Currently used on a Hanko/Helsinki - Travemünde service.

NORCLIFF Built at Trogir, Croatia for *Sea-Link AB* of Sweden but due to delays order cancelled before completion. On delivery, renamed the BRAVO and chartered to the *Stora Paper Group.* In 1995 chartered to *North Sea Ferries* and renamed the NORCLIFF. She became second vessel on the Middlesbrough - Rotterdam service. The charter ended in 1996 when the service reverted to a single ship operation. She kept her *NSF* name and was chartered to a number of operators including *Finnlines (Finncarriers).* In 2001 again chartered to *Finnlines* and is used on the Finland to Spain via Antwerp service.

OIHONNA Built at Rauma, Finland for *Finncarriers.* Currently operating on the Turku - Rauma - Lübeck service.

POLARIS Built at Hamburg, Germany for *Pohl Shipping* and chartered to Finncarriers. Currently operating between Finland and Spain via Antwerp.

TRADEN Built at Rauma, Finland as the ABHA. In 1979 sold to *Bore Line* of Finland and renamed the BORE SONG. In 1991 chartered to *Erikson Rederi AB* of Åland and renamed the KEY BISCAYNE. Later that year she was sub-chartered to *Seaboard Marine* of the USA and renamed the SEABOARD HORIZON. She was used on services in the Caribbean. In 1993 she returned to *Bore Line* and was renamed the BORE SONG. She was chartered to *Finncarriers*. In 1997 she was renamed the TRANSNORDICA. In 2000 she was sold to *Rederi AB Engship* of Finland and renamed the TRADEN. She was chartered to *Botnia Link*. In 2001 she was replaced by the larger TRANSPARADEN. In 2002 she was again chartered to *Finnlines* and placed on their new Hull - Gdynia service.

TRANSBALTICA Built at Ulsan, South Korea as the AHLERS BALTIC the for *Ahlers Line* and chartered to *Finncarriers*. In 1995 acquired by *Poseidon Schiffahrt AG* of Germany and renamed the TRANSBALTICA. She continued to be chartered to *Finncarriers* and was acquired by them when they purchased *Poseidon Schiffahrt AG* (now *Finnlines Deutschland AG*) in 1997. Currently operating on the Helsinki/Hamina - Felixstowe/Amsterdam/Antwerp service.

TRANSFINLANDIA Built at Lübeck, Germany for *Poseidon Schiffahrt AG* of Germany. Currently operating on the Helsinki/Kotka/Turku/Rauma - Lübeck service.

UNITED CARRIER, UNITED TRADER Built at Rissa, Norway for *Birka Line* of Finland and chartered to *Transfennica*. During 2000 they were used on their Kemi/Oulu - Antwerp/Felixstowe service. In 2001 the route and vessels used were transferred to *Finnlines*.

UNITED EXPRESS Built at Rissa, Norway for *United Shipping* of Finland and chartered to *Transfennica*. During 2000 she was used on their Kemi/Oulu - Antwerp/Felixstowe service. In 2001 the route and vessels used were transferred to *Finnlines*.

MANN LINES

THE COMPANY *Mann Lines* is owned by *Mann & Son (London) Ltd* of Great Britain. It replaced in 2001 *ArgoMann Ferry Service*, a joint venture between *Argo Reederei* of Germany and *Mann & Son*.

MANAGEMENT Managing Director Allan Binks, **Operations Director** Bill Binks.

ADDRESS *UK* Mann & Son (London) Ltd, The Naval House, Kings Quay Street, Harwich CO12 3JJ, Germany Mann Lines GmbH, Birkenstrasse 15, 28195 Bremen.

TELEPHONE Administration & Reservations *UK* +44 (0)1255 245200, ***Germany*** +49 (0)421 163850

FAX Administration & Reservations *UK* +44 (0)1255 245219, ***Germany*** +49 (0)421 1638520

INTERNET Email mannlines@manngroup.co.uk michael.footitt@manngroup.co.uk

Website www.mannlines.com *(English)*

ROUTE OPERATED Harwich (Navyard) *(dep: 22.00 Fri)* - Cuxhaven *(arr: 17.00 Sat, dep: 19.00 Sat)* - Tallinn *(arr: 15.00 Mon, dep: 21.00 Mon)* - Turku *(arr: 08.00 Tue, dep: 17.30 Tue)* - Bremerhaven *(arr: 18.00 Thu, dep: 21.00 Thu)* - Harwich *(arr: 16.00 Fri)*; *(1)*; one per week.

1	ESTRADEN	18205t	99	20k	162.7m	12P	130C	170T	A	FI

Built at Rauma, Finland as the ESTRADEN for *Rederi Ab Engship* of Finland and chartered to *ArgoMann*. Later in 1999 renamed the AMAZON. In 2001 charter was taken over by *Mann Lines* and later in the year she resumed the name ESTRADEN.

NORFOLKLINE

THE COMPANY, MANAGEMENT, ADDRESS, TELEPHONE & INTERNET See Section 1.

ROUTES OPERATED Felixstowe *(dep: 06.00 Tue-Fr, 12.00 Daily, 19.00 Mon-Fri, 23.59 Daily)* - Scheveningen *(dep: 07.00 Tue-Fri, 13.00 Sun, 14.00 Mon-Sat, 19.30 Mon-Sat, 23.59 Sun-Fri)* (7 hrs; *(1,2,3,4)*; 4 per day), Immingham - Esbjerg (5 per week), Harwich - Esbjerg (6/7 per week). UK - Denmark services operated in conjunction with *DFDS Tor Line* who provide all vessels.

1	MAERSK ANGLIA	13017t	00	18.6k	142.5m	12P	-	114T	A	NL
2	MAERSK EXPORTER	13017t	96	18.6k	142.5m	12P	-	114T	A	NL
3	MAERSK FLANDERS	13073t	00	18.6k	142.5m	12P	-	114T	A	NL
4	MAERSK IMPORTER	13017t	96	18.6k	142.5m	12P	-	114T	A	NL

MAERSK ANGLIA Built at Guangzhou, China for *Norfolkline*. Entered service as the GUANGZHOU 7130011 (unofficially the CHINA II) but renamed shortly afterwards. Operates on the Scheveningen - Felixstowe service.

MAERSK EXPORTER, MAERSK IMPORTER Built at Shimizu, Japan for *Norfolkline*. Used on the Felixstowe - Scheveningen service.

MAERSK FLANDERS Built at Guangzhou, China for *Norfolkline*. Used on the Felixstowe - Scheveningen service.

NORSEMERCHANT FERRIES

THE COMPANY, MANAGEMENT AND ADDRESS. See Section 1.

TELEPHONE Administration +44 (0)28 9077 9090, **Reservations *Belfast (Liverpool service)*** +44 (0)28 9077 9090, ***(Heysham service)*** +44 (0)28 9078 6000, **Liverpool *(Belfast service)*** +44 (0)151 944 1010, ***(Dublin service)*** +44 (0)151 955 4030, ***Heysham*** +44 (0)1524 865050, ***Dublin*** +353 (0)1 819 2955.

FAX Administration *Belfast* +44 (0)28 9078 1599, **Reservations *Belfast (Liverpool service)*** +44 (0)28 9077 5520, ***(Heysham service)*** +44 (0)28 9078 6070, ***Heysham*** +44 (0)1524 865070, ***Liverpool (Belfast service)*** 44 (0)151 922 0344, ***(Dublin service)*** 44 (0)151 955 4083, ***Dublin*** +353 (0)1 819 2941.

INTERNET Email enquiries@norsemerchant.com **Website** www.norsemerchant.com *(English)*

ROUTES OPERATED Heysham *(dep: 10.30 Tue-Sat, 21.00 Daily)* - Dublin *(dep: 08.45 Tue-Sat, 19.00 Sun, 23.00 Mon-Sat)* (8 hrs; *(5,6)*; 2 per day), Heysham *(dep: 09.30 Sun, Tue-Sat, 19.15 Mon-Fri, 22.00 Sun, 23.15 Mon-Sat)* - Belfast *(dep: 07.00 Tue-Sat, 18.30 Mon-Fri, 21.00 Sun, 21.30 Mon-Sat)*; (8 hrs; *(1,2,4)*; 3 per day). *NorseMerchant Ferries* also operate passenger/freight services from Liverpool to Belfast and Dublin. See Section 1.

1	MERCHANT BRAVERY	9368t	78	17k	133.0m	12P	-	94T	A	BA
2	MERCHANT BRILLIANT	9368t	79	17k	133.0m	12P	-	94T	A	BA
3•	MERCHANT VENTURE	6056t	79	17k	119.4m	12P	-	48T	A	IM
4	RIVER LUNE	7765t	83	15k	121.4m	12P	-	90T	A	BA
5	SAGA MOON	7746t	84	15k	134.8m	12P	-	66T	A	GI
6	VARBOLA	7800t	98	17k	122.3m	12P	-	84T	A	ES

MERCHANT BRAVERY Built at Oslo, Norway. Launched as the STEVI for *Steineger & Wiik* of Norway and, on delivery, chartered to *Norient Line* of Norway, being renamed the NORWEGIAN CRUSADER. In 1980 chartered to *Ignazio Messina* of Italy for Mediterranean service and renamed the JOLLY GIALLO. In 1982 the charter ended and she was briefly renamed the NORWEGIAN CRUSADER before being purchased by *Ignazio Messina* and resuming the name JOLLY GIALLO. In 1993 sold to *Merchant Ferries*, renamed the MERCHANT BRAVERY and placed on the Heysham - Warrenpoint (Dublin since 1995) service. In 1999 transferred to *Belfast Freight Ferries'* Heysham - Belfast service.

Maersk Anglia *(Philippe Holthof)*

Brave Merchant *(Gordon Hislip)*

MERCHANT BRILLIANT Built at Kyrksæterøra, Norway as the NORWEGIAN CHALLENGER *for Steineger & Wiik* of Norway and chartered to *Norient Line* of Norway. In 1982, chartered to *Ignazio Messina* of Italy for Mediterranean service and renamed the JOLLY BRUNO. Later in 1982 she was purchased by *Ignazio Messina*. In 1993 sold to *Merchant Ferries*, renamed the MERCHANT BRILLIANT and placed on the Heysham - Warrenpoint (Dublin since 1995) service. In 1999 transferred to *Belfast Freight Ferries'* Heysham - Belfast service.

MERCHANT VENTURE Built at Castelo, Portugal as the FARMAN and chartered to *GNMTC* of Italy for Mediterranean services. In 1982 she was sold to *Medlines* for similar service and renamed the MED ADRIATICO. In 1985 she was sold, renamed the ARGENTEA and chartered to *SGMAT*, continuing to operate in the Mediterranean. In 1987 sold to *Cenargo* and chartered to *Merchant Ferries* who renamed her first the MERCHANT ISLE and then the MERCHANT VENTURE. She was purchased by *Merchant Ferries* in 1993. Until 1993 she was used on the Fleetwood - Warrenpoint service; in 1993 the UK terminal was moved to Heysham and in 1995 the Irish terminal was moved to Dublin. In autumn 1998 she was placed on the charter market. In Autumn 1999 she was chartered to *P&O Irish Sea* and used on the Fleetwood - Larne service. She was later replaced by EUROPEAN NAVIGATOR and then used on Cairnryan – Larne service until end of 1999 when her charter ended and she was returned to her owners. In 2000 she operated for *Merchant Ferries* between Heysham and Belfast until the autumn when she was replaced by the DART 3 (see *Dart Line*) and laid up.

RIVER LUNE Built at Galatz, Romania for *Almira Shipping* of Liberia (part of the Norwegian *Balder* group) as the BALDER VIK and initially used on services between Italy and the Middle East. Subsequently she was employed on a number of charters including *North Sea Ferries* and *Norfolk Line*. In 1986 she was acquired by *Navimpex* of Romania, renamed the BAZIAS 7 and initially used on Mediterranean and Black Sea services. In 1987 she was chartered to *Kent Line* for service between Chatham and Zeebrugge. In 1988 she was sold to *Stena Rederi AB* of Sweden and chartered for service between Finland and Germany. In 1989 she was briefly renamed the STENA TOPPER before being further renamed the SALAR. During the ensuing years she undertook a number of charters. In 1993 she briefly resumed the name STENA TOPPER before being chartered to *Belfast Freight Ferries* and renamed the RIVER LUNE. In October 1996 she was sold to *Belfast Freight Ferries*. In 1999 she was transferred to *Merchant Ferries'* Heysham - Dublin service. In 2000 she returned to the Heysham - Belfast route.

SAGA MOON Built at Travemünde, Germany as the LIDARTINDUR for *Trader Line* of the Faroe Islands for services between Tórshavn and Denmark. In 1986 chartered to *Belfast Freight Ferries* renamed the SAGA MOON. In 1990 she was purchased by *Belfast Freight Ferries*. In 1995 she was lengthened by 18m to increase trailer capacity from 52 to 72 units and trade cars from 25 to 50; the lift was replaced by an internal fixed ramp. In 1998 she was transferred to *Merchant Ferries'* Heysham - Dublin service and in 2001 back to the Heysham - Belfast service. Resumed service between Heysham and Dublin in 2002.

VARBOLA Built at Huelva, Spain as the VARBOLA for *Estonian Shipping Company*. On completion, chartered to *Dart Line* and placed on the Dartford - Vlissingen route. In 1999 she was renamed the DART 6. At the end of August 1999, the charter was terminated and she was renamed the VARBOLA. She undertook a number of short term charters, including *Merchant Ferries*. In 2000 long-term chartered to *Merchant Ferries* to operate between Heysham and Dublin.

NORTHLINK ORKNEY AND SHETLAND FERRIES

THE COMPANY, MANAGEMENT, ADDRESS, TELEPHONE, FAX & INTERNET See Section 1.

ROUTE OPERATED ***From October 2002*** Aberdeen - Kirkwall (Orkney) - Lerwick (Shetland). Timings not yet available.

1	HASCOSAY	6136t	71	17k	118.4m	12P	-	50T	A	NO

HASCOSAY Built Kristiansand, Norway as the JUNO. In 1979 sold to *Finnfranline* of France, renamed the NORMANDIA and chartered to *Finncarriers* for service between Finland and France. In 1982 chartered to *Sucargo* and used on services between France and Algeria and the Middle East. In 1986 sold to *Mikkola* of Finland, renamed the MISIDIA and chartered to *Transfennica* for services between Finland and Northern Europe. In 1990 sold to *Kristiania Eiendom* of Norway and renamed the EURO

NOR. In 1991 she was chartered to *Commodore Ferries* and renamed the COMMODORE CLIPPER. In 1996 she was replaced by the COMMODORE GOODWILL and renamed the SEA CLIPPER. She was placed on the charter market. In 1998 she was chartered to the *Estonian Shipping Company (ESCO)* and operated between Germany and Estonia; she was renamed the TRANSBALTICA. In 2001 she resumed the name SEA CLIPPER and chartered to *Fjord Line*. In 2002 she was sold to *NorthLink* and renamed the HASCOSAY. She was modified to enable her to accommodate *NorthLink's* cassette system for livestock transport in addition to commercial vehicles. Chartered to *Caledonian MacBrayne* to operate between Ullapool and Stornoway during summer 2002. In October 2002 due to enter service with *NorthLink*.

P&O IRISH SEA

THE COMPANY AND ADDRESS See Section 1.

MANAGEMENT Chairman Graeme Dunlop, **Managing Director** J H Kearsley, **Commercial Manager** Philip Simpson.

TELEPHONE Administration +44 (0)1253 615700, **Reservations *UK*** 0870 6000 868, ***Irish Republic*** +353 (0)1 855 0522.

FAX Administration & Reservations *Cairnryan* +44 (0)1581 200282, ***Larne*** +44 (0)28 2827 2477, ***Fleetwood*** +44 (0)1253 615740.

INTERNET Website www.poisfreight.com *(English)*

ROUTES OPERATED Troon *(dep: 02.30 Mon-Sat, 12.00 Sun)* - Larne *(dep: 10.00 Sat, 19.00 Sun-Fri)* (4 hrs 30 mins; *(5)*; 1 per day), ***Until July 2002*** Cairnryan *(dep: 01.45 Tue-Sat, 04.15* Mon-Sat, 07.30 Daily, 09.15 Tue-Fri, 11.45* Daily, 15.30 Daily, 17.30 Mon-Fri, 19.45* Daily, 23.30 Mon-Fri)* - Larne *(dep: 03.30* Tue-Sat, 08.00* Daily, 11.30 Daily, 13.30 Mon-Fri, 15.45* Daily, 19.30 Daily, 21.30 Mon-Fri, 23.00 Sun, 23.59 Mon-Fri) (*operated by ro-pax vessel EUROPEAN CAUSEWAY)* (2 hrs 15 mins; *(2,6)*; up to 9 per day), ***From July 2002*** Cairnryan *(dep: 01.45 Tue-Sat, 04.15* Mon-Sat, 07.30* Daily, 10.30* Mon-Sat, 13.30* Daily, 16.30* Daily, 20.00* Daily, 23.59* Sun-Fri)* - Larne *(dep: 01.45 Tue-Sat, 04.15* Mon-Sat, 07.30* Daily, 10.30* Mon-Sat, 13.30* Daily, 16.30* Daily, 20.00* Daily, 21.45 Mon-Fri, 23.59* Sun-Fri) (*operated by ro-pax vessels EUROPEAN CAUSEWAY and EUROPEAN HIGHLANDER)* (2 hrs -2 hrs 15 mins; *(2 or 6)*; up to 9 per day), Fleetwood *(dep: 03.00 Tue-Sat, 10.00 Daily, 22.00 Daily)* - Larne *(dep: 10.00 Daily, 16.00 Mon-Fri, 22.00 Daily)* (7 hrs; *(3,7,8)*; 3 per day), Liverpool *(dep: 10.30 Tue-Sat, 22.30 Daily)* - Dublin *(dep: 10.30 Tue-Sat, 22.00 Mon-Sat, 23.00 Sun)* (8 hrs; *(9,10)*; 2 per day), Rosslare *(dep: 22.00 Tue, 21.30 Thu, 16.00 Sat)* - Cherbourg *(dep: 14.00 Sun, 22.00 Wed, 19.00 Fri)* (18 hrs; *(8)*; 3 per week), Liverpool *(dep: 03.00 Mon-Sat)* - Larne *(dep: 15.00 Sun-Fri)* (8 hrs; *(1)*; 1 per day). Note: there will be a requirement for one freight vessel to remain on the Cairnryan - Larne route when then the EUROPEAN HIGHLANDER enters service; at the time of going to press it is not known whether this will be the EUROPEAN ENDEAVOUR or EUROPEAN PATHFINDER.

Vessels are sometimes moved between routes. A limited number of private cars and their passengers is conveyed on the day sailings between Fleetwood and Larne, Troon and Larne, Liverpool and Dublin and on all sailings between Rosslare and Cherbourg under the 'Value Route' branding.

1	EUROPEAN DIPLOMAT	16776t	78	17k	151.0m	74P	-	122T	A2	UK
2	EUROPEAN ENDEAVOUR	8097t	78	18.4k	117.8m	107P	-	74T	BA2	BD
3	EUROPEAN LEADER	12879t	75	17k	157.2m	50P	-	114T	A	BD
4•	EUROPEAN MARINER	5897t	77	15k	116.3m	12P	-	62T	A	BA
5	EUROPEAN NAVIGATOR	9085t	77	18k	144.1m	42P	-	62T	A	BD
6	EUROPEAN PATHFINDER	8023t	75	18.5k	117.8m	52P	-	64T	BA	BD
7	EUROPEAN PIONEER	14387t	75	17.7k	141.8m	76P	-	114T	A	BD
8	EUROPEAN SEAFARER	10957t	75	18k	141.8m	50P	-	80T	A	BD
9	NORBANK	17464t	93	22k	166.7m	114P	-	150T	A	NL
10	NORBAY	17464t	94	22k	166.7m	114P	-	150T	A	UK
11	NORTHERN STAR	11086t	91	20.8k	136.0m	0P	-	86T	A	CY

EUROPEAN DIPLOMAT Built at Ulsan, South Korea as the STENA TRANSPORTER, for *Stena Rederi* of Sweden. In 1979 she was renamed the FINNROSE and chartered to *Finnlines*. She later served with *Atlanticargo* on their service between Europe and USA/Mexico. In 1980 she returned to *Stena Line* and resumed her original name. Later in 1980 she was chartered to *European Ferries* for their Felixstowe - Rotterdam freight-only service and renamed the BALTIC FERRY. In 1982 she served in the Falkland Islands Task Force. In 1986 she was converted to ro-pax format and moved to the Felixstowe - Zeebrugge passenger service. In 1992 she was renamed the PRIDE OF SUFFOLK. In 1994 she was purchased by *P&O European Ferries*. In 1995 the Felixstowe - Zeebrugge passenger service ceased, most of her additional passenger accommodation was removed, passenger capacity was reduced and she was transferred to the Felixstowe - Rotterdam freight service. In 2001 transferred to the *P&O Irish Sea's* Liverpool - Dublin route and renamed the EUROPEAN DIPLOMAT. In 2002 transferred to the Rosslare - Cherbourg route.

EUROPEAN ENDEAVOUR Built at Bremerhaven, Germany as the EUROPEAN ENTERPRISE for *European Ferries*. In 1988 she was renamed the EUROPEAN ENDEAVOUR. She was used on freight services between Dover and Calais and Dover and Zeebrugge. If space was available, a small number of passengers was sometimes conveyed on the Zeebrugge service, although the sailings were not advertised for passengers. This ceased with the withdrawal of passenger services on this route at the end of 1991. During the summer period she provided additional freight capacity on the Dover - Calais service and has also served on other routes. In autumn 1995 she was transferred to the Cairnryan - Larne service. In 1998 accommodation was raised to provide extra freight capacity. In March 1999 began also operating to Ardrossan but this ceased later in the year. May be withdrawn from service when the EUROPEAN HIGHLANDER enters service on Cairnryan - Larne route in July 2002.

EUROPEAN LEADER Built at Hamburg, Germany for *Stena Line* as the BUFFALO and due to be chartered to *P&O* for *Pandoro* Irish Sea services. Before completion she was purchased by *P&O*. In 1989 she was lengthened by 12.5m and in 1998 she was further lengthened by 15m and renamed the EUROPEAN LEADER. She is now used on the Fleetwood - Larne service.

EUROPEAN MARINER Built at Bremerhaven, Germany as the SALAHALA and chartered to *Gilnavi* of Italy for Mediterranean services. In 1990 she was purchased by *Cenargo* and chartered to *Merchant Ferries* who renamed her the MERCHANT VALIANT. She was used on the Fleetwood - Warrenpoint service until 1993 when she was chartered to *Pandoro* and placed on their Ardrossan - Larne service. Purchased by *P&O* in 1995 and renamed the LION. In early 1998 renamed the EUROPEAN HIGHLANDER. In July 2001, the service moved to Troon and she was renamed the EUROPEAN MARINER. In 2002 replaced by the EUROPEAN NAVIGATOR. Laid up for sale.

EUROPEAN NAVIGATOR Hull launched at Korneuburg, Austria as the STENA TRADER and moved to Galatz in Romania. Superstructure was conveyed separately on a barge and was due to be placed on the hull there. However, due to heavy rains, the barge was unable to pass under some bridges for a considerable period. Whilst waiting for the superstructure to arrive, the hull was sold to the *United Baltic Corporation* of Great Britain and was towed to Rendsburg where a new superstructure was built. In 1978 she entered service as the GOYA and was used on services between Britain and Spain. In 1979 sold to *Federal Commerce* of Canada for Canadian service and renamed the FEDERAL NOVA. In 1981 briefly renamed the CARIBBEAN SKY before being sold to *Linea Manuare* of Venezuela, renamed the MANUARE VII and used on services to the USA. In 1983 she was sold to new owners who chartered her to *Navigation Central* and renamed her the OYSTER BAY. Later that year she was chartered to *European Ferries*, renamed the VIKING TRADER and used on services between Portsmouth and France. In 1989 transferred to *Pandoro* and in 1996 renamed the LEOPARD. She was renamed the EUROPEAN NAVIGATOR in 1998. Used on the Liverpool - Dublin service until March 1999 when she was transferred to the Cairnryan - Larne route. Later in 1999 she returned to the Fleetwood - Larne, to operate the third daily service which had been inaugurated by the chartered MERCHANT VENTURE. In 2002 moved to the Larne - Troon service.

EUROPEAN PATHFINDER Built at Bremerhaven, Germany as the EUROPEAN CLEARWAY for *European Ferries* ro-ro freight services. She was built at to a standard design rather than custom-built. She was used on freight services between Dover and Calais and Dover and Zeebrugge. In 1992 she was moved to the Portsmouth - Le Havre route. In 1993 she was transferred to *Pandoro* to inaugurate a new Cherbourg - Rosslare service. In 1996 she was renamed the PANTHER. In early

1998 she was renamed the EUROPEAN PATHFINDER. In 2001 she was moved to the Cairnryan - Larne service to replace the EUROPEAN TRADER. May be withdrawn from service when the EUROPEAN HIGHLANDER enters service on Cairnryan - Larne route in July 2002.

EUROPEAN PIONEER Built at Hamburg, Germany for *Stena Line* as the BISON and due to be chartered to *P&O* for *Pandoro* Irish Sea services. Before completion she was purchased by *P&O*. Between 1989 and 1993 she was operated by *B&I Line* of Ireland on a joint service with *Pandoro* between Dublin and Liverpool. An additional deck was added in 1995. In late 1997 she was renamed the EUROPEAN PIONEER. She is now used on the Fleetwood - Larne service.

EUROPEAN SEAFARER Built at Hamburg, Germany. Ordered by *Stena Line* as the UNION TRADER but completed as the UNION MELBOURNE for the *Northern Coasters Ltd* of the UK and lengthened before entering service. Chartered to the *Union Steamship Company* of New Zealand and used on services to Australia. In 1980 she was sold to another *P&O* subsidiary and renamed the PUMA. In early 1998 she was renamed the EUROPEAN SEAFARER. Used on the Fleetwood - Larne service in recent years, in 2001 she was transferred to the Rosslare - Cherbourg service. In 2002 replaced by the EUROPEAN DIPLOMAT and returned to the Fleetwood - Larne service.

NORBANK Built at Krimpen an der IJssel, Rotterdam, Netherlands for *North Sea Ferries* for the Hull - Rotterdam service. She was owned by *Nedlloyd* and in 1996 was sold to *P&O* but retains Dutch crew and registry. In May 2001 moved to the Felixstowe - Europoort route. In January 2002 transferred to *P&O Irish Sea*.

NORBAY Built at Krimpen an der IJssel, Rotterdam, Netherlands for *North Sea Ferries* for the Hull - Rotterdam service. Owned by *P&O*. In January 2002 transferred to *P&O Irish Sea*.

NORTHERN STAR Built at Kawajiri, Japan as the KOSEI MARU for *Kanko Kisen KK Line* of Japan for domestic services. In 1998 she was sold to *Jay Management Corporation* of Cyprus and renamed the IOLAOS. In November 1998 she was chartered to *East Coast Ferries*, renamed the LOON-PLAGE and placed on their Hull - Dunkerque service. The service ceased in January 1999 and after a brief charter to *DFDS Tor Line*, she was renamed the CELTIC STAR, chartered *to P&O European Ferries (Irish Sea)* and placed on the Liverpool - Dublin route. In January 2002 she was renamed the NORTHERN STAR and inaugurated a new Liverpool - Larne service.

P&O NORTH SEA FERRIES

THE COMPANY, MANAGEMENT, ADDRESS, TELEPHONE See Section 1.

INTERNET Website www.ponsffreight.com *(English)*

ROUTES OPERATED Middlesbrough (Teesport) *(dep: 20.00 Mon-Thu, 17.00 Sat)* - Rotterdam (Europoort) *(dep: 21.00 Mon-Thu, 19.00 Sat)* (15 hrs; *(4,5)*; 5 per week), Middlesbrough (Teesport) *(dep: 21.00 Mon-Fri, 21.00 Sat)* - Zeebrugge *(dep: 20.30 Mon-Sat)* (15 hrs; *(6,7)*; 6 per week), Hull *(dep: 19.00* Daily, 21.00 Mon, Wed, Fri)* - Zeebrugge *(dep: 19.00* Daily, 21.00 Tue, Thu, Sat)* (13 hrs; *(3,*passenger vessels)*; 10 per week), Felixstowe *(dep: 04.00 Tue-Sat, 11.30 Mon-Sat, 22.30 Sun-Fri)* - Rotterdam (Europoort) *(dep: 11.30 Daily, 18.00 Mon-Fri, 23.30 Sun-Fri)* (7 hrs 30 mins; *(1,2,8)* 3 per day), Felixstowe *(dep: 11.00 Sun, Tue-Fri, 21.30 Sun, 23.00 Mon-Fri)* - Zeebrugge *(dep: 09.00 Mon, 11.00 Sun, Tue-Sat, 23.59 Mon-Fri)* (6 hrs; *(9,10)*; 2 per day.

1	EUROPEAN FREEWAY	21162t	77	16.5k	184.6m	166P	-	180T	A2	UK
2	EUROPEAN TIDEWAY	21162t	77	16.5k	184.6m	166P	-	180T	A2	UK
3	NORCAPE	14807t	79	19.4k	151.0m	12P	-	124T	A	NL
4	NORKING	17884t	80	19k	170.9m	12P	-	155T	A	FI
5	NORQUEEN	17884t	80	19k	170.9m	12P	-	155T	A	FI
6	NORSKY	19992t	99	20k	180.0m	12P	-	194T	A	NL
7	NORSTREAM	19992t	99	20k	180.0m	12P	-	194T	A	NL
8	PRIDE OF FLANDERS	16776t	78	17k	151.0m	74P	-	122T	A2	UK
9	RODONA	6568t	80	15k	136.0m	12P	-	84T	A	SW
10	SAPPHIRE	6568t	80	15k	136.1m	12P	-	84T	A	SW

EUROPEAN FREEWAY Built at Ulsan, South Korea for *Stena Rederi* as the ALPHA ENTERPRISE and chartered to *Aghiris Navigation* of Cyprus. In 1979 she was renamed the SYRIA and chartered to *Hellas Ferries* for services between Greece and Syria. In 1981 she was lengthened by 33.6m. In 1982 she was chartered to *European Ferries* and used on freight services between Felixstowe and Rotterdam. In 1983 she was renamed the STENA TRANSPORTER and in 1986 the CERDIC FERRY. In 1992 she was renamed the EUROPEAN FREEWAY and, in 1994, purchased by *P&O European Ferries*.

EUROPEAN TIDEWAY Built at Ulsan, South Korea. Launched as the STENA RUNNER by *Stena Rederi* of Sweden. On completion, renamed the ALPHA PROGRESS and chartered to *Aghiris Navigation* of Greece. In 1979 renamed the HELLAS and operated by *Soutos-Hellas Ferry Services* on services between Greece and Syria. In 1982 she was lengthened by 33.6m. In 1982 she was chartered to *European Ferries* and used on freight services between Felixstowe and Rotterdam. The following year she was returned to *Hellas Ferries*. In 1985 she returned to *European Ferries* and the Rotterdam service. In 1986 she was renamed the DORIC FERRY. In 1992 she was renamed the EUROPEAN TIDEWAY and, in 1994, purchased by *P&O European Ferries*. In 2001 replaced by the NORBANK and laid up. In 2002 returned to the Felixstowe - Rotterdam route when the NORBANK was transferred to *P&O Irish Sea*.

NORCAPE Built at Tamano, Japan. Launched as the PUMA but, on completion chartered to *B&I Line* and renamed the TIPPERARY for their Dublin - Liverpool service. In 1989 sold to *North Sea Ferries*, renamed the NORCAPE and introduced onto the Ipswich - Rotterdam service. In 1995 service ceased and she was moved to the Hull - Zeebrugge freight service. She retains Dutch crew and registry.

NORKING, NORQUEEN Built at Rauma, Finland as the BORE KING and the BORE QUEEN for *Bore Line* of Finland for Baltic services. In 1991 chartered to *North Sea Ferries* for their Teesport - Zeebrugge service and renamed the NORKING and NORQUEEN respectively. During winter 1995/96 they were lengthened by 28.8 metres and re-engined. In 1999 transferred to the Teesport - Rotterdam service.

NORSKY, NORSTREAM Built at Rauma, Finland for *Bore Line* of Finland and chartered to *P&O North Sea Ferries*. They operate on the Teesport - Zeebrugge service.

PRIDE OF FLANDERS Built at Ulsan, South Korea as the MERZARIO ESPANIA for *Stena Rederi* of Sweden and immediately chartered to *Merzario Line* for their service between Italy and Saudi Arabia. In the same year she was renamed the MERZARIO HISPANIA. In 1979 she was chartered to *European Ferries* for their ro-ro freight service between Felixstowe and Rotterdam and renamed the NORDIC FERRY. In 1982 she served in the Falkland Islands Task Force. In 1986 she was modified to carry 688 passengers and, with sister vessel the BALTIC FERRY (now PRIDE OF SUFFOLK), took over the Felixstowe - Zeebrugge passenger service. In 1992 she was renamed the PRIDE OF FLANDERS. In 1994, purchased by *P&O European Ferries*. In 1995 the Felixstowe - Zeebrugge passenger service ceased, her additional passenger accommodation was removed, passenger capacity was reduced and she was transferred to the Felixstowe - Rotterdam freight service.

RODONA Built at Karslkrona, Sweden as the BALDER DONA for *Dag Engström* of Sweden and undertook a number of charters in the Caribbean and Mediterranean. In 1984 she was renamed the RODONA and chartered to *Seaboard Shipping* of the USA and used on Caribbean services. In 1987 she was chartered to the *Ford Motor Company* for conveyance of cars and trailers between Dagenham and Zeebrugge. In 1995 *Cobelfret Ferries* took over the operation of this service and she was used on both the Purfleet - Zeebrugge and Dagenham - Zeebrugge services. In 1999 she was chartered to *P&O North Sea Ferries* to operate between Felixstowe and Zeebrugge.

SAPPHIRE Built at Karlskrona, Sweden as the BALDER VINGA for *Dag Engström* of Sweden and undertook a number of charters in the Caribbean and Mediterranean. In 1984 she was renamed the ROVINGA and chartered to *Seaboard Shipping* of the USA and used on Caribbean services. In 1985 she was renamed the AZUA. In 1987 she briefly reverted to the name ROVINGA before being renamed the SAPPHIRE and chartered to the *Ford Motor Company* for conveyance of privately owned trailers between Dagenham and Zeebrugge. Since 1995, as the RODONA.

P&O SCOTTISH FERRIES

THE COMPANY, MANAGEMENT AND ADDRESS See Section 1.

TELEPHONE Administration +44 (0)1224 589111, **Reservations** +44 (0)1224 572615.

FAX Administration & Reservations +44 (0)1224 574411.

INTERNET Email passenger@poscottishferries.co.uk **Website** www.posf.co.uk *(English)*

ROUTES OPERATED Aberdeen - Lerwick (14 hrs; *(1)*; up to 3 per week). There are no fixed sailing times. One southbound trip returns via Stromness or Kirkwall taking approximately 20 hours. Service ends in October 2002.

1	ST ROGNVALD	5297t	70	16 k	103.8m	12P	-	41L	A	UK

ST ROGNVALD Built at Lübeck, Germany. Launched as the RHONETAL but renamed the NORCAPE on delivery and chartered to *North Sea Ferries* for their Hull - Rotterdam service; in 1972 she inaugurated their Hull - Zeebrugge service. In 1974 she returned to her owners and resumed the name RHONETAL. In 1975 sold to *Meridional D'Armements* of France for services to Corsica and renamed the RHONE. In 1987 sold to *Conatir* of Italy for Mediterranean services and renamed the MARINO TORRE. In 1989 taken on six months charter to *P&O Scottish Ferries*. In 1990 she was purchased by them and renamed the ST ROGNVALD. She initially operated alongside and then replaced the ST MAGNUS (1206t, 1970). Earlier calls at Leith, Hanstholm (Denmark) and Stavanger (Norway) were discontinued.

SAMMARINA SHIPPING & TRADING

THE COMPANY *Sammarina Shipping & Trading Ltd* is a Romanian company.

MANAGEMENT Managing Director S Samara, **Marketing Manager** Captain Dan Caligas.

ADDRESSES ***Romania*** 20 Grivita Str, 8700 Constanta, Romania, ***UK*** No 10 Berth Portacabin, Sheerness Docks, Sheerness, Kent ME12 1RS, ***Belgium*** J Verschaeveweg, Kaai 410, 8380 Zeebrugge, Belgium.

TELEPHONE Administration *Romania* +40 (0)41 611323, 619682, 619506, **Reservations *UK*** +44 (0)1795 669850 ***Belgium*** +32 (0)50 45 25 61.

FAX Administration *Romania* +40 (0)41 616271, **Reservations *UK*** +44 (0)1795 669847, ***Belgium*** +32 (0)50 45 25 62.

INTERNET Email Administration *(Romania)* sammarina@impromex.ro

ROUTE OPERATED Service currently suspended.

1	SAMMARINA A	8161t	84	17k	128.3m	OP	151C	65T	A	RO
2	SAMMARINA M	8110t	82	17k	128.3m	OP	151C	65T	A	RO

SAMMARINA A Built at Galatz, Romania as the PALTINIS for *Navrom* of Romania. Used on services from Romania to other Mediterranean countries and chartered out. In 1997 sold to *Sammarina Shipping & Trading Ltd* and renamed the SAMMARINA A. Inaugurated a Sheerness - Ostend service in spring 2001. The service ended in October 2001 and she was laid up. A Sheerness - Zeebrugge service started in early 2002 and ended in April 2002.

SAMMARINA M Built at Galatz, Romania as the PASCANI for *Navrom* of Romania. Used on services from Romania to other Mediterranean countries and chartered out. In 1997 sold to *Sammarina Shipping & Trading Ltd* and renamed the SAMMARINA M. Maybe used again on the route again in the future.

SCA TRANSFOREST

THE COMPANY *SCA Transforest* is a Swedish company.

MANAGEMENT Managing Director (UK) Bo Frölander.

ADDRESS Interforest Terminal London Ltd, 44 Berth, Tilbury Dock, Essex RM18 7HR.

TELEPHONE Administration & Reservations +44 (0)1375 48 85 00.

FAX Administration & Reservations +44 (0)1375 48 85 03.

INTERNET Email bo.frolander@transforest.sca.se **Website** www.transforest.sca.se *(English)*

ROUTE OPERATED Umeå *(dep: Mon, Thu)* - Husum *(dep: Mon, Thu)* - Sundsvall *(dep: Tue, Fri)* - Iggesund *(dep: Tue, Fri)* - Oskarshamn *(dep: Sat)* - Tilbury *(arr/dep: Sat, Tue)* - Rotterdam (Europoort) *(arr/dep: Sun, Wed)* - Umeå *(arr: Mon, Thu)* (8/9 day round trip; *(1,2,3)*; 2 per week).

1	OBBOLA	20171t	96	16k	170.6m	OP	-	-	A	SW
2	ORTVIKEN	20171t	97	16k	170.4m	OP	-	-	A	SW
3	ÖSTRAND	20171t	96	16k	170.6m	OP	-	-	A	SW

OBBOLA, ORTVIKEN, ÖSTRAND Built at Seville, Spain for *Gorthon Lines* and chartered to *SCA Transforest*. They are designed for the handling of forest products in non-wheeled 'cassettes' but can also accommodate ro-ro trailers; however no trailer capacity is quoted. The ORTVIKEN was lengthened during autumn 2000 and the OBBOLA and ÖSTRAND were lengthened during 2001.

SEA-CARGO

THE COMPANY *Sea-Cargo AS* of Norway is a joint venture between *Nor-Cargo AS* (a Norwegian company jointly owned by *Ofotens og Vesteraalen Dampskipsselskab, Det Stavangerske Dampskipsselskab* and *Troms Fylkes Dampskipsselskab*) and *SeaTrans DS* of Norway.

MANAGEMENT *Sea-Cargo UK Ltd* Managing Director Barry Jenks.

ADDRESS *Norway* Sea-Cargo AS, PO Box 353, Nesttun, N-5853 Bergen, Norway, ***Grimsby*** Sea-Cargo UK, 1 Prince Albert Gardens, Grimsby DN31 3HT, ***Aberdeen*** Nor-Cargo Ltd, Matthews Quay, Aberdeen Harbour, Aberdeen, AB11 5PG.

TELEPHONE Administration & Bookings *Bergen* +47 55 10 84 84, ***Grimsby*** +44 (0)1472 251269, ***Aberdeen*** +44 (0)1224 596481.

FAX Administration & Reservations *Bergen* +47 55 91 22 33, ***Grimsby*** +44 (0)1472 267966, ***Aberdeen*** +44 (0)1224 582360.

INTERNET Email mail@sea-cargo.no **Website** www.sea-trans.no *(English, Norwegian)*

ROUTES OPERATED Circuit 1 Bergen *(dep: Fri)* - Odda *(dep: Fri)* - Tanager *(dep: Sat)* - Aberdeen *(arr: Sun)* - Grimsby *(arr: Mon, dep: Tue)* - Aberdeen *(dep: Wed)* - Tanager *(arr: Thu)* - Haugesund *(arr: Thu)* - Odda *(arr: Fri)* - Bergen *(arr: Fri)* (1 week; *(1)*; weekly), **Circuit 2** Bergen *(dep: Tue)* - Tananger *(dep: Wed)* - Aberdeen *(arr: Thu)* - Amsterdam *(arr: /dep: Fri)* - Aberdeen *(arr:/dep: Sat)* - Tananger *(arr: Mon)* - Haugesund *(arr: Mon)* - Bergen *(arr: Tue)* (1 week; *(2)*; weekly), **Circuit 3** Bergen *(dep: Fri)* - Tanager *(dep: Sat)* - Amsterdam *(arr: Mon, dep: Tue)* - Tanager *(arr: Thu)* - Haugesund *(arr: Thu)* - Bergen *(arr: Fri)* (1 week; *(3)*; weekly) (**Note** Circuit 3 is strictly outside the scope of this book but is included for completeness).

1	COMETA	4610t	81	16k	102.2m	OP	-	26T	AS	NO
2	SC ABERDEEN	4234t	79	15.5k	109.0m	OP	-	24T	AS	NO
3	TRANS CARRIER	8407t	93	14.5k	125.2m	OP	-	78T	A	BA

COMETA Built at Rissa, Norway for *Nor-Cargo*.

SC ABERDEEN Built at Rissa, Norway for *Nor-Cargo*. Launched as the ERIC JARL but renamed the ASTREA before entering service. In 1986 she sank and, after raising and refitting she was, in 1992,

European Envoy *(Gordon Hislip)*

Stena Hollandica *(Ferry Publications Library)*

renamed the TUNGENES. In 2001 she was renamed the SC ABERDEEN.

TRANS CARRIER Built at Kraljevica, Croatia as the KORSNÄS LINK for *SeaLink AB* of Sweden and due to be time chartered to *Korsnäs AB*, a Swedish forest products company. However, due to the war in Croatia, delivery was seriously delayed and she was offered for sale. In 1994 sold to the *Swan Group* and renamed the SWAN HUNTER. She was placed on the charter market. In 1997 she was chartered to *Euroseabridge* and renamed the PARCHIM. In 1999 the charter ended and she resumed the name SWAN HUNTER. In 1999 she was sold to *SeaTrans* and renamed the TRANS CARRIER.

SEAFRANCE

THE COMPANY, MANAGEMENT & ADDRESS See Section 1.

TELEPHONE Reservations +44 (0)1304 203030.

FAX Reservations +33 321 464861

INTERNET Email freightdover@wanadoo.fr **Website** www.seafrancefreight.com *(English, French)*

ROUTE OPERATED Calais *(dep: 01.15 Mon-Sat, 05.15 Mon-Sat, 09.15 Tue-Sat, 13.15, 17.15, 21.15 Sun-Fri)* - Dover *(dep: 02.15 Mon-Sat, 06.15 Mon-Sat, 10.15 Tue-Sat, 14.15, 18.15, 22.15 Sun-Fri)* (1 hr 30 mins; *(1)*; 6 per day).

1	SEAFRANCE NORD PAS-DE-CALAIS	13727t	87	21.5k	160.1m	80P	-	102L	BA2	FR

SEAFRANCE NORD PAS-DE-CALAIS Built at Dunkerque, France for *SNCF* for the Dunkerque (Ouest) - Dover train ferry service. Before being used on this service (which required the construction of a new berth at Dover (Western Docks)) in May 1988, she operated road freight services from Calais to Dover Eastern Docks. The train ferry service continued to operate following the opening of the Channel Tunnel in 1994, to convey road vehicles and dangerous loads which were banned from the tunnel. However, it ceased in December 1995 and, after a refit, in February 1996 she was renamed the SEAFRANCE NORD PAS-DE-CALAIS and switched to the Calais - Dover service, primarily for road freight vehicles and drivers but also advertised as carrying up to 50 car passengers. Since the entry into service of a third multi-purpose ferry, she has operated on a freight-only basis. There are plans to increase her passenger capapcity to 200.

SEATRUCK FERRIES

THE COMPANY *Seatruck Ferries Ltd* is a British private sector company, owned by *Crescent plc*.

MANAGEMENT Managing Director Kevin Hobbs, **Sales Director** Alastair Eagles.

ADDRESS *Warrenpoint (HQ)* Seatruck House, The Ferry Terminal, Warrenpoint, County Down BT34 3JR. ***Heysham*** North Quay, Heysham Port, Heysham, Morecambe, Lancs LA3 2UL.

TELEPHONE Administration +44 (0)28 4175 4411, **Reservations *Warrenpoint*** +44 (0)28 4175 4400, ***Heysham*** +44 (0)1524 853512.

FAX Administration +44 (0)28 4175 4545, **Reservations *Warrenpoint*** +44 (0)28 4177 3737, ***Heysham*** +44 (0)1524 853549.

INTERNET Email alistair@seatruck-ferries.co.uk **Website** www.seatruckferries.com *(English)*

ROUTES OPERATED Heysham *(dep: 08.00 Tue-Sat, 21.00 Daily)* - Warrenpoint *(dep: 08.00 Tue-Sat, 17.00 Sun, 20.00 Mon-Sat)* (8 hrs; *(1,2)*; 2 per day).

1	MOONDANCE	5881t	78	15k	116.3m	12P	-	62T	A	BA
2	RIVERDANCE	6041t	77	15k	116.3m	12P	-	62T	A	BA

MOONDANCE Built at Bremerhaven, Germany as the EMADALA for *Emadala Shipping* and chartered to *Gilnavi Line* of Italy for Mediterranean service. In 1987 she was purchased by *Gilnavi Line*. In 1990 sold to *Cenargo* of Great Britain and chartered to *Merchant Ferries* for their Heysham - Warrenpoint service and renamed the MERCHANT VICTOR. She was withdrawn from that service in

1993 and was chartered out to a number of operators. In 1997 she was chartered to *Seatruck Ferries* and renamed the MOONDANCE. In 1998 she was purchased by *Seatruck Ferries*. Following collapse of ramp at Warrenpoint in January 2001, she briefly operated between Heysham and Larne.

RIVERDANCE Built at Bremerhaven, as the MASHALA for *Mashala Shipping* and chartered to *Gilnavi* of Italy for Mediterranean services. After a long period out of service in the mid-nineteen eighties, in 1987 she was sold, renamed the HALLA and chartered for Caribbean service. In 1988 she was renamed the TIKAL. In 1989 she was sold to *Schiaffino Line* of France, renamed the SCHIAFFINO and put into service between Ramsgate and Ostend. In 1990 the company was taken over by *Sally Ferries* and in 1991 she was chartered to *Belfast Freight Ferries*. In 1993 she was renamed the SALLY EUROBRIDGE. In January 1994, she was chartered to *North Sea Ferries* to operate between Hull and Zeebrugge and renamed the EUROBRIDGE. In summer 1994 she returned to *Sally Ferries*, resumed the name SALLY EUROBRIDGE and became the second vessel on the Ramsgate - Vlissingen service; in the autumn the British terminal was switched to Dartford. In 1995 she was chartered to *Norfolk Line*, renamed the EUROBRIDGE and also sold by *Sally Ferries*. In 1996 she was chartered to *Seatruck Ferries* and renamed the RIVERDANCE. In 1997 she was purchased by *Seatruck Ferries*. Following collapse of ramp at Warrenpoint in January 2001, she briefly operated between Heysham and Larne.

SMYRIL LINE

THE COMPANY, MANAGEMENT, ADDRESS, TELEPHONE, FAX & INTERNET See Section 1.

ROUTES OPERATED Tórshavn (Faroes) *(dep: 00.01 Thu)* - Lerwick *(arr: 15.00 Thu, dep: 17.00 Thu)* - Hanstholm *(arr: 18.00 Fri, dep: 00.01 Sat)* - Lerwick *(arr: 06.00 Sun, dep: 07.00 Sun)* - Tórshavn *(arr: 04.00 Mon)*.

1	CLARE	5617t	72	17k	114.9m	12P	-	62T	A	NO

CLARE Built at Bremerhaven, Germany as the WESERTAL for *Reinecke* of Germany. After delivery she was renamed the MEYER EXPRESS and resumed the name WESERTAL in 1973. She was chartered out to a number of operators including *North Sea Ferries* and *Olau Line*. In 1998 she was briefly renamed the. In 1993 she was sold to Italian Interests and renamed the VINZIA E. She was chartered to *Stena Sealink Line* and operated between Newhaven and Dieppe. In 1994 she was chartered to DFDS subsidiary *Dan-Liet Line* (later *DFDS Baltic Line*) and renamed the DANA BALTICA. She operated between Denmark and Lithuania. In 1996 she was renamed the CLARE and again placed on the charter market. 1997 she briefly served on *NorSea Link*, a joint venture between *Scandlines (DSB Rederi)* and *Norse Irish Ferries* between Kristiansand and Eemshaven in the north of the Netherlands. In 1998 she was again chartered to *DFDS* to institute freight only services between Newcastle and IJmuiden. After further brief charters she was, in 1999, briefly chartered to *CargoConnect Transport + Logistics* and placed on a new service between Hull and Hamburg. In 2001, she was chartered to *Smyril Line* to operate between Tórshavn and Hanstholm. In 2002, Lerwick was added to her itinerary.

STENA LINE

THE COMPANY, MANAGEMENT, ADDRESS, TELEPHONE AND INTERNET See Section 1.

ROUTE OPERATED Hoek van Holland *(dep: 19.15)* - Killingholme *(dep: 19.00)* (12 hrs; *(1,2)*; 1 per day).

1	STENA SEARIDER	21019t	69	17k	178.9m	120P	-	198T	AS2	IM
2	STENA SEATRADER	17991t	73	17.5k	181.6m	221P	-	174T	AS2	UK

STENA SEARIDER Built at Helsinki, Finland as the FINNCARRIER for *Finnlines* of Finland for service between Finland, Denmark and Germany. In 1975 renamed the POLARIS. In 1984 sold to *Rederi AB Nordö* of Sweden to operate between Malmö (Sweden) and Travemünde (Germany) and renamed the SCANDINAVIA. In 1987 she was rebuilt to increase capacity from 122 trailers to 200. In 1989 the name of the company was changed to *Nordö Link* and she was renamed the SCANDINAVIA LINK. In 1990 she was sold to *Stena Line*, renamed the STENA SEARIDER and used on their Gothenburg (Sweden) - Travemünde service. In 1991 she was chartered out for service in the Caribbean and renamed the SEARIDER. In 1992 she was chartered to *Norse Irish Ferries* and renamed the NORSE MERSEY. In 1995 she was replaced by a new vessel of the same name and returned to *Stena Line*, resumed the name STENA SEARIDER and resumed operating between Gothenburg and Travemünde and Gothenburg and Kiel. In May 1997, she was transferred to the Harwich - Hoek van Holland service. In autumn 2000 she inaugurated (with the chartered ROSEBAY - see the TRANSPARADEN, *Botnia Link*) a new service from Hoek van Holland to Killingholme (near Immingham).

STENA SEATRADER Built at Nakskov, Denmark as the SVEALAND for *Lion Ferry AB* of Sweden and chartered to *Statens Järnvägar (Swedish State Railways)* for the train ferry service between Trelleborg (Sweden) and Sassnitz (Germany (DDR)). The charter ceased in 1980 and in 1982 she was sold to *Rederi AB Nordö* of Sweden. She was lengthened by 33.7 metres, renamed the SVEALAND AV MALMÖ and used on their lorry/rail wagon service between Malmö and Travemünde. In 1986 she was rebuilt with a higher superstructure and in 1987 she was renamed the SVEA LINK, the service being renamed *Nordö Link*. In 1990 she was sold to *Stena Line*, renamed the STENA SEATRADER and introduced onto the Hoek van Holland - Harwich service. In spring 2001 she replaced the chartered ROSEBAY on the Hoek van Holland - Killingholme service.

TRANSEUROPA FERRIES

THE COMPANY *TransEuropa Ferries NV* is a Belgian subsidiary of *TransEuropa Shipping Lines*, a Slovenian private sector company. Channel operations started in 1977, in conjunction with *Sally Ferries*, replacing them on November 1998.

MANAGEMENT *TransEuropa Shipping* Managing Director Stergulc Rihard, ***TransEuropa Ferries NV*, General Manager Belgium & UK** Mr Dominique Penel, **Sales Promoter, Europe** Mr Peter Sys.

ADDRESS *TSL Slovenia* Vojkovo nabrezje 38, 6000 Koper, Slovenia, ***TEF UK*** Ferry Terminal, Ramsgate New Port, RAMSGATE, Kent CT11 8RP ***TEF Belgium*** Slijkensesteenweg 2, 8400 Ostend, Belgium.

TELEPHONE *TSL Slovenia* +386 (0)5 664 17 77, ***TEF UK*** +44 (0)1843 853833, ***TEF Belgium*** +32 (0)59 34 02 50.

FAX *TSL Slovenia* +386 (0)5 639 50 36, ***TEF UK*** +44 (0)1843 853668, ***TEF Belgium*** +32 (0)59 34 02 51.

INTERNET Website www.t-s-l.si *(English)*

ROUTE OPERATED Ramsgate *(dep: 01.00 Mon-Sat, 03.30 Tue-Fri, 05.00 Mon-Thu, Sat, 10.00 Tue-Thu, 13.30 Sun, 14.00 Mon-Fri, 17.30 Mon-Sat, 18.30 Sun, 20.00 Sun-Fri, 21.30 Sun-Fri)* - Ostend (Belgium) *(dep: 01.00 Mon-Sat, 02.30 Tue-Thu, 05.00 Mon, 07.30 Tue-Thu, 13.00 Daily, 16.00 Mon-Fri, 17.30 Sun-Fri, 18.00 Sat, 20.30 Sun-Fri, 22.30 Sun-Thu)* (4 hrs; *(1,2,3,4,5,6)*; up to 8 per day).

1	EUROVOYAGER	12110t	78	22k	118.4m	1500P	54C	54L	BA2	CY
2	LABURNUM	5044t	70	19.5k	117.8m	800P	202C	20L	BA	CY
3	LARKSPUR	14458t	76	17.5k	143.8m	1040P	-	58L	BA2	CY
4	OLEANDER	13061t	80	23k	132.0m	1300P	330C	48L	BA2	CY
5	PRIMROSE	12046t	76	22k	118.9m	1200P	354C	54L	BA2	CY
6	ROSEANNE	7744t	82	17k	112.8m	12P	-	78L	AS	CY

EUROVOYAGER Built at Hoboken, Belgium as the PRINS ALBERT for *RMT* of Belgium for the Ostend - Dover service. During 1986 she had an additional vehicle deck added. In 1994 the British port became Ramsgate. Withdrawn after 28th February 1997 and laid up. In 1998 she was sold to *Hawthorn Shipping Co Ltd*, renamed the EUROVOYAGER. In July, she entered service with *Sally Freight*. In November the *Sally Freight* service ended and she immediately began operating for *TSL*.

LABURNUM Built at Schiedam, Netherlands as the FREE ENTERPRISE V for Dover - Calais and Dover - Zeebrugge services. In 1982 she was transferred to Portsmouth to operate summer extra services to Cherbourg. During 1985/6 she operated on the Dover - Zeebrugge service while the FREE ENTERPRISE VI and the FREE ENTERPRISE VII were being rebuilt. In 1986 she was transferred to the Dover - Boulogne service and in 1988 she was renamed the PRIDE OF HYTHE. In 1992 the Dover - Boulogne service ended and she was laid up. In 1993 she was sold to *Charterhall Shipping* and renamed the LABURNUM. She was operated for *TLS* until 2002 between Italy and Albania. In 1995 the service was taken over by *TESL*. In 2000 she was transferred to *TESL's* Ramsgate - Ostend service.

LARKSPUR Built at Bremerhaven, Germany as the GEDSER for *Gedser-Travemünde Ruten* of Denmark for their service between Gedser (Denmark) and Travemünde (Germany). In 1986 she was purchased by *Thorsviks Rederi A/S* of Norway and chartered to *Sally Ferries*, re-registered in the Bahamas, renamed the VIKING 2 and entered service on the Ramsgate - Dunkerque service. In early 1989 she was renamed the SALLY SKY and during winter 1989/90 she was 'stretched' to increase vehicle capacity. At the end of 1996 she was withdrawn from the Dunkerque service. In 1997 she was renamed the EUROTRAVELLER, transferred to *Holyman-Sally Ferries* and, in March, was introduced onto the Ramsgate - Ostend route. In 1998, when *Holyman-Sally Ferries* came to an end, she operated in a freight-only role for *Sally Line* under the *Sally Freight* name. Passenger services were resumed in May, under the name of *Sally Direct*. All *Sally Line* operations ended in November 1998 and she was withdrawn for sale and laid up. In 1999 sold to *Forsythia Maritime Co Ltd* and renamed the LARKSPUR. She was given a major refit at Dunkerque, including the provision of 60 drivers' cabins with private facilities. She entered service with *TEF* in August 2000.

OLEANDER Built at Bremerhaven, Germany for *European Ferries (Townsend Thoresen)* as the PRIDE OF FREE ENTERPRISE for the Dover - Calais service, also operating on the Dover - Zeebrugge service during the winter. She was renamed the PRIDE OF BRUGES in 1988 and, following the delivery of the new PRIDE OF CALAIS, she was transferred all year to the Dover - Zeebrugge service. In 1992, after the closure of that routes to passengers, she returned to the Dover - Calais route. Plans to operate her in a freight-only mode in 1997 were changed and she ran as a full passenger vessel. In 1998, transferred to *P&O Stena Line*. Plans to transfer her to the Newhaven - Dieppe route were dropped and she remained at Dover. In 1999 renamed the P&OSL PICARDY. In early 2000 she was laid up for sale in Dunkerque. In 2001 she was sold to *Seaborne Navigation Co Ltd* and renamed the OLEANDER. Expected to enter service in spring 2002 after major renovation work in Dunkerque, including the provision of 60 drivers' cabins with private facilities.

PRIMROSE Built at Hoboken, Belgium as the PRINCESSE MARIE-CHRISTINE for *Regie voor Maritiem Transport* of Belgium for the Ostend - Dover service. During 1985 she had an extra vehicle deck added, increasing vehicle capacity. Passenger capacity was increased by 200 by the conversion of an upper deck 'garage' into passenger accommodation. In January 1994 the British port became Ramsgate. In 1994 chartered briefly to *Sally Ferries* and operated between Ramsgate and Dunkerque. Since then a spare vessel and withdrawn in early 1997. In 1998 sold to *Cypress Co Ltd* of the UK and renamed the PRIMROSE. In 1999 she began operating for *TSL* between Ramsgate and Ostend after a major refit at Dunkerque.

ROSEANNE Built at Vigo, Spain as the REINA DEL CANTABRICO for *Labiad Andalusia* of Spain and chartered to *Matina Line* for services between Europe and West Africa. In 1983 renamed the SALAH LABIAD but resumed her original name in 1985. In 1987 she was sold, renamed the FAROY and chartered to *Elbe-Humber Roline* for their service between Immingham and Cuxhaven. In 1989 sold to *Denval* and renamed the ROSEANNE; she was chartered to *P&O European Ferries* and used on their Felixstowe - Zeebrugge service. In 1991 chartered to *Norfolk Line*. In 1996 this charter ended and she was chartered to *Lineas Suardiaz* of Spain. In 2000 chartered to *TSL* and placed on the Ostend - Ramsgate service.

TRANSFENNICA

THE COMPANY *Transfennica Ltd* is a Finnish private sector company.

MANAGEMENT President Rolf G W Eriksson, **Director (UK)** Jim Deeprose, **Operations Manager (UK)** Andrew Prior.

ADDRESS ***Finland*** Eteläranta 12, FIN-00130 Helsinki, Finland, ***UK*** Finland House, 47 Berth, Tilbury Freeport, Tilbury, Essex RM18 7EH.

TELEPHONE Administration & Reservations ***Finland*** +358 (0)9 13262, ***UK*** +44 (0)1375 363 900.

FAX Administration & Reservations ***Finland*** +358 (0)9 652377, ***UK*** +44 (0)1375 840 888.

INTERNET Email ***Finland*** info@transfennica.com ***UK*** info.uk@transfennica.com

Website www.transfennica.com *(English)*

ROUTES OPERATED ***Circuit One*** Tilbury *(dep: 17.00 Mon)* - Hanko *(arr: 07.00 Thu, dep: 17.00 Thu)* - Rauma *(arr: 07.00 Fri, dep: 14.00 Fri)* - Tilbury *(arr: 06.00 Mon)*, ***Circuit Two*** Tilbury *(dep: 17.00 Fri)* - Hamina *(arr: 10.00 Mon, dep: 19.00 Mon)* - Hanko *(arr: 07.00 Tue, dep: 14.00 Tue)* - Tilbury *(arr: 07.00 Fri)* *((1,2)*; 2 per week Finland - UK). Note 'dep:' times are closure times for freight. Ship will actually leave a little later.

1	CAROLINE RUSS	10471t	99	21k	153.5m	12P	-	120T	A2	AT
2	SEAGARD	10471t	99	21k	153.5m	12P	-	134T	A2	FI

CAROLINE RUSS Built at Hamburg, Germany for *Ernst Russ* of Germany and chartered to *Transfennica.*

SEAGARD Built at Hamburg, Germany for *Bror Hussel* of Finland and chartered to *Transfennica.*

TRUCKLINE FERRIES

THE COMPANY *Truckline Ferries* is *Brittany Ferries'* freight division.

MANAGEMENT Managing Director David Longden, **Freight Director** John Clarke.

ADDRESS New Harbour Road, POOLE, Dorset BH15 4AJ.

TELEPHONE Administration & Enquiries +44 (0)8709 013300, **Reservations** +44 (0)8709 040200.

FAX Administration & Reservations +44 (0)1202 679828, **Telex** 41744, 41745.

INTERNET Website www.truckline.co.uk *(English)*

ROUTES OPERATED Cherbourg (***Winter*** *dep: 09.30 Wed, Fri, Sun, 18.30 Tue, Thu, Sat, 23.45 Mon, Wed, Fri, Sun,* ***Summer*** *02.00 Mon, Sat, Sun, 09.30 Tue, Thu, 14.30 Fri, Sat, Sun, 18.30 Mon, Wed, 23.45 Tue, Thu)* - Poole *(****Winter*** *dep: 16.00 Mon, Wed, Fri, Sun, 08.30, 23.45 Tue, Thu, Sat,* ***Summer*** *dep: 16.00 Tue, Thu, 08.30, 23.45 Mon, Wed, 07.30, 23.45 Fri, Sat, Sun)* (4 hrs 30 mins; *(1)*; 1/2 per day). Note Operates with *Brittany Ferries* passenger vessel BARFLEUR to provide three or four sailings every 24 hrs. Caen *(dep: 14.00 Sun, Mon, Fri, Sat, 00.30 Wed, Thu)* - Portsmouth *(dep: 13.00 Wed, 23.30 Sun, Mon, Thu-Sat)* (7 hr 15 min; *(2)*; 6 per week).

1	COUTANCES	6507t	78	17k	125.2m	58P	-	58T	BA	FR
2	PURBECK	6507t	78	17.5k	125.5m	58P	-	58T	BA	BA

COUTANCES Built at Le Havre, France for *Truckline Ferries* for their Cherbourg - Poole service. In 1986 lengthened to increase vehicle capacity by 34%.

PURBECK Built at Le Havre, France for *Truckline Ferries* for their Cherbourg - Poole service. In 1986 she was lengthened to increase vehicle capacity by 34%. In 1992 transferred to the Roscoff - Plymouth and Santander - Plymouth services. In 1994 she was sold to *Channel Island Ferries* (parent company of *British Channel Island Ferries*) to operate freight services between Poole and The Channel Islands. Later in 1994, chartered to *Commodore Ferries* following the cessation of *BCIF's*

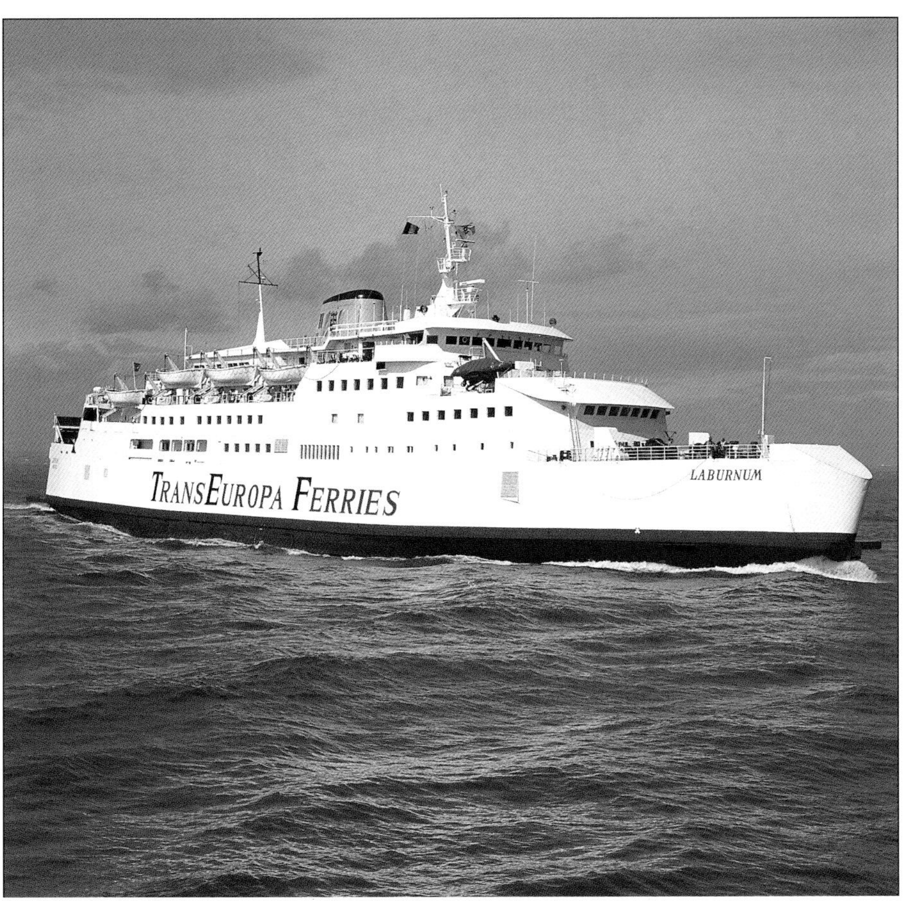

Laburnum *(Mike Louagie)*

operations. In 1995 she was chartered to *Sally Ferries* for use on their Dartford - Vlissingen service until replaced by the DART 5 later in the year. During summer 1996 she was chartered to *Irish Ferries* to operate supplementary freight services between Dublin and Holyhead. In autumn 1996 she returned to *Sally Ferries* and in 1997 she was transferred to *Holyman Sally Ferries*. In summer 1997 she was chartered to *Truckline Ferries* to operate between Caen and Portsmouth. Later in 1997, she was chartered to *Gaelic Ferries* to inaugurate a new Cork - Cherbourg service. During the French truckers' blockade in late 1997, she operated between Cork and Santander (Spain). In 1998 she was chartered to *Falcon Seafreight* and operated between Folkestone and Boulogne. In summer 1999 she was chartered to *Truckline Ferries* to operate between Caen and Portsmouth.

SOLENT ENTERPRISE
FOR PRIVATE HIRE

Spirit of Gosport *(John Bryant)*

section 4 chain, cable etc ferries

gb & ireland

In addition to the ferries listed above, there are a number of short chain ferries, cable ferries and ferries operated by unpowered floats.

BOURNEMOUTH-SWANAGE MOTOR ROAD AND FERRY COMPANY

Address ***Company*** Shell Bay, Studland, Swanage, Dorset. **Tel** +44 (0)1929 450203, **Fax** +44 (0)1929 450498), ***Ferry*** Floating Bridge, Ferry Way, Sandbanks, Poole, Dorset BH13 7QN. **Tel** +44 (0)1929 450203.

Route Sandbanks - Studland (Dorset).

1	BRAMBLE BUSH BAY	93	78.6m	400P	48C	BA

BRAMBLE BUSH BAY chain ferry, built at Hessle, UK for the *Bournemouth-Swanage Motor Road and Ferry Company.*

CUMBRIA COUNTY COUNCIL

Address Community, Economy & Environment Department, Citadel Chambers, Carlisle CA3 8SG. **Tel** +44 (0)1228 606744, **Fax** +44 (0)1228 606577.

INTERNET Email john.robinson@cumbriacc.gov.uk **Website** www.cumbria.gov.uk *(English (County Council web site - little about ferry))*

Route Bowness-on-Windermere - Far Sawrey.

1	MALLARD	90	25.9m	140P	18C	BA

MALLARD Chain Ferry built at Borth, Dyfed for *Cumbria County Council.*

DARTMOUTH – KINGSWEAR FLOATING BRIDGE CO LTD

Address Dart Marina, Sandquay Road, Dartmouth, Devon TQ6 9PH. **Tel** +44 (0)1803 833351.

Route Dartmouth - Kingswear (Devon) across River Dart (higher route) (forms part of A379).

1	HIGHER FERRY	60	42.7m	136P	18C	BA

HIGHER FERRY Built by *Philip Ltd* at Dartmouth UK. Diesel electric paddle propelled vessel guided by cross-river cables.

ISLE OF WIGHT COUNCIL (COWES FLOATING BRIDGE)

Address Ferry Office, Medina Road, Cowes, Isle of Wight PO31 7BX. **Tel** +44 (0)1983 293041

Route Cowes - East Cowes.

1	NO 5	76	33.5m	-	15C	BA

NO 5 Chain ferry built at East Cowes for *Isle of Wight County Council*, now *Isle of Wight Council*.

KING HARRY STEAM FERRY COMPANY

Address Feock, Truro, Cornwall TR3 6QJ. **Tel** +44 (0)1872 862312, **Fax** +44 (0)1872 863355.

INTERNET Email kingharryferry@feock.fsbusiness.co.uk **Website** www.kingharryferry.co.uk *(English)*

Route Across River Fal, King Harry Ferry (Cornwall).

1	KING HARRY FERRY	74	44.2m	100P	28C	BA

KING HARRY FERRY Chain ferry built at Falmouth, UK for *King Harry Steam Ferry Company*.

REEDHAM FERRY

Address Reedham Ferry, Ferry Inn, Reedham, Norwich NR13 3HA. **Tel** +44 (0)1493 700429, **Fax** +44 (0)1493 700999.

Route Acle - Reedham - Norton (across River Yare, Norfolk).

1	REEDHAM FERRY	84	11.3m	12P	3C	BA

REEDHAM FERRY Chain ferry built at Oulton Broad, UK for *Reedham Ferry*. Maximum weight, 12 tons.

SOUTH HAMS DISTRICT COUNCIL

Address Lower Ferry Office, The Square, Kingswear, Dartmouth, Devon TQ6 0AA. **Tel** +44 (0)1803 752342, **Fax** +44 (0)1803 752227.

Route Dartmouth - Kingswear (Devon) across River Dart (lower route).

1	THE TOM AVIS	94	33.5m	50P	8C	BA
2	THE TOM CASEY	89	33.5m	50P	8C	BA

THE TOM AVIS Float propelled by tugs built at Fowey, UK for *South Hams District Council*.

THE TOM CASEY Float propelled by tugs built at Portland, UK for *South Hams District Council*.

TORPOINT FERRY

Address 2 Ferry Street, Torpoint, Cornwall PL11 2AX. **Tel** +44 (0)1752 812233, **Fax** +44 (0)1752 816873.

INTERNET Website www.torpointferry.org.uk *(English)*

Route Devonport (Plymouth) - Torpoint (Cornwall) across the Tamar. Pre-booking is not possible and the above number cannot be used for that purpose.

1	LYNHER	61	70.7m	350P	48C	BA
2	PLYM	68	70.7m	350P	54C	BA
3	TAMAR	60	70.7m	350P	48C	BA

LYNHER, PLYM, TAMAR Chain ferries built at Southampton, UK (PLYM built at Bristol) for the *Torpoint Ferry*. The three ferries operate in parallel, each on its own 'track'.

Vessels to be built

4	NEWBUILDING 1	03	-	350P	73C	BA
5	NEWBUILDING 2	03	-	350P	73C	BA
6	NEWBUILDING 3	03	-	350P	73C	BA

NEWBUILDING 1, NEWBUILDING 2, NEWBUILDING 3 To be built for *Torpoint Ferry* to replace existing vessels. Orders not placed at time of going to press.

section 5 major passenger only ferries

gb & ireland

There are a surprisingly large number of passenger only ferries operating in the British Isles, mainly operated by launches and small motor boats. There are, however, a few 'major' operators who operate only passenger vessels (of rather larger dimensions) and have not therefore been mentioned previously.

Clyde Marine Motoring CRUISER (119t, 1974, 24.4m, 249 passengers (ex POOLE SCENE, 2001), FENCER (18t, 1976, 11.0m, 33 passengers), KENILWORTH (44t, 1936, 18.3m, 97 passengers (ex HOTSPUR II (Southampton - Hythe ferry) 1979)), ROVER (48t, 1964, 19.8m, 120 passengers), THE SECOND SNARK (45t, 1938, 22.9m, 120 passengers). **Route operated** Gourock - Kilcreggan - Helensburgh (generally the KENILWORTH is used on the ferry services and other vessels on excursions). **Tel** +44 (0)1475 721281, **Fax** +44 (0)1475 888023, **Website** www.clyde-marine.co.uk *(English)*

Dart Pleasure Craft EDGCUMBE BELLE (35t, 1957, 17.7m, 150 passengers), KINGSWEAR BELLE (43t, 1972, 18.0m, 257 passengers). **Route operated** Dartmouth - Kingswear. Note Pleasure craft owned by this operator are also used for the ferry service on some occasions. **Tel** +44 (0)1803 834488, **Fax** +44 (0)1803 835248, **Email** sales@riverlink.co.uk **Website** www.riverlink.co.uk *(English)*

Doolin Ferry Company/O'Brien Shipping DONEMARK (70t, 1978, 19.8m, 65 pass), HAPPY HOOKER (77t, 1989, 19.8m, 96 passengers), QUEEN OF ARAN (113t, 1976, 20.1m, 96 passengers), ROSE OF ARAN (113t, 1976, 20.1m, 96 passengers), TRANQUILITY (62t, 1988, 15.8m, 96 passengers). **Route operated** Doolin - Inishere, Doolin - Inishmaan, Doolin - Inishmore. OILEAN ARANN (416t, 1992, 39.6m, 190 passengers). **Route operated** Galway - Inishere, Galway - Inishmaan, Galway - Inishmore. **Tel** +353 (0)65 7074455, **Fax** +353 (0)65 7074417, **Email** doolinferries@eircom.net **Web Site** www.doolinferries.com *(English)*

Gosport Ferry GOSPORT QUEEN (159t, 1966, 30.5m, 250 passengers), PORTSMOUTH QUEEN (159t, 1966, 30.5m, 250 passengers), SOLENT ENTERPRISE (274t, 1971, 32.0m, 250 passengers (ex GAY ENTERPRISE 1979) (mainly used on excursion work), SPIRIT OF GOSPORT (250t, 2001, 32.6m, 300 passengers). **Route operated** Gosport - Portsmouth. **Tel** +44 (0)23 9252 4551, **Email** info@gosportferry.co.uk **Web Site** www.gosportferry.co.uk *(English)*

Hovertravel DOUBLE O SEVEN (1989, 24.5m, 98 passengers) (BHC AP1-88/100 hovercraft), FREEDOM 90 (1990, 24.5m, 98 passengers) (BHC AP1-88/100S hovercraft (converted from AP1-88/100 in 2000)), FREJA VIKING (1985, 24.5m, 82 passengers) (BHC AP1-88/100S hovercraft (converted from BHC AP1-88/100 in 2001)), IDUN VIKING (1983, 24.5m, 98 passengers) (BHC AP1-88/100 hovercraft), LIV VIKING (1985, 24.5m, 82 passengers) (BHC AP1-88/100 hovercraft). **Route operated** Southsea - Ryde. **Tel** +44 (0)1983 811000, **Fax** +44 (0)1983 562216, **Email** info@hovertravel.co.uk, **Website** www.hovertravel.co.uk *(English)*

Island Ferries ARAN EXPRESS (117t, 1984, 27.4m, 180 passengers), ARAN FLYER (170t, 1988, 33.5m, 208 passengers), ARAN SEABIRD (164t, 1976, 27.7m, 181 passengers), CEOL NA FARRAIGE (200t, 2001, 35.4m, 294 passengers), DRAÍOCHT NA FARRAIGE (200t, 1999, 35.4m, 294 passengers). **Routes operated** Rossaveal (Co Galway) - Aran Islands. **Tel** +353 (0)91 568903 (572273 after 19.00), **Fax** +353 (0)91 568538, **Email** island@iol.ie, **Website** www.aranislandferries.com *(English)*

Lower Thames & Medway Passenger Boat Co Ltd MARTIN CHUZZLEWIT (25.6t, 1995, 18.3m, 60 passengers (tri-maran)), PRINCESS POCAHONTAS (180t, 1962, 33.5m, 207 passengers (ex FREYA II 1989, LABOE I 1985, LABOE 1984 (excursion vessel)). **Route operated** Gravesend (Kent) - Tilbury (Essex). **Tel** +44 (0)1732 353448, **Mobile** +44 (0)7831 300148, **Email** enquiry@princess-pocahontas.com **Web Site** www.princess-pocahontas.com *(English). Service suspended at the time of going to press.*

Lundy Company OLDENBURG (288t, 1958, 43.6m, 267 passengers). **Routes operated** Bideford - Lundy Island, Ilfracombe - Lundy Island. Also North Devon Coastal Cruises. **Tel** +44 (0)1237 470422, **Fax** +44 (0)1237 477779, **Email** infor@lundyisland.co.uk **Web Site** www.lundyisland.co.uk *(English)*

Mersey Ferries ROYAL DAFFODIL (ex OVERCHURCH 1999) (468t, 1962, 46.6m, 860 passengers), ROYAL IRIS OF THE MERSEY (ex MOUNTWOOD 2002) (464t, 1960, 46.3m, 750 passengers), WOODCHURCH (464t, 1960, 46.6m, 750 passengers). **Routes operated** Liverpool (Pier Head) - Birkenhead (Woodside), Liverpool - Wallasey (Seacombe). Also regular summer cruises from Pier Head to Salford along Manchester Ship Canal. **Tel** ***Admin*** +44 (0)151 639 0609, ***Reservations*** +44 (0)151 330 1444, **Fax** +44 (0)151 639 0578, **Email** info@merseyferries.co.uk **Website** www.merseyferries.co.uk *(English)*

Nexus (trading name of Tyne & Wear PTE) PRIDE OF THE TYNE (222t, 1993, 25.6m, 350 passengers), SHIELDSMAN (93t, 1976, 24.1m, 350 passengers). **Route operated** North Shields - South Shields. Also cruises South Shields - Newcastle. **Tel** +44 (0)191 454 8183, **Fax** +44 (0)191 427 9510, **Web Site** www.nexus.org.uk *(English)*

Strathclyde Passenger Transport RENFREW ROSE (65t, 1984, 21.9m, 50 passengers), YOKER SWAN (65t, 1984, 21.9m, 50 passengers). **Route operated** Renfrew - Yoker. Note although this a passenger only service, the vessels are built as small front loading car ferries and are able to convey one vehicle if necessary. This facility is sometimes used for the conveyance of ambulances. **Tel** +44 (0)141 885 2123, **Fax** +44 (0)141 432 1025, **Email** liz.parkes@spt.co.uk **Website** www.spt.co.uk *(English)*

Thames Clippers (part of Collins River Enterprises) ABEL MAGWITCH (25.6t, 1999, 18.3m, 60 passengers (tri-maran)), HURRICANE CLIPPER (2002, 37.8m, 27.5k, 220 passengers), SKY CLIPPER (60t, 1992, 25.0m, 62 passengers) (ex VERITATUM 1995, SD10 2000), STORM CLIPPER (60t, 1992, 25.0m, 62 passengers) (ex DHL WORLDWIDE EXPRESS 1995, SD11 2000). Routes operated Savoy Pier (Embankment) - Canary Wharf, Canary Wharf - Rotherhithe (Holiday Inn) (usually the ABEL MAGWITCH). **Tel** +44 (0)20 7977 6892, **Fax** +44(0) 20 7481 8300, **Email** sean@thamesclippers.com **Website** www. thamesclippers.com *(English)*

Waverley Excursions BALMORAL (735t, 1949, 62.2m, 800 passengers), WAVERLEY (693t, 1947, 73.2m, 950 passengers). **Routes operated** Excursions all round British Isles. However, regular cruises in the Clyde, Bristol Channel and south coast provide a service which can be used for transport purposes and therefore both vessels are, in a sense, ferries. The WAVERLEY is the only seagoing paddle steamer in the world. **Tel** +44 (0)141 221 8152, **Fax** +44 (0)141 248 2150, **Email** info@waverleyexcursions.co.uk **Website** www.waverleyexcursions.co.uk *(English)*

White Horse Ferries GREAT EXPECTATIONS (66t, 1992, 21.3m, 62 passengers) (catamaran), HOTSPUR IV (50t, 1946, 19.5m, 125 passengers). **Route operated** Southampton - Hythe (Hants). ***Head Office*** **Tel**. +44 (0)1793 618566, **Fax** +44 (0)1793 488428, ***Local Office*** **Tel** +44 (0)23 8084 0722, **Fax** +44 (0)23 8084 6611, **Email** post@hytheferry.co.uk **Website** www.hytheferry.co.uk *(English)*

TT-Line
Nils Holgersson
Lübeck
Peter Pan
Nassau

Peter Pan, Nils Holgerson and **Robin Hood** *(TT Line)*

section **6** major passenger ferries

northern europe

ÅNEDIN LINE

THE COMPANY *Ånedin Line* is the trading name of *Rederi AB Allandia*, a Swedish company.

MANAGEMENT Managing Director Magnus Straunch, **Marketing Manager** Torsten Sundberg.

ADDRESS PO Box 1151, S-11181 Stockholm, Sweden.

TELEPHONE Administration +46 (0)8-456 2200, **Reservations** +46 (0)8-456 2200.

FAX Administration & Reservations +46 (0)8-10 07 41.

ROUTE OPERATED Cruises from Stockholm to Mariehamn (Åland) (22 hrs; *(1)*; 1 per day).

INTERNET Email m.straunch@rederiallandia.se **Website** www.anedinlinjen.com *(Swedish)*

1	BIRGER JARL	3564t	53	15k	92.4m	400P	0C	0L	-	SW

BIRGER JARL Built at Stockholm, Sweden as the BIRGER JARL for *Stockholms Rederi AB Svea* of Sweden to operate between Stockholm and Turku and Stockholm and Helsinki. She was a crane loading car ferry with capacity for 25 cars, since removed. In 1973 she was sold to *Jacob Line*, to operate between Pietarsaari (Finland) and Skellefteå (Sweden); she was renamed the BORE NORD. In 1974 she started a service from Turku to Visby (Gotland) but this was short lived and, for a time, she served as an accommodation vessel at Stavanger. In 1977 she was sold to *Mini Carriers* of Finland who renamed her the MINISEA and announced plans for a new Finland - Sweden service. These plans did not materialise and in 1978 she was acquired by the *Caribbean Shipping Company* of Panama, chartered to *Rederi AB Allandia*, renamed the BALTIC STAR and started operating 24 hour cruises. In 1997, following changes to Swedish customs regulations, these became 22 hour cruises, allowing a regular departure time each day. In 2002 renamed the BIRGER JARL and re-registered in Sweden.

BASTØ FOSEN

THE COMPANY *Bastø Fosen* is a Norwegian private sector company, a subsidiary of *Fosen Trafikklag* of Trondheim.

MANAGEMENT Managing Director Olav Brein, **Operations Manager** Kirsti Been Tofte.

ADDRESS PO Box 94, 3191 Horten, Norway.

TELEPHONE Administration +47 33 03 17 40, **Reservations** not applicable.

FAX Administration & Reservations +47 33 03 17 49.

INTERNET Email basto@fosen.no **Website** www.basto-fosen.no *(Norwegian)*

ROUTE OPERATED Moss - Horten (across Oslofjord, Norway) (30 mins; *(1,2,3)*; up to every 45 mins).

1	BASTØ I	5505t	97	14k	109.0m	550P	220C	18L	BA	NO
2	BASTØ II	5505t	97	14k	109.0m	550P	220C	18L	BA	NO

BASTØ I, BASTØ II Built at Frengen, Norway for *Bastø Fosen*.

BIRKA CRUISES

THE COMPANY *Birka Cruises* is an Åland Islands company.

MANAGEMENT Managing Director Michael Larkner.

ADDRESS Box 15131, S-104 65 Stockholm, Sweden.

TELEPHONE Administration +46 (0)8-702 7200, **Reservations** +46 (0)8-702 7230.

FAX Administration & Reservations +46 (0)8-643 9246.

INTERNET Email info@birkacruises.com **Website** www.birkacruises.com *(Swedish, English)*

ROUTES OPERATED Stockholm - Mariehamn (Åland) - Stockholm (cruise) (22 hrs 45 mins; *(1)*; 1 per day (except when Riga/Gdynia/Tallinn cruises operate), Stockholm - Visby (Gotland) - Riga (Latvia) - Stockholm, Stockholm - Visby Gdynia (Poland) or Stockholm - Tallinn (Estonia) - Visby - Stockholm (70 hrs 45 mins (cruise); *(1)*; weekly, mid June to mid-August).

1p	BIRKA PRINCESS	22412t	86	21k	142.9m	1500P	0C	0L	-	FI

BIRKA PRINCESS Built at Helsinki, Finland for *Birka Cruises*. As built, she had capacity for 10 cars, loaded via a side door. During winter 1998/99 she was the subject of a major refit to modernise her, increase her passenger capacity and install catalytic converters on all engines to make her the most environmentally friendly cruise ferry in the world; the vehicle facility was removed.

BORNHOLMSTRAFIKKEN

THE COMPANY *BornholmsTrafikken* is a Danish state owned company.

MANAGEMENT Managing Director Mads Kofod, **Sales and Marketing Manager** Niels Kreutzmann.

ADDRESS Havnen, DK-3700 Rønne, Denmark.

TELEPHONE Administration +45 56 95 18 66, **Reservations** +45 56 95 18 66.

FAX Administration & Reservations +45 56 91 07 66.

INTERNET Email info@bornholmferries.dk **Website** www.bornholmferries.dk *(Danish, German)*

ROUTES OPERATED Conventional Ferries Rønne (Bornholm, Denmark) - Copenhagen (7 hrs; *(1,2)*; 1 or 2 per day), Rønne - Ystad (Sweden) (2 hrs 30 mins; *(1,2)*; 1 or 2 per day), Rønne - Sassnitz (Germany) (3 hrs 30 mins; *(1,2)*; up to 10 per week (joint with *Scandlines AG* - this operator operates the service in the summer). **Fast Ferry** Ystad (Sweden) - Rønne (1 hr 20 mins; *(3)*; up to 5 per day).

1	JENS KOFOED	12131t	79	19.5k	121.0m	1500P	262C	26T	BA	DK
2	POVL ANKER	12131t	78	19.5k	121.0m	1500P	262C	26T	BA	DK
3»	VILLUM CLAUSEN	6402t	99	40k	86.6m	1000P	180C	-	BA	DK

JENS KOFOED, POVL ANKER Built at Aalborg, Denmark for *BornholmsTrafikken*. Used on the Rønne - Copenhagen, Rønne - Ystad and Rønne - Sassnitz services.

VILLUM CLAUSEN Austal Auto-Express 86 catamaran built at Fremantle, Australia for *BornholmsTrafikken*. Used on the Rønne - Ystad service.

BOTNIA LINK

THE COMPANY *Botnia Link* is a Swedish private sector company.

MANAGEMENT Managing Director Börje Lassfolk.

ADDRESS *Sweden* Skeppsbron 31, Box 345, SE-871 Härnösand, Sweden, ***Finland*** 30 Harnosand Reininkatu 3, PO Box 257, FI-651 01, Vaasa, Finland.

TELEPHONE Administration & Reservations *Sweden* +46 (0)611-55 05 55, ***Finland*** +358 (0)6-322 66 00.

FAX Administration & Reservations *Sweden* +46 (0)611-55 05 34, ***Finland*** + 358 (0)6-322 66 01.

INTERNET Email info.se@botnialink.se **Website** www.botnialink.se *(Swedish, Finnish, English)*

ROUTE OPERATED Vaasa (Finland) - Umeå (Sweden) (4 hrs; *(1)*; 3/4 per week), Vaasa - Härnösand (Sweden) (7 hrs; *(1)*; 4/5 per week), Umeå - Härnösand (8 hrs; *(1)*; 1 per week).

1	TRANSPARADEN	13700t	76	17k	135.8m	100P	-	115T	A	FI

TRANSPARADEN Built at Hamburg, Germany as the TRANSGERMANIA for *Poseidon Schiffahrt OHG* of Germany interests for *Finncarriers-Poseidon* services between Finland and West Germany. In 1991 chartered to *Norse Irish Ferries* and used on their freight service between Liverpool and Belfast. In 1992 she was returned to *Finncarriers* and in 1993 sold to Cypriot interests for use in the Mediterranean and renamed the ROSEBAY. In 1994 chartered to *Stena Line* to inaugurate a new service between Harwich and Rotterdam (Frisohaven). In 1995 the service was switched to Hoek van Holland following the construction of a new linkspan. She also, during the summer, carried cars towing caravans, motor caravans and their passengers. In 1997 she was chartered to *Sally Freight* and renamed the EUROSTAR, operating between Ramsgate and Ostend. Later in 1997 she was renamed the EUROCRUISER. In 1998 she returned on charter to *Stena Line* and resumed the name ROSEBAY. In 1999 she was temporarily transferred to the Irish Sea. In autumn 2000 she was transferred to the Killingholme - Hoek van Holland service but was withdrawn in 2001 when the delivery of the new STENA HOLLANDICA enabled the STENA SEARIDER to replace her. She was then sold to *Rederi AB Engship* of Sweden, renamed the TRANSPARADEN and chartered to *Botnia Link*.

COLOR LINE

THE COMPANY *Color Line ASA* is a Norwegian private sector stock-listed limited company. The company merged with *Larvik Scandi Line* of Norway (which owned *Larvik Line* and *Scandi Line*) in 1996. *Larvik Line's* operations were incorporated into *Color Line* in 1997; *Scandi Line* continued as a separate subsidiary until 1999, when it was also incorporated into *Color Line*. The marketing name *Color Scandi Line* was dropped at the end of 2000.

MANAGEMENT Managing Director Trygve Sigerset, **Marketing Manager** Elisabeth Anspach.

ADDRESS *Commercial* Postboks 1422 Vika, 0115 OSLO, Norway, ***Technical Management*** Color Line Marine AS, PO Box 2090, N-3210 Sandefjord, Norway.

TELEPHONE Administration +47 22 94 44 00, **Reservations** +47 810 00 811.

FAX Administration +47 22 83 04 30, **Reservations** +47 22 83 07 76.

INTERNET Website www.colorline.com *(Norwegian, English)*

ROUTES OPERATED Conventional Ferries Oslo (Norway) - Kiel (Germany) (19 hrs 30 mins; *(5,7)*; 1 per day), Oslo - Hirtshals (Denmark) (8 hrs 30 mins; *(3)*; 1 per day), Kristiansand (Norway) - Hirtshals (4 hrs 30 mins; *(2)*; 2 per day), Larvik (Norway) - Frederikshavn (Denmark) (6 hrs 15 mins; *(6,9)*; 2 or 3 per day), Sandefjord (Norway) - Strömstad (Sweden) (2 hrs 30 mins; *(1,4)*; up to 6 per day). **Fast Ferry (under the name 'Color Line Express') Summer only** Kristiansand - Hirtshals (2 hrs 30 mins; *(8)*; 3 per day).

1	BOHUS	8772t	71	19.5k	122.7m	1480P	280C	34T	BA	NO
2	CHRISTIAN IV	21699t	82	20k	153.1m	1860P	480C	56T	BAS2	NO
3	COLOR FESTIVAL	34314t	85	22k	168.0m	2000P	330C	80T	BA	NO
4	COLOR VIKING	19763t	85	17.5k	134.0m	2000P	320C	40T	BA2	BA
5	KRONPRINS HARALD	31914t	87	21.5k	166.3m	1432P	700C	90T	BA	NO
6	PETER WESSEL	29704t	81	19k	168.5m	2100P	570C	136T	BA	BO
7	PRINSESSE RAGNHILD	35438t	81	21k	205.3m	1875P	770C	70T	BA	NO
8»	SILVIA ANA L	7895t	96	41k	125.0m	1043P	238C	4L	A	BA
9	SKAGEN	12333t	75	20k	129.8m	1200P	430C	28Tr	BA2	NO

BOHUS Built at Aalborg, Denmark as the PRINSESSAN DESIREE for *Rederi AB Göteborg-Frederikshavn Linjen* of Sweden (trading as *Sessan Linjen*) for their service between Gothenburg and Frederikshavn. In 1981 the company was taken over by *Stena Line* and she became surplus to requirements. During 1981 she had a number of charters including *B&I Line* of Ireland and *Sealink* UK. In 1982 she was chartered to *Sally Line* to operate as second vessel on the Ramsgate - Dunkerque service between June and September. She bore the name VIKING 2 in large letters on her hull although she was never officially renamed and continued to bear the name PRINSESSAN DESIREE on her bow and stern. In September 1982 she returned to *Stena Line* and in 1983 she was transferred to subsidiary company *Varberg-Grenaa Line* for their service between Varberg (Sweden) and Grenaa (Denmark) and renamed the EUROPAFÄRJAN. In 1985 she was renamed the EUROPAFÄRJAN II. In 1986, following a reorganisation within the *Stena Line* Group, ownership was transferred to subsidiary company *Lion Ferry AB* and she was named the LION PRINCESS. In 1993 she was sold to *Scandi Line* and renamed the BOHUS. In 1999 *Scandi Line* operations were integrated into *Color Line*.

CHRISTIAN IV Built at Bremerhaven, Germany as the OLAU BRITANNIA for *Olau Line* of Germany for their service between Vlissingen (Netherlands) and Sheerness (England). In 1989 sold to *Nordström & Thulin* of Sweden for delivery in spring 1990. She was subsequently resold to *Fred. Olsen Lines* of Norway and, on delivery, renamed the BAYARD and used on their service between Kristiansand and Hirtshals. In December 1990 she was acquired by *Color Line* and in 1991 renamed the CHRISTIAN IV. She continues to operate on that route.

COLOR FESTIVAL Built at Helsinki, Finland as the SVEA for *Johnson Line* for the *Silja Line* Stockholm - Mariehamn - Turku service. During winter 1991/92 she was extensively rebuilt and in 1991 renamed the SILJA KARNEVAL; ownership was transferred to *Silja Line*. In 1993 she was sold to *Color Line* and renamed the COLOR FESTIVAL. She is used on the Oslo - Hirtshals service.

COLOR VIKING Built at Nakskov, Denmark as the PEDER PAARS for *DSB (Danish State Railways)* for their service between Kalundborg (Sealand) and Århus (Jutland). In 1990 purchased by *Stena Line* of Sweden for delivery in 1991. In 1991 renamed the STENA INVICTA and entered service on the *Sealink Stena Line* Dover - Calais service. She was withdrawn from the route in February 1998, before the formation of *P&O Stena Line* but ownership was transferred to that company. In summer 1998, she was chartered to *Silja Line* to operate between Vaasa and Umeå under the marketing name 'WASA JUBILEE'. In autumn 1998 she was laid up at Zeebrugge. She remained there until autumn 1999 when she was chartered to *Stena Line* to operate between Holyhead and Dublin. In 2000 she was chartered to *Color Line* and renamed the COLOR VIKING and in April entered service on the Sandefjord - Strömstad service. In 2002 purchased by *Color Line*.

KRONPRINS HARALD Built at Turku, Finland for *Jahre Line* of Norway for the Oslo - Kiel service. In 1991 ownership was transferred to *Color Line*.

PETER WESSEL Built at Landskrona, Sweden for *Rederi AB Gotland* of Sweden. A sister vessel of the VISBY (see *Destination Gotland*), it was intended that she should be named the GOTLAND. However, she was delivered as the WASA STAR and chartered to *Vaasanlaivat* of Finland and used on their Vaasa - Sundsvall service. In 1982 she was chartered to *Karageorgis Line* of Greece for service between Patras (Greece) and Ancona (Italy). This charter was abruptly terminated in 1983 following a dispute over payment of charter dues. She returned the Baltic and was laid up until February 1984 when she was sold to *Larvik Line*. She was renamed the PETER WESSEL. In 1988 she was lengthened. In 1996 acquired by *Color Line*. She remains on the Larvik - Moss -

Frederikshavn route.

PRINSESSE RAGNHILD Built at Kiel, Germany for *Jahre Line* of Norway for the Oslo - Kiel service. In 1991 ownership transferred to *Color Line*. In 1992 rebuilt in Spain with an additional mid-ships section and additional decks.

SILVIA ANA L Bazan Alhambra monohull vessel built at San Fernando, Spain for *Buquebus* of Argentina. Initially operated between Buenos Aires (Argentina) and Piriapolis (Uruguay). In 1997 chartered to *Color Line* to operate between Kristiansand and Hirtshals. During winter 1997/98 she again operated in South America but returned to *Color Line* in spring 1998. This was repeated during winters 1998/9 and 1999/2000 but during winter 2000/2001 she remained laid up in Europe. In 2001 she was sold to *MDFC Aircraft* of the Irish Republic and chartered to *Color Line* for four years.

SKAGEN Vehicle/train ferry built at Aalborg, Denmark as the BORGEN for *Fred. Olsen Lines* of Norway for Norway - Denmark services. In December 1990 acquired by *Color Line* and in 1991 renamed the SKAGEN. Until 1997 she operated mainly between Hirtshals and Kristiansand although in later years rail wagons were longer conveyed. In recent years she also operated between Hirtshals and Moss but this service ceased in 2000 and she then served Kristiansand only. In spring 2001 she was transferred to the Larvik - Frederikshavn service. Although mainly operated for freight, the service is also available to car passengers and a special lower rate is available on most sailings.

DESTINATION GOTLAND

THE COMPANY *Destination Gotland AB* is a Swedish private sector company owned by *Rederi AB Gotland*. It took over the operations of services to Gotland from 1st January 1998 on a six-year concession. Originally jointly owned by *Rederi AB Gotland* and *Silja Line*, *Silja Line* involvement in the company ceased at the end of 1998.

MANAGEMENT Managing Director Sten-Christer Fursberg, **Marketing Manager** Per-Erling Evensen.

ADDRESS PO Box 1234, 621 23 Visby, Gotland, Sweden.

TELEPHONE Administration +46 (0)498-20 18 00, **Reservations** +46 (0)498-20 10 20.

FAX Administration & Reservations +46 (0)498-20 13 90.

INTERNET Email per-erling.evensen@destinationgotland.se **Website** www.destinationgotland.se *(Swedish, English)*

ROUTES OPERATED Conventional Ferries Visby (Gotland) - Nynäshamn (Swedish mainland) (5 hrs 30 mins; *(2,3)*; 1/2 per day), Visby - Oskarshamn (Swedish mainland) (4 hrs 30 mins; *(2,3)*; 1/2 per day). **Fast Ferry** Visby (Gotland) - Nynäshamn (2 hrs 50 mins; *(1)*; up to 2 per day), Visby - Oskarshamn (Swedish mainland) (2 hrs 25 mins; *(3)*; very limited service) (no fast ferry services mid December - mid March).

1»	GOTLAND	5632t	99	35k	112.5m	700P	140C	-	A	SW
2	THJELVAR	16829t	81	19k	140.8m	1500P	440C	84T	BA2	SW
3	VISBY	23775t	80	20k	146.1m	1800P	510C	60L	BA2	SW

GOTLAND Alstom Leroux Corsair 11500 monohull vessel built at Nantes, France for *Rederi AB Gotland* and chartered to *Destination Gotland*.

THJELVAR Built at Helsinki, Finland as the TRAVEMÜNDE for *Gedser-Travemünde Ruten* of Denmark for their service between Gedser (Denmark) and Travemünde (Germany). In 1986 the company's trading name was changed to *GT Linien* and in 1987, following the take-over by *Sea-Link AB* of Sweden, it was further changed to *GT Link*. The vessel's name was changed to the TRAVEMÜNDE LINK. In 1988 she was purchased by *Rederi AB Gotland* of Sweden, although remaining in service with *GT Link*. Later in 1988 she was chartered to *Sally Ferries* and entered service in December on the Ramsgate - Dunkerque service. She was renamed the SALLY STAR. In 1997 she was transferred to *Silja Line*, to operate between Vaasa and Umeå during the summer period and operated under the marketing name WASA EXPRESS (although not renamed). She returned to *Rederi AB Gotland* in autumn 1997, was renamed the THJELVAR and entered service

Prinsesse Ragnhild *(Philippe Holthof)*

Nordlandia *(Dominic McCall)*

with *Destination Gotland* in January 1998.

VISBY Built at Landskrona, Sweden as the VISBY for *Rederi AB Gotland* of Sweden for their services between the island of Gotland and the Swedish mainland. In 1987, the franchise to operate these services was lost by the company and awarded to *Nordström & Thulin* of Sweden. A subsidiary called *N&T Gotlandslinjen AB* was formed to operate the service. The VISBY was chartered to this company and managed by *Johnson Line*, remaining owned by *Rederi AB Gotland*. In early 1990 she was chartered to *Sealink* and renamed the FELICITY. After modifications at Tilbury, she was, in March 1990, introduced onto the Fishguard - Rosslare route. Later in 1990 she was renamed the STENA FELICITY. In summer 1997 she was returned to *Rederi AB Gotland* for rebuilding, prior to her entering service with *Destination Gotland* in January 1998. She was renamed the VISBY.

Under Construction

4	NEWBUILDING 1	29000t	02	28.5k	195.8m	1500P	500C	118T	BA	SW
5	NEWBUILDING 2	29000t	02	28.5k	195.8m	1500P	500C	118T	BA	SW

NEWBUILDING 1, NEWBUILDING 2 Under construction at Guangzhou, China for *Rederi AB Gotland*. Expected to be used on *Destination Gotland* services.

DFDS SEAWAYS

THE COMPANY *DFDS Seaways A/S* is the passenger division of *DFDS Group*, a Danish private sector company.

MANAGEMENT Managing Director DFDS A/S Thorleif Blok, **Managing Director DFDS Seaways A/S** Thor Johannesen.

ADDRESS Sankt Annæ Plads 30, DK-1295 Copenhagen K, Denmark.

TELEPHONE Administration +45 33 42 33 42, **Reservations** +45 33 42 30 00.

FAX Administration & Reservations +45 33 42 33 41.

INTERNET Website www.dfdsseaways.com *(Danish, Dutch, English, German, Norwegian, Swedish)*

ROUTE OPERATED Copenhagen - Helsingborg (Sweden) - Oslo (Norway) (16 hrs; *(1,2)*; 1 per day), ***From 1st October 2002*** Copenhagen - Trelleborg - Gdansk (Poland) (13 hrs; *(DANA ANGLIA (see Section 1))*; alternate days). See Section 1 for services operating to Britain.

1	CROWN OF SCANDINAVIA	35498t	94	21.5k	171.0m	2136P	450C	66T	BA	DK
2	PEARL OF SCANDINAVIA	40022t	89	21.5k	176.6m	2200P	620C	82T	BA	DK

CROWN OF SCANDINAVIA Launched at Split, Croatia for *Euroway* for their Lübeck - Travemünde - Malmö service. However, political problems led to serious delays and, before delivery, the service had ceased. She was purchased by *DFDS*, renamed the CROWN OF SCANDINAVIA and introduced onto the Copenhagen - Oslo service.

PEARL OF SCANDINAVIA Built at Turku, Finland as the ATHENA for *Rederi AB Slite* of Sweden (part of *Viking Line*) and used on 24 hour cruises from Stockholm to Mariehamn (Åland). In 1993 the company went into liquidation and she was sold to *Star Cruises* of Malaysia for cruises in the Far East. She was renamed the STAR AQUARIUS. Later that year she was renamed the LANGKAPURI STAR AQUARIUS. In February 2001 sold to *DFDS* and renamed the AQUARIUS. After rebuilding, she was renamed the PEARL OF SCANDINAVIA and introduced onto the Copenhagen - Oslo service.

REDERIJ DOEKSEN

THE COMPANY *Rederij G Doeksen & Zonen bv* is a Dutch public sector company. Ferries are operated by subsidiary *Terschellinger Stoomboot Maatschappij*, trading as *Rederij Doeksen*.

MANAGEMENT Managing Director P Melles, **Marketing Manager** C Dekker.

ADDRESS Willem Barentskade 21, Postbus 40, 8880 AA West Terschelling, Netherlands.

TELEPHONE Administration +31 (0)562 442141, **Reservations** +31 (0)562 446111.

FAX Administration & Reservations +31 (0)562 443241.

INTERNET Email info@rederij-doeksen.nl **Website** www.rederij-doeksen.nl *(Dutch)*

ROUTES OPERATED Conventional Ferries Harlingen (Netherlands) - Terschelling (Frisian Islands) (2 hrs; *(1,3)*; up to 6 per day), Harlingen - Vlieland (Frisian Islands) (1 hr 45 mins; *(5)*; 3 per day). **Fast Passenger Ferries** Harlingen - Terschelling (50 mins; *(2,4)*; up to 3 per day), Harlingen - Vlieland (50 mins; *(2,4)*; 2 per day), Vlieland - Terschelling (30 mins; *(2,4)*; 2 per day).

1	FRIESLAND	3583t	89	14k	69.0m	1750P	122C	12L	BA	NL
2»p	KOEGELWIECK	439t	92	33k	36.7m	317P	0C	0L	-	NL
3	MIDSLAND	1812t	74	15.5k	77.9m	1200P	55C	6L	BA	NL
4»p	NAJADE	164t	99	32k	31.8m	184P	0C	0L	-	NL
5	OOST-VLIELAND	1350t	70	15k	62.6m	1100P	45C	4L	BA	NL

FRIESLAND Built at Krimpen an der IJssel, Rotterdam, Netherlands for *Rederij Doeksen*. Used on the Harlingen - Terschelling route.

KOEGELWIECK Harding 35m catamaran built at Rosendal, Norway for *Rederij Doeksen* to operate between Harlingen and Terschelling, Harlingen and Vlieland and Terschelling and Vlieland.

MIDSLAND Built at Emden, Germany as the RHEINLAND for *AG Ems* of Germany. In 1993 purchased by *Rederij Doeksen* and renamed the MIDSLAND. Used mainly on the Harlingen - Terschelling route but also used on the Harlingen - Vlieland service. She is now a reserve vessel.

NAJADE SBF Shipbuilders 31m monohull built at Henderson, Australia for *Rederij Doeksen* to operate between Harlingen and Terschelling, Harlingen and Vlieland and Terschelling and Vlieland.

OOST-VLIELAND Built at Emden, Germany as the OSTFRIESLAND for *AG Ems* of Germany. In 1981 purchased by *Rederij Doeksen* and renamed the SCHELLINGERLAND. In 1994 renamed the OOST VLIELAND. Now mainly used on the Harlingen - Vlieland service.

Under construction

6F	NEWBUILDING 1	-	02	14k	45.6m	12P	-	6L	BA	NL

NEWBUILDING 1 Catamaran under construction at Harwood, New South Wales, Australia for *Rederij Doeksen*. To operate freight services from Harlingen to Terschelling and Vlieland. Due to enter service in August 2002.

Orders to be placed

7	NEWBUILDING 2	-	03	-	62.0m	1300P	68C	-	BA	NL
8	NEWBUILDING 3	-	04	-	62.0m	1300P	68C	-	BA	NL

NEWBUILDING 2, NEWBUILDING 3 Catamarans to be ordered to replace the OOST-VLIELAND and MIDSLAND

ECKERÖ LINE

THE COMPANY *Eckerö Line Ab Oy* is a Finnish company, 100% owned by *Eckerö Linjen* of Åland, Finland. Until January 1998, the company was called *Eestin-Linjat.*

MANAGEMENT Managing Director Jarl Danielsson, **Marketing Director** Håkan Nordström.

ADDRESS Hietalahdenranta 13, FIN-00180 Helsinki, Finland.

TELEPHONE Administration +358 (0)9 22885421, **Reservations** +358 (0)9 2288544.

FAX Administration & Reservations +358 (0)9 22885222.

INTERNET Email info@eckeroline.fi **Website** www.eckeroline.fi *(Swedish, Finnish, English, German)*

ROUTE OPERATED Helsinki - Tallinn (Estonia) (3 hrs 30 mins; *(1)*; 1 per day).

1	NORDLANDIA	21473t	81	21k	153.4m	2048P	530C	40T	BA	FI

NORDLANDIA Built at Bremerhaven, Germany as the OLAU HOLLANDIA for *Olau Line* of Germany for the service between Vlissingen (Netherlands) and Sheerness (England). In 1989 she was replaced by a new vessel of the same name and she was sold to *Nordström & Thulin.* She was renamed the NORD GOTLANDIA and introduced onto *Gotlandslinjen* services between Gotland and the Swedish mainland. In 1997 she was purchased by *Eckerö Linjen* of Åland for delivery in early 1998, following the ending of *Nordström & Thulin's* concession to operate the Gotland services. She was renamed the NORDLANDIA and placed on the *Eckerö Line* Helsinki - Tallinn service, operating day trips.

ECKERÖ LINJEN

THE COMPANY *Eckerö Linjen* is an Åland Islands company.

MANAGEMENT Managing Director Jarl Danielsson, **Marketing Director** Christer Lindman.

ADDRESS Torggatan 2, Box 158, FIN-22100 Mariehamn, Åland.

TELEPHONE Administration +358 (0)18 28000, **Reservations** +358 (0)18 28300.

FAX Administration & Reservations +358 (0)18 28380.

INTERNET Website www.eckerolinjen.fi *(Swedish)*

ROUTE OPERATED Eckerö (Åland) - Grisslehamn (Sweden) (2 hrs; *(1,2)*; 5 per day).

1	ALANDIA	6754t	72	17k	108.7m	1320P	225C	32T	BA	FI
2	ROSLAGEN	6652t	72	18.7k	109.3m	1200P	225C	32T	BA	FI

ALANDIA Built at Papenburg, Germany as the DIANA for *Rederi AB Slite* of Sweden for *Viking Line* services. In 1979 she was sold to *Wasa Line* of Finland and renamed the BOTNIA EXPRESS. In 1982 she was sold to *Sally Line* of Finland; later that year she was sold to *Suomen Yritysrahoitus Oy* and chartered back. In 1992 she was sold to *Eckerö Linjen* and renamed the ALANDIA. She has also been used by subsidiary company *Eckerö Line.*

ROSLAGEN Built at Papenburg, Germany as the VIKING 3 for *Rederi AB Sally* and used on *Viking Line* Baltic services. In 1976 she was sold to *Vaasanlaivat* of Finland for their service between Vaasa (Finland) and Umeå/Sundsvall (Sweden) and renamed the WASA EXPRESS. In 1982 *Vaasanlaivat* was taken over by *Rederi AB Sally* and in April 1983 she resumed her original name, was transferred to *Sally Line* and used on the Ramsgate - Dunkerque service. She remained in the Channel during winter 1983/4 on freight-only services. However, in early 1984 she returned to *Vaasanlaivat* and resumed the name WASA EXPRESS. In 1988 she was sold to *Eckerö Linjen* and renamed the ROSLAGEN. During winter 1992/3 she operated between Helsinki and Tallinn for *Estonia New Line* and returned to *Eckerö Linjen* in the spring.

AG EMS

THE COMPANY *AG Ems* is a German public sector company.

MANAGEMENT Managing Director & Chief Executive B W Brons, **Marine Superintendent** J Alberts, **Marketing Manager & Assistant Manager** P Eesmann, **Operating Manager** Konrad Huismann.

ADDRESS Am Aussenhafen, Postfach 1154, 26691 Emden, Germany.

TELEPHONE Administration & Reservations +49 (0)4921 8907-400 or +49 (0)4921 8907-406.

FAX Administration & Reservations +49 (0)4921 8907-405.

INTERNET Email info@ag-ems.de **Website** www.ag-ems.de *(German)*

ROUTES OPERATED Conventional Ferries Emden (Germany) - Borkum (German Frisian Islands) (2 hrs; *(1,3,6)*; up to 4 per day), Eemshaven (Netherlands) - Borkum (55 mins; *(1,3,6)*; up to 4 per day). **Fast Ferries** Emden - Borkum (1 hr; *(2,4)*; up to 4 per day), Eemshaven - Borkum (30 mins; *(2,4)*; 1 per week in summer).

1	MÜNSTERLAND	1859t	86	15.5k	78.7m	1200P	70C	10L	BA	GY
2p»	NORDLICHT	435t	89	33k	38.8m	272P	0C	0L	-	GY
3	OSTFRIESLAND	1859t	85	15.5k	78.7m	1200P	70C	10L	BA	GY
4p»	POLARSTERN	-	01	40k	45.0m	405P	0C	0L	-	GY
5p	WAPPEN VON BORKUM	287t	76	11.5k	42.8m	358P	0C	0L	-	GY
6	WESTFALEN	1812t	72	15.5k	77.9m	1200P	65C	10L	BA	GY

MÜNSTERLAND, OSTFRIESLAND Built at Leer, Germany for *AG Ems*.

NORDLICHT Fjellstrand 38m passenger only catamaran built Mandal, Norway for *AG Ems*.

POLARSTERN Oceanfast Ferries (Australia) 45m passenger only catamaran built at Henderson, Australia for another operator as the CARAIBE JET. This order was cancelled before delivery and she was sold to *AG Ems* after a period of lay-up.

WAPPEN VON BORKUM Built at Oldersum, Germany as the HANNOVER for *Friesland Fahrlinie* of Germany. In 1979 sold to *AG Ems* and renamed the STADT BORKUM. In 1988 sold to *ST-Line* of Finland, operating day trips from Rauma. In 1994 returned to *AG Ems* and renamed the WAPPEN VON BORKUM.

WESTFALEN Built at Emden, Germany for *AG Ems*. Rebuilt in 1994.

FINNLINES

THE COMPANIES *Finnlines plc* is a Finnish private sector company.

MANAGEMENT President Asser Ahleskog, **Vice-President** Simo Airas.

ADDRESS PO Box 197, Salmisaarenkatu 1, FIN-00180 Helsinki, Finland. ***Sales and marketing of Finnlines Passenger Services*** Nordic Ferry Center Oy, Lönnrotinkatu 21, FIN-00120 Helsinki, Finland.

TELEPHONE Administration +358 (0)10 34350. **Reservations** ***(Nordic Ferry Center Oy)*** +358 (0)9-2510 200.

FAX Administration +358 (0)10 3435200, **Reservations** +358 (0)9-2510 2022.

INTERNET *Finnlines* Email info@finnlines.fi ***Nordic Ferry Center*** info@ferrycenter.fi

Website *Finnlines* www.finnlines.fi *(English, Finnish)*

Nordic Ferry Center www.ferrycenter.fi/finnlines/en/index.shtml *(English)*

ROUTES OPERATED All year Helsinki - Travemünde (32 hrs; *(1,2,3,4,5)*; 1/2 per day) **Note** frequencies refer to services which convey passengers.

Pearl of Scandinavia *(Martin Jensen)*

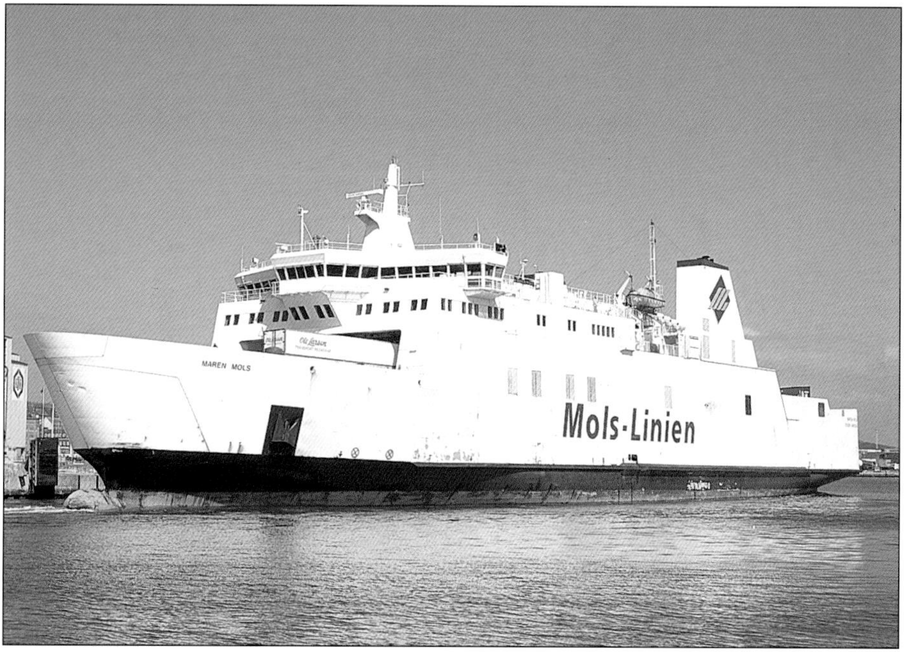

Maren Mols *(Dominic McCall)*

1	FINNCLIPPER	30500t	99	22k	188.3m	440P	-	184T	BA	FI
2	FINNHANSA	32531t	94	21.3k	183.0m	90P	-	236T	A2	FI
3	FINNPARTNER	32534t	94	21.3k	183.0m	90P	-	236T	A2	FI
4	FINNTRADER	32534t	95	21.3k	183.0m	90P	-	236T	A2	FI
5	TRANSEUROPA	32534t	95	21.3k	183.0m	90P	-	236T	A2	GY

FINNCLIPPER. 'Ro-pax' vessel built at Cadiz, Spain. Ordered by *Stena Ro-Ro* of Sweden. In 1998 sold, before delivery, to *Finnlines*. Entered service on the Helsinki - Travemünde route in 1999.

FINNHANSA, FINNPARTNER, FINNTRADER 'Ro-pax' vessels built at Gdansk, Poland for *Finnlines Oy* of Finland to provide a daily service conveying both freight and a limited number of cars and passengers on a previously freight-only route.

TRANSEUROPA 'Ro-pax' vessel built at Gdansk, Poland for *Poseidon Schiffahrt* of Germany to operate on a joint service between Lübeck and Helsinki. In 1997 *Poseidon Schiffahrt* was acquired by *Finnlines* and in 2001 renamed *Finnlines Deutschland AG.*

FINNLINK

Finnlines also operate a service between Kapellskär (Sweden) and Naantali (Finland) under the name *FinnLink*. Until spring 2002 the service was freight only. However passengers were due to be conveyed from spring 2002.

THE COMPANY *FinnLink Oy* is a subsidiary of *Finnlines*.

MANAGEMENT Managing Director Christer Backman.

ADDRESS Satamatic 11, FIN-21100, Naantali, Finland.

TELEPHONE Administration & Reservations +358 (0)10 436 7620.

FAX Administration & Reservations 358 (0)10 436 7660.

INTERNET Email finnlink@finnlink.fi **Website** www.finnlink.fi *(English, Finnish)*

ROUTE OPERATED Kapellskär (Sweden) - Naantali (Finland) (6 hrs; *(6,7,8)*; 3 per day).

6	FINNSAILOR	20783t	87	20.3k	157.6m	119P	-	146T	A	FI
7	FINNARROW	25996t	96	21k	168.0m	200P	800C	154T	BA2	FI
8	FINNEAGLE	30500t	99	22k	188.3m	440P	-	176T	BA2	FI

FINNSAILOR Built at Gdansk, Poland for *Finnlines* of Finland for freight service between Finland and Germany. In 1996 converted to ro-pax format to inaugurate a new passenger/freight service between Helsinki to Norrköping (Sweden) for subsidiary *FinnLink*. In 1997, this service was transferred to the Kapellskär - Naantali route and passengers (other than lorry drivers) ceased to be conveyed. Later in 1997 she was transferred to the Helsinki - Lübeck route. In 2000 she was chartered to *Nördo Link* to operate between Travemünde and Malmö. In 2002 she returned to *FinnLink*.

FINNARROW Built at Kodja, Indonesia as the GOTLAND for *Rederi AB Gotland* for charter. In 1997 briefly chartered *Tor Line* and then to *Nordic Trucker Line*, to operate between Oxelösund and St Petersburg (a ro-ro service). In June 1997 she was chartered to *SeaWind Line*, enabling a twice daily passenger service to be operated. In late 1997 she was sold to *Finnlines* and renamed the FINNARROW. She started operating twice weekly between Helsinki and Travemünde. During summer 1998 she was transferred to *FinnLink*; a bow door was fitted.

FINNEAGLE As the FINNCLIPPER of *Finnlines*. Although expected to join her sister on the Helsinki - Travemünde route, on delivery in late 1999 she entered service with *FinnLink*. During winter 1999/2000 she was converted to double-deck loading.

FJORD LINE

THE COMPANY *Fjord Line* is 100% owned by *Bergen-Nordhordland Rutelag AS (BNR)*, a Norwegian company.

MANAGEMENT Managing Director Ove Solem, **Marketing Manager** Nils Henrik Geitle.

ADDRESS Skoltegrunnskaien, PO Box 6020, N-5020 Bergen, Norway.

TELEPHONE Administration +47 55 54 87 00, **Reservations** +47 55 54 88 00.

FAX Administration & Reservations +47 55 54 86 01.

INTERNET Email fjordline@fjordline.com **Website** www.fjordline.co.UK *(Norwegian, Danish, English)*

ROUTE OPERATED Bergen - Egersund (Norway) - Hanstholm (Denmark) (15 hrs 30 mins; *(1)*; 3 per week), Egersund - Hanstholm (6 hrs 45 mins; *(1)*; 7 per week in summer). Also UK route - see Section 1.

1	BERGEN	16794t	93	20k	134.5m	882P	160C	82T	BA	NO

BERGEN Built at Rissa, Norway for *Rutelaget Askøy-Bergen* and used on *Fjord Line* service.

HH-FERRIES

THE COMPANY *HH-Ferries* is a Danish/Swedish private sector company. In 2002 it was acquired by *Stena AB* of Sweden.

MANAGEMENT Managing Director Lars Meijer, **Marketing Manager** Jon Cavalli-Björkman.

ADDRESS Atlantgatan 2, S-252 25 Helsingborg, Sweden.

TELEPHONE Administration +46 (0)42-26 80 00, **Reservations *Denmark*** +45 49 26 01 55, ***Sweden*** +46 (0)42-19 8000.

FAX Administration & Reservations *Denmark* +45 49 26 01 56, ***Sweden*** +46 (0)42-28 10 70.

INTERNET Email admin@hhferries.se **Website** www.hhferries.se *(Swedish, Danish, English)*

ROUTE OPERATED Helsingør - Helsingborg (20 mins; *(1,2)*; every 30 minutes).

1	MERCANDIA IV	4296t	89	13k	95.0m	420P	170C	18L	BA	DK
2	MERCANDIA VIII	4296t	87	13k	95.0m	420P	170C	18L	BA	DK

MERCANDIA IV Built at Sunderland, UK as the SUPERFLEX NOVEMBER for *Vognmandsruten* of Denmark. In 1989 sold to *Mercandia* and renamed the MERCANDIA IV. In 1990 she began operating on their *Kattegatbroen* Juelsminde - Kalundborg service. In 1996 she was transferred to their *Sundbroen* Helsingør - Helsingborg service. In 1997 the service and vessel were leased to *HH-Ferries*. In 1999 she was purchased by *HH-Ferries*. She has been equipped to carry dangerous cargo.

MERCANDIA VIII Built at Sunderland, UK as the SUPERFLEX BRAVO for *Vognmandsruten* of Denmark and used on their services between Nyborg and Korsør and Copenhagen (Tuborg Havn) and Landskrona (Sweden). In 1991 she was chartered to *Scarlett Line* to operate on the Copenhagen and Landskrona route. In 1993 she was renamed the SVEA SCARLETT but later in the year the service ceased and she was laid up. In 1996 she was purchased by *Mercandia*, renamed the MERCANDIA VIII and placed on their *Sundbroen* Helsingør - Helsingborg service. In 1997 the service and vessel was leased to *HH-Ferries*. In 1999 she was purchased by *HH-Ferries*.

HURTIGRUTEN

SERVICE The *'Hurtigruten'* is the *'Norwegian Coastal Express Service'*. It is part cruise, part passenger ferry, part cargo line and part car ferry (although this is a fairly minor part of the operation). In recent years the service has been operated by a consortium of two operators - *Ofotens og Vesteraalen Dampskipsselskab* and *Troms Fylkes Dampskipsselskab*. These are to merge in 2002 to form a new company called *Nord Norges Dampskipsselskap*.

ADDRESS ***Ofotens og Vesteraalen Dampskipsselskab*** Postboks 43, 8501 Narvik, Norway, ***Troms Fylkes Dampskipsselskab*** 9005 Tromsø, Norway.

TELEPHONE Administration ***Ofotens og Vesteraalen D/S*** +47 76 96 76 96, ***Troms Fylkes D/S*** +47 77 64 82 00, **Reservations** ***Norway*** 810 30 000, ***UK*** +44 (0)20 7371 4011.

FAX Administration & Reservations ***Ofotens og Vesteraalen D/S*** +47 76 96 76 11, ***Troms Fylkes D/S*** +47 77 64 82 40, ***Reservations (UK)*** +44 (0)20 7371 4070.

INTERNET Email booking@ovds.no booking@tfds.no **Website** www.hurtigruten.no *(English, Norwegian, German, Dutch, Spanish, Finnish, French, Italian and Swedish)*

ROUTE OPERATED Bergen - Kirkenes with many intermediate calls. Daily departures throughout the year. The round trip takes just under 11 days.

1	FINNMARKEN	14000t	02	18k	133.0m	647P	50C	OL	SC	NO
2•	HARALD JARL	2621t	60	16k	87.4m	410P	4C	OL	C	NO
3	KONG HARALD	11204t	93	18k	121.8m	691P	50C	OL	SC	NO
4	LOFOTEN	2621t	64	16k	87.4m	410P	4C	OL	C	NO
5	MIDNATSOL	6167t	82	18k	108.6m	550P	40C	OL	SC	NO
6	NARVIK	6257t	82	18k	108.6m	550P	40C	OL	SC	NO
7	NORDKAPP	11386t	96	18k	123.3m	691P	50C	OL	SC	NO
8	NORDLYS	11204t	94	18k	121.8m	691P	50C	OL	SC	NO
9	NORDNORGE	11384t	97	18k	123.3m	691P	50C	OL	SC	NO
10	POLARLYS	11341t	96	18k	123.0m	691P	50C	OL	SC	NO
11	RICHARD WITH	11205t	93	18k	121.8m	691P	50C	OL	SC	NO
12	TROLLFJORD	14000t	02	18k	135.7m	626P	50C	OL	SC	NO
13	VESTERÅLEN	6261t	83	18k	108.6m	550P	40C	OL	SC	NO

FINNMARKEN Built at Ulsteinvik, Norway for *Ofotens og Vesteraalen D/S* to replace the LOFOTEN.

HARALD JARL Built at Trondheim, Norway for *Nordenfjeldske D/S*. In 1988 she was sold to *Troms Fylkes Dampskibsselskap*. In 2002 withdrawn and laid up for sale.

KONG HARALD Built at Stralsund, Germany for *Troms Fylkes D/S*.

LOFOTEN Built at Oslo, Norway for *Vesteraalens D/S*. In 1984 she was sold to *Finnmark Fylkesrederi og Ruteselskap*. In 1996 she was sold to *Ofotens og Vesteraalen D/S*. In 2002 replaced by the FINNMARKEN but is to continue to operate cruises and is to substitute for the NORDNORGE during winter 2002/3 when she goes to South America to operate cruises.

MIDNATSOL Built at Ulsteinvik, Norway for *Troms Fylkes D/S*.

NARVIK Built at Trondheim, Norway for *Ofoten D/S*. Since 1984 owned by *Ofotens og Vesteraalen D/S*.

NORDKAPP Built at Ulsteinvik, Norway for *Ofotens og Vesteraalen D/S*.

NORDLYS Built at Stralsund, Germany for *Troms Fylkes D/S*.

NORDNORGE Built at Ulsteinvik, Norway for *Ofotens og Vesteraalen D/S*. During winter 2002/3 to operate cruises down the coast to Chile and to Antarctica.

POLARLYS Built at Ulsteinvik, Norway for *Troms Fylkes D/S*.

RICHARD WITH Built at Stralsund, Norway for *Ofotens og Vesteraalen D/S.*

TROLLFJORD Built at Rissa, Norway for *Troms Fylkes D/S* to replace the HARALD JARL.

VESTERÅLEN Built at Harstad, Norway for *Vesteraalens D/S.* Since 1984 owned by *Ofotens og Vesteraalen D/S.*

Under Construction

14	NEWBUILDING	14000t	03	18k	135.7m	626P	-	-	SC	NO

NEWBUILDING Under construction at Rissa, Norway for *Troms Fylkes D/S.* To replace the MIDNATSOL.

LATLINES

THE COMPANY *LatLines* is a Latvian company.

MANAGEMENT President Ligmunds Fankovsuis, **Marketing Manager** Ervins Kaverskis.

ADDRESS 1 Zivju str, Riga LV-1015, Latvia.

TELEPHONE Administration *Latvia* +371 7349527, ***Germany*** +49 (0)451 7099697, **Reservations *Latvia*** +371 7353523, ***Germany*** +49 (0)451 7099685.

FAX Administration *Latvia* +371 7349575, ***Germany*** +49 (0)451 7099687, **Reservations *Latvia*** +371 7353071, ***Germany*** +49 (0)451 7099687.

INTERNET Email latlines@latlines.lv **Website** www.latlines.lv *(Latvian, English, German, Russian)*

ROUTE OPERATED Lübeck (Germany) - Riga (Latvia) (32 hrs; *(1)*; 2 per week).

1	SEA SYMPHONY	4972t	76	17k	119.2m	210P	885C	64T	A	CY

SEA SYMPHONY Built at Livorno, Italy as the BUONO SPERENZA, a freight ro-ro, for *Lloyd Triestino* of Italy and used on services between Europe and West Africa. In 1994 she was chartered to *Truck Ferries* and renamed the ELEFSIS, operating between Italy and Greece. In 1995 she was sold to *Poseidon Lines* and renamed the SEA SONATA; later that year she was renamed the SEA SYMPHONY. She was used on services between Italy, Greece and Albania. In 1996 she was modified to ro-pax format. In 2001, chartered to *LatLines* and placed on a new Lübeck - Riga service.

LISCO BALTIC SERVICE

THE COMPANY *AB Lisco Baltic Service* is a Lithuanian company, 76% owned by *DFDS Tor Line*; they purchased this holding from Lithuanian Government in 2001. Passenger and cargo services are marketed by *AB Lisco Baltic Service* and ticket sales in Lithuania by *Krantas Shipping.*

ADDRESS 24 J. Janonio Str, KLAÌPEDA LT-5813, Lithuania.

TELEPHONE Administration *LISCO Baltic Service (Klaìpeda)* + 370 6 393101, **Reservations *LISCO (Klaìpeda):*** + 370 6 393288, ***Krantas (Klaìpeda)*** + 370 6 395048, ***DFDS Tor Line/LISCO Baltic Service (Karlshamn)*** + 46 (0)45433680, ***LISCO Baltic Service GmbH (Kiel)*** + 49 (0)43120976444 - cargo, + 49 (0)43120976420 - passengers.

FAX Administration *LISCO Baltic Service (Klaìpeda)* + 370 6 393121, ***Reservations: LISCO (Klaìpeda)*** + 370 6 393287, ***Krantas (Klaìpeda):*** + 370 6 395041, ***DFDS Tor Line/LISCO Baltic Service (Karlshamn)*** + 46 (0) 45433689, ***LISCO Baltic, Service GmbH (Kiel)***: + 49 (0) 43120976555.

INTERNET Email - Administration ml5@lisco.lt **Reservations *LISCO (Klaìpeda)*** booking@lisco.lt ***Krantas (Klaìpeda)*** Cargo.de@krantas.lt ***DFDS Tor Line/LISCO Baltic Service (Karlshamn)*** Karlshamn@dfdstorline.com, ***LISCO Baltic Service GmbH (Kiel)***: cargo@lisco-baltic-service.de passage@lisco-baltic-service.de

Website: www.lisco.lt *(English,German)*

ROUTES OPERATED Klaìpeda (Lithuania) - Kiel (Germany) (30 hrs; *(1,2,6)*; 8 per week) (joint with *Scandlines Euroseabridge* under the 'Kiel-Klaìpeda-Express' name), Klaìpeda - Karlshamn (Sweden) (15 hrs; *(4.5)*; 4 per week), Klaìpeda - Sassnitz (Germany) (18 hrs; *(3)*; 3 per week (joint with *Scandlines Euroseabridge*).

1	GREIFSWALD	24084t	88	15.5k	190.9m	120P	100C	116T	A2	LB
2	KAUNAS	25606t	89	16k	190.9m	214P	460C	116T	A2	LT
3F	KLAIPEDA	21890t	87	16k	190.9m	45P	250C	116T	A	LT
4	PALANGA	11630t	79	19k	126.5m	126P	300C	70T	A	LT
5F	SIAULIAI	6894t	85	13k	125.9m	12P	350C	38T	A	LT
6	VILNIUS	22341t	87	16k	190.9m	120P	460C	116T	A2	LT

GREIFSWALD Built at Wismar, East Germany as a train ferry for *DSR* of Germany (DDR) to operate on the service between Mukran and Klaìpeda (Lithuania). In 1994 she was rebuilt to introduce road vehicle and additional passenger capacity. In 1996 she was transferred to the new *Euroseabridge* Travemünde - Klaìpeda service. During winter 1998/99 she was chartered to *Stena Line* to operate between Gothenburg and Kiel. She was then chartered to the British *Ministry of Defence* for use in the Balkans. In November 1999 she was transferred to the Kiel - Klaìpeda route. In early 2001 the charter was ended and she was chartered to *Transocean Line* of Denmark and operated between Århus (Denmark) and Halmstad (Sweden). This service ended after a few weeks. In the autumn chartered to *TransRussia Express*. Later in 2001 chartered to *Lisco* for the Klaìpeda - Kiel route.

KAUNAS, VILNIUS train ferries built at Wismar, East Germany for *Lisco* of the former Soviet Union and used by to operate between Klaìpeda and Mukran in Germany (DDR). This was part of series of vessels built at to link the USSR and Germany (DDR), avoiding Poland. In 1994 they were modified to increase passengers capacity in order to offer a limited passengers facilities and placed on Klaìpeda – Kiel service.

KLAÌPEDA train ferry as KAUNAS and VILNIUS – but not converted to full ro-pax format (although she does carry more than the normal 12 for a ro-ro). Operates on the Klaìpeda –Sassnitz route.

PALANGA Built at Le Havre, France; rebuilt at in 1992 to increase passengers capacity. In 1996 sold to *Lisco*, renamed the PALANGA; presently she operates on the Klaìpeda – Karlshamn service.

SIAULIAI Built in Rostock Germany (DDR) as the KOMPOZITOR BORODIN for *Lisco*. In 1992 renamed the SIAULIAI. At present she operates on the Klaìpeda – Karlshamn service.

AB Lisco Baltic Service also own the TOR NERINGA which is currently on long time charter to *DFDS Tor Line* serving Klaìpeda – Copenhagen/Fredericia route. She is shown under *DFDS Tor Line* in Section 3. It is possible that this route could be transferred to *Lisco Baltic Service* control at some stage

MOLS-LINIEN

THE COMPANY *Mols-Linien A/S* is a Danish private sector company; previously a subsidiary of *J Lauritzen A/S*, it was, in 1988 sold to *DIFKO No LXII (Dansk Investeringsfond)*. Since 1994 shares in the company have been traded on the stock exchange. In January 1999 a 40% share in the company was acquired by *Scandlines Danmark A/S*. Their *Scandlines Cat-Link* Århus - Kalundborg service became part of *Mols-Linien* in February 1999 and the service was switched from Kalundborg to Odden in April 1999. The Ebeltoft - Odden ro-pax service was transferred to the Århus - Kalundborg route in January 2000.

MANAGEMENT Managing Director Preben Wolff, **Marketing Manager** Christian Hingelberg.

ADDRESS Færgehavnen, DK-8400 Ebeltoft, Denmark.

TELEPHONE Administration +45 89 52 52 00, **Reservations** +45 70 10 14 18.

FAX Administration +45 89 52 52 90, **Reservations** +45 89 52 52 92.

INTERNET Email Mols-Linien@Mols-Linien.dk **Website** www.Mols-Linien.dk *(Danish)*

ROUTES OPERATED Ro-pax Ferries Århus (Jutland) - Kalundborg (Sealand) (2 hr 40 mins; *(3,6)*;

7 per day). **Fast Ferries** Århus - Odden (Sealand) (1 hr 5 mins; *(1)*; every 3 hrs), Ebeltoft (Jutland) - Odden (45 mins; *(2,5)*; hourly).

1»•	MADS MOLS	5619t	98	43k	91.3m	800P	220C	-	A	DK
2»	MAI MOLS	3971t	96	43.4k	76.1m	450P	120C	-	BA	DK
3	MAREN MOLS	14221t	96	19k	136.4m	600P	344C	82L	BA2	DK
4»	MAX MOLS	5617t	98	43k	91.3m	800P	220C	-	A	DK
5»	MIE MOLS	3971t	96	43.4k	76.1m	450P	120C	-	BA	DK
6	METTE MOLS	14221t	96	19k	136.4m	600P	344C	82L	BA2	DK

MADS MOLS InCat 91 metre catamaran, built speculatively at Hobart, Tasmania, Australia. In spring 1998, following *InCat's* acquisition of a 50% share in *Scandlines Cat-Link A/S, S*he was chartered to that company and named the CAT-LINK V. She is the current holder of the Hales Trophy for fastest crossing of the Atlantic during her delivery voyage between the USA and Falmouth, UK. In 1999 the charter was transferred to *Mols-Linien* and she was renamed the MADS MOLS. At the beginning of 2000 she was laid up; re-entered service in April 2000.

MAI MOLS Danyard SeaJet 250 catamaran built at Aalborg, Denmark for *Mols-Linien.*

MAREN MOLS, METTE MOLS Ro-pax vessels built at Frederikshavn, Denmark for *Mols-Linien.* Initially operated on the Ebeltoft - Odden route. In January 2000 switched to the Århus - Kalundborg route.

MAX MOLS InCat 91 metre catamaran, built speculatively at Hobart, Tasmania, Australia. In spring 1998, following *InCat's* acquisition of a 50% share in *Scandlines Cat-Link A/S, S*he was sold to that company and named the CAT-LINK IV. In 1999 purchased by *Mols-Linien* and renamed the MAX MOLS. In 2000 chartered to *Marine Atlantic* of Canada to operate between Port aux Basques (Newfoundland) and North Sydney (Nova Scotia). Returned to *Mols-Linien* in autumn 2000. In 2002 chartered to *Rigas Juras Lines* (See late news)

MIE MOLS Danyard SeaJet 250 catamaran built at Aalborg, Denmark for *Mols-Linien.*

REEDEREI NORDEN-FRISIA

THE COMPANY *Aktiengesellschaft Reederei Norden-Frisia* is a German public sector company.

MANAGEMENT President/CEO Dr Stegmann, **Managing Director/CFO** Prok. Graw.

ADDRESS Postfach 1262, 26534 Norderney, Germany.

TELEPHONE Administration +49 (0)4932 9130.

FAX Administration +49 (0)4932 91310.

INTERNET Email info@reederei-frisia.de **Website** www.reederei-frisia.de *(German)*

ROUTES OPERATED ***Car Ferries & Passenger Ferries*** Norddeich (Germany) - Norderney (German Frisian Islands) (1 hr; *(2,4,5)*; up to 15 per day), Norddeich - Juist (German Frisian Islands) (1 hr 20 mins; *(3,6)*; up to 15 per day), ***Passenger only fast ferry*** Norderney - Helgoland (1 hr 30 mins; *(1)*), Laugeoog - Helgoland (1 hr 15 min; *(1)*), Waugerooge - Helgoland (1 hr 15 min; *(1)*).

1p»	CAT NO 1	963t	99	40k	52.4m	432P	-	-	AL	GY
2	FRISIA I	1020t	70	12.3k	63.7m	1500P	53C	-	-	GY
3	FRISIA II	1125t	78	12k	63.3m	1340P	53C	-	-	GY
4	FRISIA IV	1600t	02	12k	71.0m	1400P	60C	-	-	GY
5	FRISIA V	1007t	65	11k	63.8m	1442P	53C	-	-	GY
6	FRISIA VI	768t	68	12k	54.9m	1096P	35C	-	-	GY
7F	FRISIA VII	363t	84	12k	53.0m	12P	30C	-	-	GY
8•	FRISIA VIII	1058t	62	12.5k	63.7m	1340P	53C	-	-	GY
9p	FRISIA IX	571t	80	11k	51.0m	785P	-	-	-	GY
10p	FRISIA X	187t	72	12k	36.3m	290P	-	-	-	GY

Dronning Margrethe II *(Mike Louagie)*

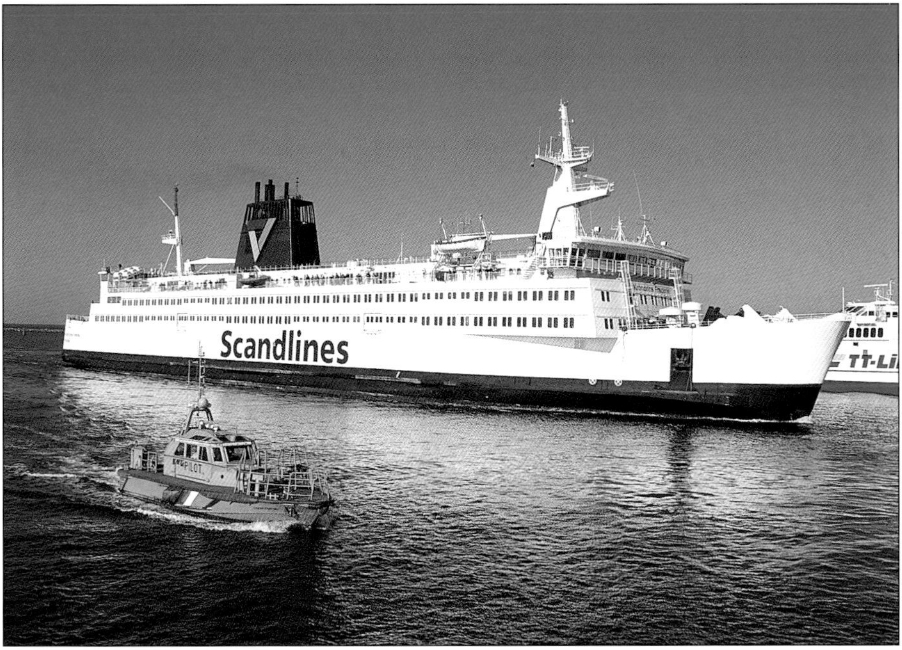

Kronprins Frederik *(Mike Louagie)*

CAT NO I Built at Fremantle, Western Australia for *Reederei Norden-Frisia* to inaugurate new services to Helgoland.

FRISIA I, FRISIA II, FRISIA V, FRISIA VI, FRISIA VIII Built at Papenburg, Germany for *Reederei Norden-Frisia.* Passenger capacities relate to the summer seasons. Capacity is reduced during the winter.

FRISIA IV Built at Emden, Germany for *Reederei Norden-Frisia* to replace the FRISIA VIII.

FRISIA VI Built at Papenburg, Germany for *Reederei Norden-Frisia.* Conveys freight to Norderney and Juist.

FRISIA IX, FRISIA X Built at Oldersum, Germany for *Reederei Norden-Frisia.* The FRISIA IX was built at to convey 9 cars at the bow end but is now used mainly in passenger only mode. These ships are generally used for excursions.

NORDIC JET LINE

THE COMPANY *Nordic Jet Line* is an international company, registered in Estonia. Main shareholders are *Förde Reederei Seetouristik* of Germany, *Finnmark Fylkesrederi og Ruteselskap* of Norway and *Kværner Investments* of Norway.

MANAGEMENT Managing Director Mikael Granrot, **Deputy Managing Director** Hans Jonasson.

ADDRESS ***Estonia*** Sadama 25-4, 15051 Tallinn, Estonia, ***Finland*** Kanavaterminaali K5, 00160 Helsinki, Finland.

TELEPHONE Administration ***Estonia*** +372 (0)6 137200, ***Finland*** +358 (0)9 68177150, **Reservations** ***Estonia*** +372 (0)6 137000, ***Finland*** +358 (0)9 681770.

FAX Administration & Reservations ***Estonia*** +372 (0)6 137222, ***Finland*** +358 (0)9 6817111.

INTERNET Email marketing@njl.fi **Website** www.njl.fi *(English, Finnish, Estonian, German)*

ROUTE OPERATED Helsinki (Finland) - Tallinn (Estonia) (1 hr 30 mins; *(1,2)*; up to 6 per day (all year except during winter ice period)).

1»	BALTIC JET	2273t	99	36k	60.0m	430P	52C	-	A	NO
2»	NORDIC JET	2273t	98	36k	60.0m	430P	52C	-	A	NO

BALTIC JET, NORDIC JET Kværner Fjellstrand JumboCat 60m catamarans built at Omastrand, Norway for *Nordic Jet Line.* Alternative traffic mix is 38 cars and 2 buses.

POLFERRIES

THE COMPANY *Polferries* is the trading name of *Polska Zegluga Baltycka SA (Polish Baltic Shipping Company)*, a Polish state owned company.

MANAGEMENT General Director & President of the Board Jan Warchol, **Shipping Policy Director and Board Member** Grazyna Bak **Financial Director** Wojciech Rogowski **Technical Director** Elzbieta Juszczak.

ADDRESS ul Portowa 41, PL 78-100 Kolobrzeg, Poland.

TELEPHONE Administration +48 (0)94 3525211, **Passenger Reservations** ***Swinoujscie*** +48 (0)91 3216140, ***Gdansk*** +48 (0)58 3431887, **Freight Reservations** ***Swinoujscie*** +48 (0)91 3216161, ***Gdansk*** +48 (0)58 3430212.

FAX Administration +48 (0)94 3526612, **Passenger Reservations** ***Swinoujscie*** +48 (0)91 3216168, ***Gdansk*** +48 (0)58 3436574, **Freight Reservations** ***Swinoujscie*** +48 (0)91 3216169, ***Gdansk*** +48 (0)58 3430975.

INTERNET Email info@polferries.pl **Passenger Reservations** ***Swinoujscie*** boas.pax@polferries.pl ***Gdansk*** pax.gdansk@polferries.pl **Freight Reservations** ***Swinoujscie*** boas.cargo@polferries.pl, ***Gdansk*** cargo.gsansk@polferries.pl **Website** www.polferries.pl *(Polish, English)*

ROUTES OPERATED Swinoujscie - Ystad (8 hrs; *(1)*; 1 per day), Swinoujscie - Copenhagen (9 hrs 45 mins; *(2)*; 5 per week), Swinoujscie - Rønne (6 hrs; *(2)*; 1 per week (seasonal)), Gdansk - Nynäshamn (Sweden) (19 hrs; *(3,4)*; 3 per week).

1	NIEBOROW	8697t	73	17.5k	118.8m	420P	225C	24T	BA	BA
2	POMERANIA	12087t	78	15.4k	127.7m	800P	273C	30T	BA	BA
3	ROGALIN	10241t	72	16.5k	126.9m	510P	146C	20T	BA	BA
4	SILESIA	10553t	79	17k	127.6m	487P	277C	34T	BA	BA

NIEBOROW Built at Rendsburg, Germany for *Prinzenlinien* of Germany as PRINZ HAMLET for the Harwich - Hamburg service. In 1981 *Prinzenlinien* was acquired by *DFDS*. In 1987 she was renamed the PRINS HAMLET, re-registered in Denmark and transferred to the seasonal Newcastle - Esbjerg and Newcastle - Gothenburg summer services. During winter 1987/88 she operated for *B&I Line* of Ireland between Rosslare and Pembroke Dock. At the end of the 1988 summer season she was acquired by a *Stena Line* subsidiary, chartered to *Polferries* and renamed the NIEBOROW. In 1994 she was sold to *Polferries*. Currently used on the Swinoujscie - Ystad route.

POMERANIA Built at Szczecin, Poland for *Polferries*. In 1978 and 1979 she briefly operated between Felixstowe and Swinoujscie via Copenhagen. In recent years she was the regular vessel on the Gdansk - Helsinki service before that service was withdrawn. She was rebuilt in 1997. Used on the Swinoujscie - Copenhagen and Swinoujscie - Rønne routes.

ROGALIN Built at Nantes, France as the AALLOTAR for the *EFFOA* of Finland. Used on overnight *Silja Line* services (joint with *Svea Line* of Sweden and *Bore Line* of Finland) between Stockholm and Helsinki. Later used on the Stockholm - Mariehamn - Turku service. In 1978 she was sold to *Polferries*. She was renamed the ROGALIN and operated on various services between Poland, West Germany and Scandinavia. In 1983 she was chartered to *Farskip* of Iceland from the end of May until September, renamed the EDDA and inaugurated a service between Reykjavik (Iceland), Newcastle and Bremerhaven (Germany). In September of that year she returned to *Polferries* and resumed the name ROGALIN. This service was not repeated in 1984 and she continued to operate for *Polferries* until chartered (with crew) by *Swansea Cork Ferries* in 1987. She was renamed the CELTIC PRIDE and inaugurated a new Swansea - Cork service. This service also operated during summer 1988 but during winter 1987/88 and after the 1988 summer season she was returned to *Polferries* and resumed the name ROGALIN, operating on Baltic services. She did not serve with *Swansea Cork Ferries* in 1989 or 1990 but in 1991 she was taken on charter (again with crew) and was again renamed the CELTIC PRIDE. This charter terminated at the end of 1992 and she returned to the Baltic and resumed the name ROGALIN. Used on the Gdansk - Nynäshamn route.

SILESIA Built at Szczecin, Poland for *Polferries*. rebuilt during winter 1997/98, although not as extensively as the POMERANIA. Used on the Gdansk - Nynashamn route.

PROVINCIALE STOOMBOOTDIENSTEN IN ZEELAND

THE COMPANY *Provinciale Stoombootdiensten in Zeeland* is a Dutch public sector company.

MANAGEMENT Managing Director H E C M Thomaes.

ADDRESS Prins Hendrikweg 10, 4382 NS Vlissingen, Netherlands (***Correspondence*** Postbus 171, 4380 AD VLISSINGEN, Netherlands).

TELEPHONE Administration +31 (0)118 460900, **Reservations** not applicable.

FAX Administration +31 (0)118 468096, **Reservations** not applicable.

INTERNET Email psd@zeeland.nl **Website** www.psdzeeland.com *(Dutch)*

ROUTES OPERATED Vlissingen - Breskens (20 mins; *(1,2)*; half hourly), Perkpolder - Kruiningen (20 mins; *(3,5)*; half hourly). Both services are due to cease in November 2003 when a new tunnel opens between Ellewoutsdijk and Terneuzen.

1	KONINGIN BEATRIX	7910t	93	17k	113.6m	1000P	210C	22L	BA2	NL
2	PRINS JOHAN FRISO	7865t	97	16.5k	113.6m	1000P	210C	22L	BA2	NL
3	PRINS WILLEM-ALEXANDER	7038t	70	16.5k	113.6m	1000P	234C	22L	BA2	NL
4	PRINSES CHRISTINA	6831t	68	16.5k	113.6m	1000P	234C	22L	BA2	NL
5	PRINSES JULIANA	8166t	86	14.5k	113.6m	1000P	210C	22L	BA2	NL

KONINGIN BEATRIX Built at Vlissingen, Netherlands for *bv Veerboot Westerschelde* (a subsidiary of *De Schelde Shipyards*) and chartered to *PSD*. Purchased by *PSD* in 1997. Used on the Vlissingen - Breskens service.

PRINS JOHAN FRISO Built at Vlissingen, Netherlands for *PSD*. Used on the Vlissingen - Breskens service.

PRINS WILLEM-ALEXANDER Built at Hardinxveld, Netherlands for *PSD*. Used on the Perkpolder - Kruiningen service.

PRINSES CHRISTINA Built at Hardinxveld, Netherlands for *PSD*. Initially used on the Perkpolder - Kruiningen. Now a spare vessel.

PRINSES JULIANA Built at Hardinxveld, Netherlands for *PSD*. Initially used on the Vlissingen - Breskens service. Now used on the Perkpolder - Kruiningen service.

RG-LINE

THE COMPANY *RG-Line Oy/Ab* is a Finnish private sector company, named after its owner, Rabbe Grönblom.

ADDRESS Hovioikeudenpuistikko 11, 65100 Vaasa, Finland.

TELEPHONE Administration & Reservations +358 (0)6-3200 300.

FAX Administration & Reservations +358 (0)6-3104 551.

INTERNET Email marketing@rgline.com **Website** www.rgline.com *(Finnish, Swedish)*

ROUTE OPERATED Vaasa (Finland) - Umeå (Sweden) (4 hrs; *(1)*; 1/2 per day).

1	CASINO EXPRESS	10542t	66	18k	128.9m	1200P	265C	32T	BA	FI

CASINO EXPRESS Built at Landskrona, Sweden as the FENNIA for *Siljavarustamo-Siljarederiet* of Finland to operate *Silja Line* services between Sweden and Finland. In 1970 she was transferred to *Stockholms Rederi AB Svea*, when *Silja Line* became a marketing organisation. In 1983 she was withdrawn and operated for a short period with *B&I Line* of Ireland between Rosslare and Pembroke Dock. In 1984 she was sold to *Jakob Line*. In 1985 she was sold to *Vaasanlaivat*. In 1992 she was returned to *Jakob Line*. During winter 1992/3 she operated for *Baltic Link* between Norrköping

(Sweden) and Riga (Latvia), but returned to *Silja Line* in summer 1993 and was used on the Vaasa - Umeå and Pietarsaari - Skellefteå services. The latter service did not operate in 1999 and, on 1st July, she was transferred to the new *Vaasanlaivat*, a *Silja Line* subsidiary formed to operate the Vaasa - Umeå link. In September 1999 she was replaced by the WASA QUEEN and withdrawn. During summer 2000 she operated freight only services between Stockholm and Turku. In 2001 sold to *RG-Line*, renamed the CASINO EXPRESS and in May re-opened the Vaasa - Umeå route which had been closed by *Silja Line* subsidiary *Vaasanlaivat* in December 2000.

RÖMÖ-SYLT LINIE

THE COMPANY *Römö-Sylt Linie GmbH* is a German company, a subsidiary of *FRS (Förde Reederei Seetouristik)* of Flensburg.

MANAGEMENT Managing Director P Rathke.

ADDRESS *Germany* Am Fähranleger, D-25992 List, Germany, ***Denmark*** Kilebryggen, DK-6792 Rømø, Denmark.

TELEPHONE Administration (Germany) +49 (0)4651 870475, **Reservations (Denmark)** +45 73 75 53 03.

FAX Administration (Germany) +49 (0)4651 871446, **Reservations (Denmark)** +45 73 75 53 05.

INTERNET Email romo-sylt@post12.tele.dk **Website** www.romo-sylt.dk *(Danish, German)*

ROUTE OPERATED List (Sylt, Germany) - Havneby (Rømø, Denmark) (45 mins; *(1,2)*; variable - half hourly at peaks). Note the island of Rømø is linked to the Danish mainland by a road causeway; the island of Sylt is linked to the German mainland by a rail-only causeway on which cars are conveyed on shuttle wagons.

1	VIKINGLAND	1963t	74	11k	68.3m	420P	60C	8L	BA	GY
2	WESTERLAND	1509t	71	11k	58.3m	400P	40C	5L	BA	GY

VIKINGLAND, WESTERLAND Built at Husum, Germany for *Römö-Sylt Linie.*

SCANDLINES (DENMARK & GERMANY)

THE COMPANY *Scandlines AG* is a German company, 50% owned by *DB Cargo AG*, a subsidiary of *Deutsche Bahn AG (German Railways)* (which is owned by the Federal Government) and 50% owned by the Kingdom of Denmark. In 1998 it took over *DFO (Deutsche Fährgesellschaft Ostsee mbH)* of Germany (renamed *Scandlines Deutschland GmbH*) and *Scandlines A/S* of Denmark (renamed *Scandlines Danmark A/S*). A 50% share in *Euroseabridge GmbH* was acquired in 1998 (by *Scandlines A/S* of Denmark before the merger with *DFO*) and the remaining 50% in 1999; the name was changed to *Scandlines Euroseabridge GmbH.*

Scandlines A/S was formerly *DSB Rederi A/S* and before that the Ferries Division of *DSB (Danish State Railways)*. *DFO* was formed in 1993 by the merging of the Ferries Divisions of *Deutsche Bundesbahn (German Federal Railways)* (which operated in the Federal Republic of Germany) and *Deutsche Reichsbahn (German State Railways)* (which operated in the former DDR).

Stena Line owned *Scandlines AB* of Sweden also trades under this name but remains a separate company. Danish domestic routes are operated by subsidiary company *Scandlines Sydfynske A/S*, and are marketed as part of the *Scandlines* network.

MANAGEMENT Chairman Bernd Malmström, **Chief Executive** Ole Rendbæk.

ADDRESS *Denmark* Dampfærgevej 10, DK-2100 Copenhagen Ø, Denmark. ***Germany*** Hochhaus am Fährhafen, D-18119 Rostock-Warnemünde, Germany.

TELEPHONE Administration *Denmark* +45 33 15 15 15, ***Germany*** +49 (0)381 5435-0, **Reservations *Denmark*** +45 33 15 15 15, ***Germany*** +49 (0)1805-7226 354637.

INTERNET Email scandlines@scandlines.dk

Websites www.scandlines.dk *(Danish)* www.scandlines.com *(German, English)*

ROUTES OPERATED Conventional Ferries Helsingør (Sealand, Denmark) - Helsingborg (Sweden) (25 mins; *(6,27)*; every 20 mins) (joint with *Scandlines AB* of Sweden), *Rødby* (Lolland, Denmark) - Puttgarden (Germany) (45 mins; *(2,7,15,16,20 (7 road freight only))*; half hourly train/vehicle ferry + additional road freight only sailings), Gedser (Falster, Denmark) - Rostock (Germany) (2 hrs; *(3,9,14)*; every 2 hours (less frequent Dec - Feb), Rostock (Germany) - Trelleborg (Sweden) (5 hrs 45 mins (7 hrs night); *(10)*; 3 per day) (joint with *Scandlines AB* of Sweden), Sassnitz (Germany) - Trelleborg (3 hrs 45 mins; *(19)*; 4-5 per day) (joint with *Scandlines AB* of Sweden), ***Summer only*** Sassnitz - Rønne (Bornholm, Denmark) (3 hrs 45 mins; *(17)*; 1 or 2 per day (joint with *BornholmsTrafikken* - this company operates the service during the winter period).

Danish domestic services operated by subsidiary *Scandlines Sydfynske A/S (formerly Sydfynske Dampskibsselskab (SFDS))* and forming part of *Scandlines* network Fynshav (Als) - Bøjden (Fyn) (50 mins; *(25)*; 6-8 per day), Esbjerg (Jutland) - Nordby (Fanø) (12 mins; *(4,11,22)*; every 20-40 mins), Spodsbjerg (Langeland) - Tårs (Lolland) (45 mins; *(5,12,23)*; hourly).

Germany - Latvia & Lithuania routes operated by subsidiary *Scandlines Euroseabridge GmbH* Kiel - Klaìpeda (Lithuania) (25 hrs; *(13, Three Lisco vessels)*; 8 per week (joint with *Lisco Baltic Service* of Lithuania under the *Kiel-Klaìpeda-Express* name)), Sassnitz (Mukran) (Germany) - Klaìpeda (18 hrs; *(Lisco vessel)*; 3 per week (joint with *Lisco Baltic Service* of Lithuania)), Rostock (Germany) - Liepaja (Latvia) (24 hrs; *(28)*; 2 per week).

Denmark - Lithuania route operated by *Scandlines Balticum Seaways division* Århus (Denmark) - Aabenraa (Denmark) - Klaìpeda (Lithuania) (from 30 hrs; *(chartered vessel)*; 2 per week from Aabenraa (1 westbound via Århus), 1 per week from Århus via Aabenraa).

Sweden - Latvia route operated by *Amber Line* Karlshamn (Sweden) - Liepaja (Latvia) (17 hrs; *(8)*; 3 per week).

1	ASK	13294t	82	18k	171.0m	186P	-	104T	AS	DK
2	DEUTSCHLAND	15187t	97	19k	142.0m	900P	294C	30Lr	BA2	GY
3	DRONNING MARGRETHE II	10850t	73	16.5k	144.6m	400P	195C	20Lr	BA2	DK
4	FENJA	751t	98	11.5k	49.9m	396P	34C	4L	BA	DK
5	FRIGG SYDFYEN	1676t	84	12.5k	70.1m	338P	50C	8L	BA	DK
6	HAMLET	10067t	97	14k	111.2m	1000P	244C	34L	BA	DK
7F	HOLGER DANSKE	2779t	76	14.5k	86.8m	12P	55C	12L	BA	DK
8	KAHLEBERG	10271t	83	14.5k	140.1m	79P	-	58T	AS	LB
9	KRONPRINS FREDERIK	16071t	81	19.5k	152.0m	1082P	210C	46T	BA	DK
10	MECKLENBURG-VORPOMMERN	36185t	96	20k	199.9m	900P	90C	150Tr	A2	GY
11	MENJA	751t	98	11.5k	49.9m	396P	34C	4L	BA	DK
12	ODIN SYDFYEN	1698t	82	12.5k	70.4m	338P	50C	8L	BA	DK
13	PETERSBURG	25353t	86	16k	190.8m	144P	329C	110T	A2	LB
14	PRINS JOACHIM	16071t	80	19.5k	152.0m	1080P	-	46Lr	BA	DK
15	PRINS RICHARD	14621t	97	19k	142.0m	900P	294C	36Lr	BA	DK
16	PRINSESSE BENEDIKTE	14621t	97	19k	142.0m	900P	294C	36Lr	BA	DK
17	RÜGEN	12289t	72	17.5k	152.2m	850P	235C	30Lr	A2	GY
18»p	SÆLEN	478t	92	33k	40.0m	282P	0C	0L	-	SW
19	SASSNITZ	21154t	89	19k	171.5m	1000P	390C	50Tr	BA2	GY
20	SCHLESWIG-HOLSTEIN	15187t	97	19k	142.0m	900P	294C	30Lr	BA2	GY
21»p	●SJÖBJÖRNEN	478t	92	33k	40.0m	282P	0C	0L	-	SW
22p	SØNDERHO	93t	62	10k	26.3m	199P	0C	0L	-	DK
23	SPODSBJERG	958t	72	13k	67.3m	225P	40C	9L	BA	DK
24»p	●SVALAN	424t	90	34.5k	38.8m	281P	0C	0L	-	SW
25	THOR SYDFYEN	1479t	78	12k	71.0m	292P	48C	9L	BA	DK
26F•	TREKRONER	15195t	79	18k	198.5m	12P	-	58Tr	A	DK
27	TYCHO BRAHE	11148t	91	14k	111.2m	1250P	240C	35Lr	BA	DK
28	URD	13144t	81	17k	171.0m	100P	-	104T	AS	DK

ASK Built at Venice, Italy as the LUCKY RIDER, a ro-ro freight ferry, for *Delpa Maritime* of Greece. In 1985 she was acquired by *Stena Line* and renamed the STENA DRIVER. Later that year she was acquired by *Sealink British Ferries* and renamed the SEAFREIGHT FREEWAY to operate freight-only services between Dover and Dunkerque. In 1988 she was sold to *SOMAT* of Bulgaria for use on *Medlink* services in the Mediterranean and renamed the SERDICA. In 1990 she was sold and renamed the NORTHERN HUNTER. In 1991 she was sold to *Blæsbjerg* of Denmark, renamed the ARKA MARINE and chartered to *DSB*. She was then converted into a ro-pax vessel, renamed the ASK and introduced onto the Århus - Kalundborg service. Purchased by *Scandlines* in 1997. Withdrawn at the end of 1998. In 1999 she was, after some modification, transferred to *Scandlines Euroseabridge* and placed on the Travemünde - Klaìpeda route. In 2000 she was transferred to the Rostock - Liepaja route. Lengthened by 20m in 2001 and, in late 2001, chartered to *Nordö Link* to operate between Travemünde and Malmö.

DEUTSCHLAND Train/vehicle ferry built at Krimpen an der IJssel, Rotterdam, Netherlands for *DFO* for the Puttgarden - Rødby service.

DRONNING MARGRETHE II Train/vehicle ferry built at Nakskov, Denmark for *DSB* for the Nyborg - Korsør service. In 1981 transferred to the Rødby - Puttgarden service. An additional vehicle deck was added in 1982. Withdrawn in 1997. In 1998 became a back-up freight-only vessel on the Rødby - Puttgarden and Gedser - Rostock routes. In 1999 she replaced the fast ferry BERLIN EXPRESS (4675t, 1995) as regular vessel on the Gedser - Rostock route.

FENJA Vehicle ferry built at Svendborg, Denmark for *SFDS A/S* for the Esbjerg - Nordby service.

FRIGG SYDFYEN Vehicle ferry built at Svendborg, Denmark for *Sydfyenske Dampskibsselskab (SFDS)* of Denmark for the service between Spodsbjerg and Tårs. In 1996, this company was taken over by *DSB Rederi*.

HAMLET Road vehicle ferry built Rauma, Finland for *Scandlines* (50% owned by *Scandlines AG* and 50% owned by *Scandlines AB* of Sweden) for the Helsingør - Helsingborg service. Sister vessel of the TYCHO BRAHE but without rail tracks.

HOLGER DANSKE Built at Aalborg, Denmark as a train/vehicle ferry for *DSB* for the Helsingør - Helsingborg service. In 1991 transferred to the Kalundborg - Samsø route (no rail facilities). In 1997, transferred to subsidiary *SFDS A/S*. Withdrawn at the end of November 1998 when the service passed to *Samsø Linien*. In 1999 began operating between Rødby and Puttgarden as a road freight only vessel, carrying, among others, loads which cannot be conveyed on passenger vessels.

KAHLEBERG Built at Wismar, East Germany for *DSR* of Germany (DDR). In 1991 chartered to *TR Line* (joint venture between *TT-Line* and *DSR*) for service between Rostock and Trelleborg. In 1995 *DSR* pulled out of the venture and the service became *TT-Line*. In 1997 she returned to *DSR* to operate for *Euroseabridge*. She initially operated on the Travemünde - Klaìpeda service. In 1999 she was transferred to the formerly freight only Rostock - Liepaja service. In 2000 replaced by the ASK and transferred to the *Amber Line* Karlshamn - Liepaja route as a ro-pax vessel.

KRONPRINS FREDERIK Train/vehicle ferry built at Nakskov, Denmark for *DSB* for the Nyborg - Korsør service. Withdrawn in 1997. After conversion to car/lorry ferry, she was transferred to the Gedser - Rostock route (no rail facilities).

MECKLENBURG-VORPOMMERN Train/vehicle ferry built at Bremerhaven, Germany for *DFO* for the Rostock - Trelleborg service.

MENJA Built at Svendborg, Denmark for *SFDS A/S* for the Esbjerg - Nordby service.

ODIN SYDFYEN Vehicle ferry built at Svendborg, Denmark for *Sydfyenske Dampskibsselskab (SFDS)* of Denmark for the service between Spodsbjerg and Tårs. In 1996, this company was taken over by *DSB Rederi*.

PETERSBURG Built at Wismar, East Germany as the MUKRAN for *DSR* of Germany (DDR). In 1995 she was rebuilt to introduce road vehicle and additional passenger capacity and was renamed the PETERSBURG. She inaugurated the Travemünde service in 1995 but is now used on the Sassnitz - Klaìpeda service. This service was operated jointly with the *Lisco* vessel KLAIPEDA, a sister vessel which has not been converted to ro-pax format. In 2001 she was transferred to the Kiel - Klaìpeda

Stena Germanica *(Philippe Holthof)*

Svealand *(Mike Louagie)*

service, replacing the sister vessel GREIFSWALD whose charter was ended.

PRINS JOACHIM Train/vehicle ferry, built at Nakskov, Denmark for *DSB* for the Nyborg - Korsør service. Withdrawn in 1997 and laid up. During winter 2000/2001 modified in same way as KRONPRINS FREDERIK and transferred to the Gedser - Rostock route.

PRINS RICHARD, PRINSESSE BENEDIKTE Train/vehicle ferries, built at Frederikshavn, Denmark for *DSB Rederi* for the Rødby - Puttgarden service.

RÜGEN Train/vehicle ferry built at Rostock, East Germany for *Deutsche Reichsbahn* of Germany (DDR) for services between Trelleborg and Sassnitz. In 1993 ownership was transferred to *DFO*. Since 1989 she has been used on the Sassnitz - Rønne service. In 1998 and 1999 she also operated between Ystad and Rønne but this was not repeated in 2000 or 2001.

SÆLEN Fjellstrand FlyingCat 40m catamaran. Built at Mandal, Norway as the SØLØVEN II for *Kværner Shipping* of Norway. In 1993 sold to *DS Øresund* and renamed the SÆLEN. In 2002 laid up.

SASSNITZ Train/vehicle ferry built at Frederikshavn, Denmark for *Deutsche Reichsbahn*. In 1993 ownership transferred to *DFO*. Used on the Sassnitz - Trelleborg service.

SCHLESWIG-HOLSTEIN Train/vehicle ferry built at Krimpen an der IJssel, Rotterdam, Netherlands for *DFO* for the Puttgarden - Rødby service.

SJÖBJÖRNEN Fjellstrand FlyingCat 40m catamaran. Built at Mandal, Norway as the SØLØVEN I for *Kværner Shipping* of Norway. In 1993 sold to *DS Øresund* and renamed the SØBJØRNEN. In 1996 transferred to the Swedish flag and renamed the SJÖBJÖRNEN. In 2002 laid up.

SØNDERHO Passenger only ferry built at Esbjerg for *DSB*. Used on extra peak sailings and late night and early morning sailings between Esbjerg and Nordby.

SPODSBJERG Vehicle ferry built at Husum, Denmark as the ÆRØ-PILEN for *Øernes D/S* of Denmark for services to the island of Ærø. In 1974 sold to *Sydfyenske Dampskibsselskab (SFDS)* for the service between Spodsbjerg and Tårs. In 1996, this company was taken over by *DSB Rederi*.

SVALEN Fjellstrand 38m catamaran. Built at Mandal, Norway as the MERKURIY for Russian interests. In 1995 sold to *DS Øresund*, which is now part of *Scandlines*. In 2001 laid up.

THOR SYDFYEN Vehicle ferry built at Århus, Denmark for *Sydfyenske Dampskibsselskab (SFDS)* of Denmark for the service between Spodsbjerg and Tårs. In 1996, this company was taken over by *DSB Rederi*. In 1998 she was transferred to the Fynshav - Bøjden route.

TREKRONER Built at Florø, Norway as the MILORA for *Yngvar Hvistendal* of Norway and chartered to *Foss Line* for services between Europe and Saudi Arabia. In 1983 sold to *Saleninvest* of Sweden and renamed the SCANDIC WASA. In 1985 she was sold to *DSB*. During 1986 she was lengthened and converted into a train ferry. She was re-delivered in late 1986 as the TREKRONER and, in early 1987, entered service on the 'DanLink' train ferry service ferry between Copenhagen and Helsingborg. Withdrawn in July 2000 and laid up. May be converted to a conventional 12 passenger RO-RO and placed on the *Scandlines Balticum Seaways* Århus - Aabenraa - Klaìpeda route.

TYCHO BRAHE Train/vehicle ferry, built at Tomrefjord, Norway for *DSB* for the Helsingør - Helsingborg service.

URD Built at Venice, Italy as the EASY RIDER, a ro-ro freight ferry, for *Delpa Maritime* of Greece and used on Mediterranean services. In 1985 she was acquired by *Sealink British Ferries* and renamed the SEAFREIGHT HIGHWAY to operate freight-only service between Dover and Dunkerque. In 1988 she was sold to *SOMAT* of Bulgaria for use on *Medlink* services in the Mediterranean and renamed the BOYANA. In 1990 she was sold to *Blæsbjerg* of Denmark, renamed the AKTIV MARINE and chartered to *DSB*. In 1991 she was converted into ro-pax vessel, renamed the URD and introduced onto the Århus - Kalundborg service. Purchased by *Scandlines* in 1997. Withdrawn at the end of May 1999 and, after modification, transferred to the *Balticum Seaways* (later *Scandlines Balticum Seaways*) Århus - Aabenraa - Klaìpeda route. In 2001 lengthened and moved to the Rostock - Liepaja route.

SCANDLINES (SWEDEN)

THE COMPANY *Scandlines AB* (formerly *SweFerry*) is a Swedish company, a subsidiary of *Stena Line Scandinavia AB* of Sweden.

MANAGEMENT Managing Director Åke Svensson.

ADDRESS Knutpunkten 43, S-252 78 Helsingborg, Sweden.

TELEPHONE Administration +46 (0)42-18 62 00, **Reservations *Helsingborg*** +46 (0)42-18 61 00, ***Trelleborg*** +46 (0)410-621 00.

FAX Administration +46 (0)42-18 60 49, **Reservations *Helsingborg*** +46 (0)42-18 74 10, ***Trelleborg*** +46 (0)410-620 29.

INTERNET Email man@mbox303.swipnet.se **Website** www.scandlines.se *(Swedish)*

ROUTES OPERATED Conventional Ferries Helsingborg (Sweden) - Helsingør (Denmark) (25 mins; *(1)*; every 20 mins), Trelleborg (Sweden) - Rostock (Germany) (6 hrs; *(3)*; 4 per day), Trelleborg - Sassnitz (Germany) (3 hrs 30 mins; *(5)*; 3 per day), Trelleborg (Sweden) - Travemünde (Germany) (8 hrs; *(2,4)*; 2 per day - freight-only). All routes are joint with *Scandlines AG* except Trelleborg - Travemünde.

1	AURORA AF HELSINGBORG	10918t	92	14.9k	111.2m	1250P	240C	535r	BA	SW
2	GÖTALAND	18060t	73	18.5k	183.1m	400P	118C	94Tr	AS2	SW
3	SKÅNE	42558t	98	21k	200.2m	600P	-	240Tr	AS2	SW
4	SVEALAND	25026t	99	21.5k	186.0m	327P	164C	170T	A	MA
5	TRELLEBORG	20028t	82	21k	170.2m	900P	108C	48Tr	A2	SW

AURORA AF HELSINGBORG Train/vehicle ferry built at Tomrefjord, Norway for *SweFerry* for *ScandLines* joint *DSB/SweFerry* service between Helsingør and Helsingborg. Owned by *Aurora 93 Trust* of the USA and chartered to *Scandlines*.

GÖTALAND Train/vehicle ferry built at Nakskov, Denmark for *Statens Järnvägar (Swedish State Railways)* for freight services between Trelleborg and Sassnitz. In 1990 transferred to *SweFerry*. In 1992 modified to increase passenger capacity in order to run in passenger service. She is was on the Trelleborg - Rostock service until autumn 1998 when she was replaced by the SKÅNE. She then inaugurated a new freight-only Trelleborg - Travemünde service.

SKÅNE Train/vehicle ferry built at Cadiz, Spain for an American trust and chartered to *Scandlines*. She is used on the Trelleborg - Rostock service.

SVEALAND Ro-pax vessel built at Donada, Italy as the ALYSSA for *Levantina Transporti* of Italy for charter. She was initially chartered to *CoTuNav* of Tunisia for service between Marseilles, Genoa and Tunis and in 2000 to *Trasmediterranea* of Spain for service between Barcelona and Palma de Majorca. In 2001 chartered to *Stena Line Scandinavia AB*, renamed the SVEALAND and placed as second vessel on the *Scandlines AB* freight only Trelleborg - Travemünde service.

TRELLEBORG Train/vehicle ferry built at Landskrona, Sweden for *Svelast* of Sweden (an *SJ* subsidiary). In 1990 ownership transferred to *SweFerry*. She is used on the Trelleborg - Sassnitz service.

SEAWIND LINE

THE COMPANY *SeaWind Line* is a Swedish private sector company owned by *Silja Service Oy*.

MANAGEMENT Managing Director Sören Lindman, **Marketing Manager** Ole Engblom.

ADDRESS Linnankatu 84, FIN-20100 Turku, Finland.

TELEPHONE Administration & Reservations +358 (0)2 2102 800.

FAX Administration & Reservations +358 (0)2 2102 810.

INTERNET Website www.seawind.fi *(English, Swedish, Finnish)*

ROUTE OPERATED Stockholm (Sweden) - Långnäs (Åland) - Turku (Finland) ***Until September 2002*** (10 hrs 45 mins; *(2)*; 1 passenger sailing per day plus 2 freight sailings *(1,3)*). ***From September 2002*** (10 hrs 45 mins; *(2,4)*; 2 passenger sailings per day).

1F	CUPRIA	10279t	77	17.5k	142.3m	8P	-	95Tr	A	SW
2	SEA WIND	15879t	71	18k	154.9m	260P	60C	88Tr	BAS	SW
3F	STAR WIND	13788t	77	18k	158.6m	119P	100C	66Tr	A	SW

CUPRIA Built at Naantali, Finland as the ROLITA for *Merivienti* of Italy. In 1979 chartered to *Finncarriers* of Finland, renamed the FINNFOREST and used on services between Finland and North West Europe. In 1982 sold to *EFFOA* of Finland and renamed the CANOPUS. In 1992 sold to Swedish interests and chartered to *Stora Line* for services from Sweden to NW Europe. She was renamed the CUPRIA. In 1995, chartered to *North Sea Ferries* to inaugurate a new service between Middlesbrough and Rotterdam and renamed the NORCOVE. In 1999 she was chartered to *Finncarriers* and renamed the CUPRIA. She was used on services from Finland to Spain via Antwerp. In 2001 she was chartered to *Cobelfret Ferries* for the Purfleet - Rotterdam service. In 2002 chartered to *SeaWind Line* to operate additional freight only sailings between Stockholm and Turku before the SKY WIND is delivered in September 2002

SEA WIND Train/vehicle ferry built at Helsingør, Denmark as the SVEALAND for *Stockholms Rederi AB Svea* and used on the *Trave Line* Helsingborg (Sweden) - Copenhagen (Tuborg Havn) - Travemünde freight service. Later she operated between Travemünde and Malmö, first for *Saga Line* and then for *TT-Saga Line*. In 1984 she was rebuilt to increase capacity and renamed the SAGA WIND. In 1989 she was acquired by *SeaWind Line*, renamed the SEA WIND and inaugurated a combined rail freight, trailer and lower priced passenger service between Stockholm and Turku.

STAR WIND Train/vehicle ferry built at Bergen, Norway as the ROSTOCK for *Deutsche Reichsbahn* of Germany (DDR). Used on freight services between Trelleborg and Sassnitz. In 1992 modified to increase passenger capacity in order to run in passenger service. In 1993 ownership transferred to *DFO* and in 1994 she opened a new service from Rostock to Trelleborg. In 1997 she was used when winds preclude the use of the new MECKLENBURG-VORPOMMERN. Following modifications to this vessel in late 1997, the ROSTOCK continued to operate to provide additional capacity until the delivery of the SKÅNE of *Scandlines AB*, after which she was laid up. In 1999 she was sold to *SeaWind Line*, renamed the STAR WIND and operated in freight-only mode. Initial plans to bring her passenger accommodation up to the standards required for Baltic service were dropped. Later in 2002 to be replaced by the SKY WIND and transferred to the Helsinki - Tallinn route.

Under Conversion

4	SKY WIND	16925t	86	15k	188.4m	-	-	130Tr	A	SW

SKY WIND Train/vehicle ferry built at Moss, Norway as the ÖRESUND for *Statens Järnvägar* (*Swedish State Railways*) for the 'DanLink' service between Helsingborg and Copenhagen. Has 817 metres of rail track. Service ceased in July 2000 and vessel laid up. In 2001 sold to *Sea Containers Ferries* and, in 2002 is being converted at Gdansk, Poland to passenger ferry. She will be chartered to *SeaWind Line* and, in autumn 2002, will replace the STAR WIND on the Stockholm - Turku service. Tonnage is before conversion and will change.

SILJA LINE

THE COMPANY *Silja Line* is a subsidiary of *Silja Oyj Abp* (formerly *Neptun Maritime Oyj*), a company based in Finland. In 1993 the services of *Jakob Line* and *Vaasanlaivat* were integrated into *Silja Line*. In 1998 the headquarter functions were concentrated in Finland, with marketing organisations in Sweden, Estonian and Germany. In 1999 a 51% holding in *Neptun Maritime Oyj* was acquired by *Sea Containers Ltd* of Great Britain; 1% was then disposed of to *Rederi AB Gotland* of Sweden. In 2000, that company's *SeaCat Sweden* operation (now ceased), operated by *SeaCat AB* (wholly owned by *Sea Containers*), was marketed as *Silja Line SeaCat*, along with a new Helsinki - Tallinn SeaCat service, operated by an Estonian subsidiary of *Sea Containers*.

MANAGEMENT President Nils-Gustaf Palmgren, **Deputy CEO, Passenger Services** Heikki Jehmusto, **Senior Vice President Cargo Services** Sören Lindman, **Senior Vice President, Ship Management** Christian Grönvall, **Senior Vice President, Corporate Communications** Thomas Nylund, **CFO** Steven G Robson.

ADDRESS POB 880, Mannerheimintie 2, FIN-00101 Helsinki, Finland.

TELEPHONE Administration *Finland* +358 (0)9 18041, **Reservations *Finland*** +358 (0)9 1804 422, ***Sweden*** +46 (0)8-222 140.

FAX Administration & Reservations *Finland* +358 (0)9 1804 279, ***Sweden*** +46 (0)8-667 8681.

INTERNET Email info@silja.com **Website** www.silja.com *(English, Finnish and Swedish)*

ROUTES OPERATED Conventional Ferries *All year* Helsinki (Finland) - Mariehamn (Åland) - Stockholm (Sweden) (16 hrs; *(5,6)*; 1 per day), Turku (Finland) - Mariehamn (Åland) (day)/Långnäs (Åland) (night) - Stockholm (11 hrs; *(2,3)*; 1 or 2 per day), ***Winter only*** Helsinki - Tallinn (Estonia) (3 hrs 30 mins (4 hrs 30 mins in ice period); *(1)*; 1 per day), ***Winter, Spring and Autumn only*** Turku (Finland) - Mariehamn (day)/Långnäs (night) - Kapellskär (Sweden) (11 hrs; *(2)*; 1 per day), ***Summer only*** Helsinki - Tallinn - Rostock (Germany) (24 hrs (Helsinki - Tallinn, 2 hr 30 min, Tallinn - Rostock, 19 hrs)); *(1)*; 3 per week). **Fast Ferry (Operated by *Sea Containers* and marketed by *Silja Line*)** Helsinki - Tallinn (1 hr 30 mins; *(7)*; up to 4 per day). **Cruise Service** Helsinki - Tallinn - Visby (Gotland), Helsinki - Riga (Latvia), St Petersburg (Russia) and other destinations *(4)*.

1	FINNJET	32940t	77	31k	214.9m	1790P	374C	44T	BA	FI
2	SILJA EUROPA	59912t	93	21.5k	201.8m	3000P	400C	68T	BA	FI
3	SILJA FESTIVAL	34414t	85	22k	170.7m	2000P	400C	80T	BA	SW
4p	SILJA OPERA	25076t	92	21k	158.9m	1400P	0C	0T	-	SW
5	SILJA SERENADE	58376t	90	21k	203.0m	2641P	450C	70T	BA	FI
6	SILJA SYMPHONY	58377t	91	21k	203.0m	2641P	450C	70T	BA	SW
7»	SUPERSEACAT FOUR	4697t	99	38k	100.0m	752P	164C	-	A	IT

FINNJET Built at Helsinki, Finland for *Finnlines* to operate between Helsinki and Travemünde, replacing several more vessels with intermediate calls. Her exceptionally fast speed was achieved by the use of gas turbine engines. During winter 1981/82 she was equipped with diesel engines for use during periods when traffic did not justify so many crossings per week. Later the trading name was changed to *Finnjet Line*. In 1986 the company was acquired by *EFFOA* and the trading name changed to *Finnjet Silja Line*. In winter 1997/98 she operated between Helsinki and Tallinn (Muuga Harbour). In summer 1998 she operated a weekly Travemünde - Tallinn - Helsinki - Travemünde triangular service in addition to two weekly Travemünde - Helsinki round trips. In autumn 1998 she resumed operating between Helsinki and Tallinn and since summer 1999 she has operated Helsinki - Tallinn - Rostock.

SILJA EUROPA Built at Papenburg, Germany. Ordered by *Rederi AB Slite* of Sweden for *Viking Line* service between Stockholm and Helsinki and due to be called EUROPA. In 1993, shortly before delivery was due, the order was cancelled. A charter agreement with her builders was then signed by *Silja Line* and she was introduced onto the Stockholm - Helsinki route as SILJA EUROPA. In early 1995 she was transferred to the Stockholm - Turku service. During off peak period she now operates between Turku and Kapellskär.

SILJA FESTIVAL Built at Helsinki, Finland as the WELLAMO for *EFFOA* for the *Silja Line* Stockholm - Mariehamn - Turku service. In 1990, following the sale of the FINLANDIA to *DFDS*, she was transferred to the Stockholm - Helsinki service until the SILJA SERENADE was delivered later in the year. During winter 1991/92 she was extensively rebuilt and in 1991 renamed the SILJA FESTIVAL; ownership was transferred to *Silja Line*. In 1993 she was transferred to the Malmö - Travemünde service of *Euroway*, which was at this time managed by *Silja Line*. This service ceased in 1994 and she was transferred to the Vaasa - Sundsvall service. In 1994 and 1995 she operated on this route during the peak summer period and on the Helsinki - Tallinn route during the rest of the year. The Vaasa - Sundsvall service did not operate in summer 1996 and she continued to operate between Helsinki and Tallinn. In 1997 she was transferred to the Stockholm - Turku route replacing the SILJA SCANDINAVIA (see the GABRIELLA, *Viking Line*).

SILJA OPERA Built as the SALLY ALBATROSS at Rauma, Finland for *Rederi AB Sally* of Finland, a subsidiary of *EffJohn International* to operate cruises from Helsinki. She was built on the lower portions of the previous SALLY ALBATROSS, which had been declared a total constructive loss following a fire when being refitted at a Stockholm shipyard in 1991. (This vessel had been built in 1980 at Turku for *Rederi AB Sally* (at that time part of *Viking Line*) as the VIKING SAGA and was used on the Helsinki - Stockholm service. In 1986 she was replaced by the OLYMPIA (now PRIDE OF BILBAO), modified to a cruising role and renamed the SALLY ALBATROSS). In spring 1994 she grounded whilst on a winter cruise and was badly damaged. Her cruise programme was cancelled and, when she had been repaired and modified, she was renamed the LEEWARD and chartered to *Norwegian Cruise Line* for Caribbean cruising. In 1999 she was chartered to *Star Cruises* of Singapore and renamed the SUPERSTAR TAURUS. She was used on cruises in the Far East. In 2002 returned to *Silja Line* and renamed the SILJA OPERA. She is used on cruises from Helsinki to various destinations, including Tallinn, Visby (Gotland), Riga (Latvia) and St Petersburg (Russia).

SILJA SERENADE, SILJA SYMPHONY Built at Turku, Finland for *Silja Line* for the Stockholm - Helsinki service. In 1993, SILJA SERENADE was transferred to the Stockholm - Turku service but in early 1995 she was transferred back to the Helsinki route.

SUPERSEACAT FOUR Fincantieri MDV1200 monohull vessel built at Riva Trigoso, Italy. Laid-up following delivery. In 2000 transferred to an Estonian subsidiary of *Sea Containers* to operate between Helsinki and Tallinn under the *Silja Line SeaCat* branding. The service was marketed by *Silja Line*. In March 2001 she resumed operations between Helsinki and Tallinn.

STENA LINE

THE COMPANY *Stena Line Scandinavia AB* is a Swedish private sector company.

MANAGEMENT Managing Director Bo Severed. **Marketing Manager** Fredrik Lantz, **Ship Management Director** Håkan Siewers, **Communication Director** Joakim Kenndal.

ADDRESS S-405 19 Gothenburg, Sweden (***Visitors' address*** Danmarksterminalen, Masthuggskajen).

TELEPHONE Administration +46 (0)31-85 80 00, **Reservations** +46 (0)31-704 00 00.

FAX Administration & Reservations +46 (0)31-24 10 38.

INTERNET Email info@stenaline.com **Website** www.stenaline.com *(English, Swedish)*

ROUTES OPERATED Conventional Ferries Gothenburg (Sweden) - Frederikshavn (Denmark) (3 hrs 15 mins; *(4,7)*; up to 6 per day), Gothenburg - Kiel (Germany) (14 hrs; *(6,10)*; 1 per day), Frederikshavn - Oslo (Norway) (8 hrs 45 mins; *(9)*; 1 per day), Varberg (Sweden) - Grenaa (Denmark) (4 hrs; *(8)*; 2 per day), Karlskrona (Sweden) - Gdynia (Poland) (10 hrs 30 mins; *(1)*; 1 per day). **Fast Ferry** Gothenburg - Frederikshavn (2 hrs; *(2)*; 4 per day), **Freight Ferries** Gothenburg - Frederikshavn (Train Ferry) (3 hrs 45 mins; *(11)*; 2 per day), Gothenburg - Travemünde (15 hrs; *(3,5)*; 1 per day), Karlskrona - Gdynia (10 hrs 30 mins; *(12)*; 1 per day).

1	STENA BALTICA	31189t	86	20k	161.8m	1800P	500C	72T	BA	SW
2»	STENA CARISMA	8631t	97	40k	88.0m	900P	210C	-	A	SW
3F	STENA CARRIER	8698t	78	18k	156.0m	12P	510C	124T	A	SW

4	STENA DANICA	28727t	83	19.5k	154.9m	2274P	555C	120T	BAS2	SW
5F	STENA FREIGHTER	8800t	77	18k	156.0m	12P	510C	124T	A	SW
6	STENA GERMANICA	38772t	87	20k	175.4m	2400P	550C	120T	BAS2	SW
7	STENA JUTLANDICA	29691t	96	21.5k	183.7m	1500P	550C	156T	BAS2	SW
8	STENA NAUTICA	19763t	86	19.4k	134.0m	700P	330C	70T	BA	SW
9	STENA SAGA	33750t	81	22k	166.1m	2000P	510C	76T	BA	SW
10	STENA SCANDINAVICA	38756t	88	20k	175.4m	2400P	550C	120T	BAS2	SW
11F	STENA SCANRAIL	7504t	73	16.5k	142.4m	65P	-	64Tr	A	SW
12	STENA TRAVELLER	18332t	92	18k	153.6m	250P	-	132T	BA2	SW

STENA BALTICA Built at Krimpen an der IJssel, Rotterdam, Netherlands as the KONINGIN BEATRIX for *Stoomvaart Maatschappij Zeeland* of The Netherlands for their Hoek van Holland - Harwich service (trading as *Crown Line*). In 1989 transferred to *Stena Line bv*. In June 1997 chartered by *Stena Line bv* to *Stena Line Ltd* and used on the Fishguard - Rosslare service. In August 1997, transferred to the British flag. In 2002 renamed the STENA BALTICA and transferred to the Karlskrona - Gdynia service.

STENA CARISMA Westamarin HSS 900 craft built at Kristiansand, Norway for *Stena Line* for the Gothenburg - Frederikshavn service. Work on a sister vessel, approximately 30% completed, was ceased.

STENA CARRIER Built at Ulsan, South Korea as the IMPARCA EXPRESS I for *Stena AB* and chartered to *Imparca Line* and used on Caribbean services. In 1980 renamed the STENA CARRIER. Later that year she was renamed the IMPARCA MIAMI. In 1981 she reverted to the name STENA CARRIER. In 1981 she was chartered to *Ignazio Messina* of Italy and renamed the JOLLY BRUNO. In 1982 renamed the JOLLY SMERALDO and in 1983 this charter ended and she resumed the name STENA CARRIER. In 1988 she was transferred to *Stena Line* and placed on the Gothenburg - Travemünde service.

STENA DANICA Built at Dunkerque, France for *Stena Line* for the Gothenburg - Frederikshavn service. Sister vessel STENA JUTLANDICA was transferred to the Dover - Calais service in July 1996 and renamed the STENA EMPEREUR (now P&OSL PROVENCE). This vessel is listed in Section 1.

STENA FREIGHTER Built at Ulsan, South Korea as the MERZARIO AUSONIA for *Stena AB*, chartered to *Merzario Line* of Italy and used on services between Italy and the Middle East. In 1981 she was renamed the STENA FREIGHTER. In 1982 she was chartered to *Ignazio Messina* of Italy and renamed the JOLLY GIALLO; later that year she was renamed the JOLLY TURCHESE. In 1983 this charter ended and she resumed the name STENA FREIGHTER. In 1988 she was transferred to *Stena Line* and placed on the Gothenburg - Travemünde service.

STENA GERMANICA, STENA SCANDINAVICA Built at Gdynia, Poland for *Stena Line* for the Gothenburg - Kiel service. Names were swapped during construction in order that the STENA GERMANICA should enter service first. There were originally intended to be four vessels. Only two were delivered to *Stena Line*. The third (due to be called the STENA BALTICA) was sold by the builders as an unfinished hull to *Fred. Olsen Lines* of Norway and then resold to *ANEK* of Greece who had her completed at Perama and delivered as EL VENIZELOS for service between Greece and Italy. The fourth hull (due to be called the STENA POLONICA) was never completed. During the summer period, the vessel arriving in Gothenburg overnight from Kiel operates a round trip to Frederikshavn before departing for Kiel the following evening. During winter 1998/99 they were modified to increase freight capacity and reduce the number of cabins.

STENA JUTLANDICA Train/vehicle 'ro-pax' vessel built at Krimpen an der IJssel, Rotterdam, Netherlands for *Stena Line* to operate between Gothenburg and Frederikshavn. She was launched as the STENA JUTLANDICA III and renamed on entry into service. During winter she has operated in 'freight-only' mode. However, during winter 2000/1 she continued to provide a full passenger service and this was repeated in winter 2001/2.

STENA NAUTICA Built at Nakskov, Denmark as the NIELS KLIM for *DSB (Danish State Railways)* for their service between Århus (Jutland) and Kalundborg (Sealand). In 1990 she was purchased by *Stena Rederi* of Sweden and renamed the STENA NAUTICA. In 1992 she was chartered to *B&I Line*, renamed the ISLE OF INNISFREE and introduced onto the Rosslare - Pembroke Dock service, replacing the MUNSTER (8093t, 1970). In 1993 she was transferred to the Dublin - Holyhead service. In early 1995 she was chartered to *Lion Ferry*. She was renamed the LION KING. In 1996 she was replaced by a new LION KING and renamed the STENA NAUTICA. During summer 1996 she was chartered to *Trasmediterranea* of Spain but returned to *Stena RoRo* in the autumn and remained laid up during 1997. In December 1997 she was chartered to *Stena Line* and placed on the Halmstad - Grenaa route. This route ended on 31 January 1999 and she was transferred to the Varberg - Grenaa route. During winter 2001/2 rebuilt to heighten upper vehicle deck; passenger capacity reduced.

STENA SAGA Built at Turku, Finland as the SILVIA REGINA for *Stockholms Rederi AB Svea* of Sweden. She was registered with subsidiary company *Svea Line* of Turku, Finland and was used on *Silja Line* services between Stockholm and Helsinki. In 1981 she was sold to *Johnson Line* and in 1984 sold to a Finnish Bank and chartered back. In 1990 she was purchased by *Stena RoRo* of Sweden for delivery in 1991. In 1991 she was renamed the STENA BRITANNICA and took up service on the Hoek van Holland - Harwich service for Dutch subsidiary *Stena Line bv*, operating with a British crew. In 1994 she was transferred to *Stena Line's* Oslo - Frederikshavn route and renamed the STENA SAGA.

STENA SCANRAIL Built at Capelle an der IJssel, Rotterdam, Netherlands. Launched as the STENA SEATRADER for *Stena AB* and entered service as the SEATRADER. In 1976 she was lengthened and then demise chartered to *Bahjah Navigation* of Cyprus and renamed the BAHJAN. In 1981 charter ended and she was renamed the STENA SEARIDER. In 1983 chartered to *Snowdrop Shipping* of Cyprus and renamed the SEARIDER. The charter ended the following year and she renamed the name STENA SEARIDER. Later in 1984 she was renamed the TRUCKER and in 1985 again reverted to the name STENA SEARIDER. In 1987 she was converted to a train ferry to operate between Gothenburg and Frederikshavn, chartered to *Stena Line* and renamed the STENA SCANRAIL.

STENA TRAVELLER Ro-pax vessel built at Fevaag, Norway for *Stena RoRo*. After a short period with *Stena Line* on the Hoek van Holland - Harwich service, she was chartered to *Sealink Stena Line* for their Southampton - Cherbourg route, initially for 28 weeks. At the end of the 1992 summer season she was chartered to *TT-Line* to operate between Travemünde and Trelleborg and was renamed the TT-TRAVELLER. In late 1995, she returned to *Stena Line*, resumed the name STENA TRAVELLER and inaugurated a new service between Holyhead and Dublin. In autumn 1996 she was replaced by the STENA CHALLENGER (18523t, 1991). In early 1997 she was again chartered to *TT-Line* and renamed the TT-TRAVELLER. She operated on the Rostock - Trelleborg route. During winter 1999/2000, her passenger capacity was increased to 250 and passenger facilities renovated. In early 2002 the charter ended and she was renamed the STENA TRAVELLER, chartered to *Stena Line* and placed on their Karlskrona - Gdynia service.

SUPERFAST FERRIES

THE COMPANY *SuperFast Ferries* is a Greek company, owned by *Attica Enterprises*.

MANAGEMENT Managing Director Alexander P Panagopulos, **Corporate Marketing Director** Yannis B Criticos, **General Manager, Germany of Attica Premium SA** Jens-Peter Berg.

ADDRESS *Greece* 157 Alkyonidon Avenue, Voula, GR-16673 Athens, Greece, ***Northern Europe*** Hermann-Lange-Strasse 1, DE-23558 Lübeck, Germany.

TELEPHONE Administration (Greece) +30 (0)1 891 9500, **Administration (Germany)** +49 (0)451 88006130, **Reservations** +49 (0)451 88006130.

FAX Administration (Greece) +30 (0)10 891 9509, **Administration & Reservations (Germany)** +49 (0)451-8800629.

INTERNET Email criticos@superfast.com **Website** www.superfast.com *(English, German, Finnish, Swedish)*

ROUTES OPERATED Rostock (Germany) - Hanko (Finland) (21 hrs; *(1,2)*; 1 per day)

1	SUPERFAST VII	29800t	01	29.2k	203.3m	626P	1000C	140T	BA2	GR
2	SUPERFAST VIII	29800t	01	29.2k	203.3m	626P	1000C	140T	BA2	GR

SUPERFAST VII, SUPERFAST VIII Built at Kiel, Germany for *Attica Enterprise* for use by *SuperFast Ferries* between Rostock and Hanko.

TALLINK

THE COMPANY *AS Tallink Grupp*, (formerly *AS Hansatee Grupp* trading as *Tallink*), is an Estonian company owned by the *AS Infortar (*86.0%) and others. Services are marketed outside Estonia by *Tallink Finland Oy.*

MANAGEMENT Director, Tallink Finland Oy Keijo Mehtonen.

ADDRESS PO Box 195, 00181 Helsinki, Finland.

TELEPHONE Administration +358 (0)9 228211, **Reservations** +358 (0)9 228311.

FAX Administration & Reservations +358 (0)9 228 21242.

INTERNET Email keijo.mehtonen@tallink.fi **Websites** www.tallink.ee *(Finnish, Estonian, English)*

Also www.tallink.se *(Swedish)* www.tallink.fi *(Finnish).*

ROUTES OPERATED Conventional Ferries *Until June 2002* Tallinn (Estonia) - Helsinki (Finland) (3 hrs 30 mins; *(2,4,9)*; up to 4 per day), Tallinn - Stockholm (Sweden) (14 hrs; *(5)*; alternate days), Kapellskär (Sweden) - Paldiski (Estonia) (9 hrs - 11 hrs; *(1,3)*; 2 per day), ***From June 2002*** Helsinki - Tallinn (3 hrs 30 mins; *(4,6,9)*; up to 4 per day), Stockholm - Tallinn (14 hrs; *(2,5)*; daily), Kapellskär - Paldiski (9 hrs - 11 hrs; *(1,3)*; 2 per day). **Fast Ferries** Helsinki - Tallinn (1 hr 30 mins; *(7,8)*; up to 6 per day).

1	BALTIC KRISTINA	12281t	73	19k	128.0m	578P	344C	40T	BA	ES
2	FANTAASIA	16630t	79	21.3k	136.1m	1700P	549C	46T	BA2	ES
3	KAPELLA	‡2794t	74	14.5k	110.1m	50P	-	42T	A	ES
4	MELOODIA	17955t	79	21k	138.8m	1500P	480C	52T	BA2	ES
5	REGINA BALTICA	18345t	80	21.3k	145.2m	1450P	500C	68T	BA	ES
6	ROMANTIKA	c40000t	02	22k	193.8m	2178P	300C	83T	BA	ES
7»	TALLINK AUTOEXPRESS	4859t	95	32k	78.6m	586P	150C	-	BA	ES
8»	TALLINK AUTOEXPRESS 2	5419t	97	37k	82.3m	700P	175C	-	A	ES
9	VANA TALLINN	10002t	74	18k	153.7m	1500P	300C	44L	BAS	ES

BALTIC KRISTINA Built at Turku, Finland as the BORE 1 for *Ångfartygs AB Bore* of Finland for *Silja Line* services between Turku and Stockholm. In 1980, *Bore Line* left the *Silja Line* consortium and disposed of its passenger ships. She was acquired by *EFFOA* of Finland and continued to operate on *Silja Line* service, being renamed the SKANDIA. In 1983 she was sold to *Stena Line* and renamed the STENA BALTICA. She was then resold to *Latvia Shipping* of the USSR, substantially rebuilt, renamed the ILLICH and introduced onto a Stockholm - Leningrad (now Sankt-Peterburg) service trading as *ScanSov Line.* In 1986 operations were transferred to *Baltic Shipping Company.* In 1992 she inaugurated a new service between Stockholm and Riga but continued to also serve Sankt-Peterburg. In 1995 the Swedish terminal was changed to Nynäshamn. In late 1995 arrested and laid up in Stockholm. In 1997, services were planned to restart between Kiel and Sankt-Peterburg under the auspices of a German company called *Baltic Line*, with the vessel renamed the ANASTASIA V. However, this did not materialise and she was sold to *Windward Line* of Barbados and renamed the WINDWARD PRIDE. In 1997, she was chartered to *ESCO*, and renamed the BALTIC KRISTINA. In late 1997 she sailed for *EstLine* between Stockholm and Tallinn in a freight-only role. Following a major refurbishment, she entered service with *EstLine* in May 1998, allowing a daily full passenger service to be operated. In 2000 charter transferred to *Tallink.* Placed on the Paldiski - Kapellskär service.

FANTAASIA Built at Turku, Finland as the TURELLA for *SF Line* of Finland for the *Viking Line* Stockholm - Mariehamn - Turku service and later moved to the Kapellskär - Mariehamn - Naantali service. In 1988 she was sold to *Stena Line*, renamed the STENA NORDICA and placed onto the

Silja Serenade *(Miles Cowsill)*

Koningin Beatrix *(Miles Cowsill)*

Frederikshavn - Moss (night) and Frederikshavn - Gothenburg (day) service. In 1996 the Frederikshavn - Moss service ceased and she was transferred to subsidiary *Lion Ferry* and renamed the LION KING. She operated between Halmstad and Grenaa. In December 1997 she was sold to *Tallink Line Ltd* of Cyprus and renamed the FANTAASIA. In February 1998, after substantial modification, she was placed on the *Tallink* service between Helsinki and Tallinn. In June 2002 to move to the Tallinn - Stockholm route, enabling a daily service to be reinstated.

KAPELLA Built at Kristiansand, Norway for *A/S Larvik-Frederikshavnferjen* of Norway as DUKE OF YORKSHIRE. In 1978 she was chartered to (and later purchased by) *CN Marine* of Canada (from 1986 *Marine Atlantic*) and renamed the MARINE EVANGELINE. She was used on services between Canada, USA and Newfoundland. In 1992 she was chartered to *Opale Ferries* of France and inaugurated a new Boulogne - Folkestone freight service. In 1993 the company went into liquidation and the service and charter were taken over by *Meridian Ferries*, a British company. She was renamed the SPIRIT OF BOULOGNE. In spring 1995, *Meridian Ferries* went into liquidation and she returned to her owners, resuming the name MARINE EVANGELINE. After a period of lay up she was chartered to *Stena Sealink Line*. She spent the summer on the Newhaven - Dieppe service and was then transferred to the Stranraer - Larne (from November 1995 Stranraer - Belfast) route. She returned to Newhaven in summer 1996 but was laid up during most of 1997. In late 1997 she was chartered to *Hansatee* and inaugurated a new ro-pax service between Paldiski and Kapellskär. She was renamed the KAPELLA.

MELOODIA Built at Papenburg, Germany as DIANA II for *Rederi AB Slite* for *Viking Line* services between Stockholm and Turku, Mariehamn, Kapellskär and Naantali. In 1992 sold to a *Nordbanken* and, in 1993, chartered to *TR-Line* of Germany (joint venture between *TT-Line* and *DSR*) for service between Trelleborg and Rostock. In 1994 sold to *ESCO* and chartered to *EstLine* and renamed the MARE BALTICUM. During winter 1994/95 she was completely renovated. In 1996, following the delivery of the REGINA BALTICA, she was chartered to *Tallink*, renamed the MELOODIA and placed on the Tallinn - Helsinki service. In 2002 purchased by Tallink.

REGINA BALTICA Built at Turku, Finland as the VIKING SONG for *Rederi AB Sally* of Finland and used on the *Viking Line* service between Stockholm and Helsinki. In 1985 replaced by the MARIELLA of *SF Line* and sold to *Fred. Olsen Lines*. She was named BRAEMAR and used on services between Norway and Britain as well as Norway and Denmark. Services to Britain ceased in June 1990 and she continued to operate between Norway and Denmark. She was withdrawn in 1991 and sold to *Rigorous Shipping* of Cyprus (a subsidiary of *Fred. Olsen Lines*). She was chartered to the *Baltic Shipping Company* of Russia, renamed the ANNA KARENINA and inaugurated a service between Kiel and Sankt-Peterburg (St Petersburg). In 1992 a Nynäshamn call was introduced. In 1996 the service ceased and she was returned to her owners and renamed the ANNA K. Later in 1996 she was sold to *Empremare Shipping Co Ltd* of Cyprus (a company jointly owned by *Nordström & Thulin* and *Estonian Shipping Company*), chartered to *EstLine* and renamed the REGINA BALTICA. In 2000 charter transferred to *Tallink*. Continues to operate between Stockholm and Tallinn. May be withdrawn in autumn 2002.

ROMANTIKA Built at Rauma, Finland for *Tallink Grupp* to operate for *Tallink* between Tallinn and Helsinki. Due to enter service in June 2002.

TALLINK AUTOEXPRESS Austal Ships Auto Express 79 catamaran ordered by *Sea Containers* and launched at Fremantle, Western Australia as the AUTO EXPRESS 96. On completion she was renamed the SUPERSEACAT FRANCE. However, due to a dispute between *Sea Containers* and the builders, delivery was not taken and it was announced that she was to be sold to *Stena Rederi* of Sweden, renamed the STENA LYNX IV and chartered to *Stena Line (UK)*, *I*naugurating a Newhaven - Dieppe service in February 1996. This did not happen and she was instead sold to *DSB Rederi (*now *Scandlines Danmark A/S*) and, in summer 1996, she was chartered to *Cat-Link* and renamed the CAT-LINK III. In 1999 she was sold to *Tallink* and renamed the TALLINK AUTOEXPRESS. Operates between Tallinn and Helsinki.

TALLINK AUTOEXPRESS 2 Austal Ships Auto Express 82 catamaran built at Fremantle, Western Australia as the BOOMERANG for *Polferries* and used on the Swinoujscie - Malmö route. In autumn 1999 she withdrawn and it was anticipated that she would no longer operate for *Polferries*. However in summer 2000 she returned to the Swinoujscie - Malmö route. She was laid up again in the autumn and in May 2001 was sold to Tallink and renamed the TALLINK AUTOEXPRESS 2. Operates between Tallinn and Helsinki.

VANA TALLINN Built at Helsingør, Denmark as the DANA REGINA for *DFDS* and used on their Esbjerg - Harwich service until 1983 when she was moved to the Copenhagen - Oslo route. In 1990 she was sold to *Nordström & Thulin* of Sweden, renamed the NORD ESTONIA and used on the *EstLine* Stockholm - Tallinn service. In 1992 she was chartered to *Larvik Line* to operate as a second vessel between Larvik and Frederikshavn and renamed the THOR HEYERDAHL. In 1994 she was sold to *Inreko Ships Ltd*, chartered to *Tallink* and renamed the VANA TALLINN. In November 1996 she was withdrawn and in December 1996 she was chartered to a new company called *TH Ferries* and resumed sailings between Helsinki and Tallinn. In January 1998 she was sold to *Hansatee* subsidiary *Vana Tallinn Line Ltd* of Cyprus and placed on *Tallink* service between Helsinki and Tallinn. *TH Ferries* then ceased operations. In autumn 2002 likely to be moved to the Paldiski - Kapellskär route, replacing the BALTIC KRISTINA.

TESO

THE COMPANY *TESO* is a Dutch public sector company. Its full name is *Texels Eigen Stoomboot Onderneming*.

MANAGEMENT Managing Director R Wortel.

ADDRESS Pontweg 1, 1797 SN Den Hoorn, Texel, Netherlands.

TELEPHONE Administration +31 (0)222 369600, **Reservations** n/a.

FAX Administration & Reservations +31 (0)222 369659.

INTERNET Email teso.nl@wxs.nl **Website** www.teso.nl *(Dutch, English, German, French)*

ROUTES OPERATED Den Helder (Netherlands) - Texel (Dutch Frisian Islands) (20 minutes; *(1,2)*; hourly).

1	MOLENGAT	6170t	80	13k	88.8m	1250P	126C	19L	BA2	NL
2	SCHULPENGAT	8311t	90	13.6k	110.4m	1750P	156C	25L	BA2	NL

MOLENGAT, SCHULPENGAT Built at Heusden, Netherlands for *TESO*.

TT-LINE

THE COMPANY *TT-Line GmbH & Co* is a German private sector company.

MANAGEMENT Managing Director Hanns Heinrich Conzen & Dr Arndt-Heinrich von Oertzen, **Sales Manager** Dirk Lifke.

ADDRESS Mattenwiete 8, D-20457 Hamburg, Germany.

TELEPHONE Administration *Hamburg* +49 (0)40 3601 372, ***Rostock*** +49 (0)381 6707911, **Reservations *Hamburg*** +49 (0)40 3601 442, ***Rostock*** +49 (0)381 670790.

FAX Administration & Reservations *Hamburg* +49 (0)40 3601 407, ***Rostock*** +49 (0)381 6707980.

INTERNET Email info@TTLine.com **Website** www.TTLine.de *(German)*

ROUTES OPERATED Passenger Ferries Travemünde (Germany) - Trelleborg (Sweden) (7 hrs 30 mins; *(3,4)*; 2 per day). **Ro-pax Ferries** Travemünde (Germany) - Trelleborg (Sweden) (7 hrs 30 mins; *(2,5)*; 2 per day), Rostock (Germany) - Trelleborg (Sweden) (6 hrs; *(1,6)*; 3 per day). **Fast Ferry** Rostock (Germany) - Trelleborg (Sweden) (2 hrs 45 mins; *(7)*; up to 3 per day).

1	HUCKLEBERRY FINN	30740t	88	20k	177.2m	400P	280C	146T	BAS	SW
2	NILS DACKE	26790t	95	21k	179.6m	308P	-	157T	BA	SW
3	NILS HOLGERSSON	36000t	01	22k	190.0m	744P	-	174T	BA	GY
4	PETER PAN	36000t	01	22k	190.0m	744P	-	174T	BA	SW

Nils Holgersson *(Mike Louagie)*

5	ROBIN HOOD	26800t	95	21k	179.6m	308P	-	157T	BA	GY
6	TOM SAWYER	30740t	89	20k	177.0m	400P	280C	146T	BAS	GY
7»	TT-DELPHIN	5333t	96	37.5k	82.3m	600P	175C	-	A	SW

HUCKLEBERRY FINN Built at Bremerhaven, Germany as the NILS DACKE, a ro-pax vessel. During summer 1993 rebuilt to transform her into a passenger/car ferry and renamed the PETER PAN, replacing a similarly named vessel (31356t, 1986). On arrival of the new PETER PAN in autumn she was renamed the PETER PAN IV. She was then converted back to ro-pax format, renamed the HUCKLEBERRY FINN and, in early 2002, transferred to the Trelleborg - Rostock route.

NILS DACKE, ROBIN HOOD Ro-pax vessels built at Rauma, Finland for *TT-Line*. Primarily freight vessels but accompanied cars - especially camper vans and cars towing caravans - are conveyed.

NILS HOLGERSSON, PETER PAN Built at Bremerhaven, Germany for *TT-Line* for the Travemünde - Trelleborg route.

TOM SAWYER Built at Bremerhaven, Germany as the ROBIN HOOD, a ro-pax vessel. During winter 1992/93 rebuilt to transform her into a passenger/car ferry and renamed the NILS HOLGERSSON, replacing a similarly named vessel (31395t, 1987) which had been sold to *Brittany Ferries* and renamed the VAL DE LOIRE. In 2001 converted back to ro-pax format and renamed the TOM SAWYER. Transferred to the Rostock - Trelleborg route.

TT-DELPHIN Austal Ships Auto Express 82 catamaran built at Fremantle, Western Australia for *TT-Line* to operate between Rostock and Trelleborg. Renamed the TT-DELPHIN in 2002.

UNITY LINE

THE COMPANY *Unity Line* is a Polish company, jointly owned by *Polish Steamship Company* and *Euroafrica Shipping Lines.*

MANAGEMENT Chairman of the Board Pawel Porzycki, **Managing Director** Ronald Stone.

ADDRESS Poland, 70-419 Szczecin, Plac Rodla 8.

TELEPHONE Administration +48 (0)91 35 95 795, **Reservations** +48 (0)91 35 95 692, (0)91 35 95 755.

FAX Administration +48 (0)91 35 95 885, **Reservations** +48 (0)91 35 95 673.

INTERNET Email unity@unityline.pl **Website** www.unityline.pl *(Polish, English, Swedish)*

ROUTE OPERATED Swinoujscie (Poland) - Ystad (Sweden) (6 hrs 30 mins (day), 9 hrs (night); *(1)*; 1 per day).

1	POLONIA	29875t	95	17.2k	169.9m	920P	860C	160Tr	BA	BA

POLONIA Train/vehicle ferry built at Tomrefjord, Norway for *Polonia Line Ltd* and chartered to *Unity Line*.

VIKING LINE

THE COMPANY *Viking Line AB* is an Åland (Finland) company (previously *SF Line*, trading (with *Rederi AB Slite* of Sweden) as *Viking Line*). Services are marketed by subsidiary company *Viking Line Marketing AB OY* of Finland and Sweden; this dates from the time that *Viking Line* was a consortium of three operators.

MANAGEMENT Managing Director *(Viking Line AB)* Nils-Erik Eklund, **Managing Director *(Viking Line Marketing AB OY)*** Boris Ekman.

ADDRESS *Viking Line AB* Norragatan 4, FIN-22100 Mariehamn, Åland, ***Viking Line Marketing AB OY*** PO Box 35, FIN-22101 Mariehamn, Åland.

TELEPHONE Administration +358 (0)18 26011, **Reservations** +358 (0)9 12351.

FAX Administration & Reservations +358 (0)9 1235292.

INTERNET Email incoming@vikingline.fi **Websites** www.vikingline.fi *(Finnish, Swedish, English)* www.vikingline.se *(Swedish, English)*

ROUTES OPERATED *All year* Stockholm (Sweden) - Mariehamn (Åland) - Helsinki (Finland) (14 hrs; *(4,6)*; 1 per day), Stockholm - Mariehamn (day)/Långnäs (Åland) (night) - Turku (Finland) (9 hrs 10 mins; *(2,5)*; 2 per day), cruises from Helsinki to Tallinn (Muuga Harbour) (Estonia) (20 hrs - 21 hrs round trip; *(3)*; 1 per day) (freight vehicles are conveyed on this service but not private cars; only 1 hr 30 minutes is spent in port), ***Summer only*** Kapellskär (Sweden) - Mariehamn (Åland) (2 hrs 15 mins; *(1)*; up to 3 per day), Kapellskär (Sweden) - Mariehamn (Åland) - Turku (Finland) (8 hrs 45 mins; *(7)*; 1 per day) (peak period only), ***Except summer peak period*** Cruises from Stockholm to Mariehamn (21 hrs - 24 hrs round trip (most 22 hrs 30 mins); *(7)*; 1 per day).

1	ÅLANDSFÄRJAN	6172t	72	17k	104.6m	1004P	185C	26T	BA	SW
2	AMORELLA	34384t	88	21.5k	169.4m	2480P	450C	70T	BA	FI
3	CINDERELLA	46398t	89	21.5k	190.9m	2500P	340C	82T	BA	FI
4	GABRIELLA	35492t	92	21.5k	171.0m	2420P	420C	70T	BA	FI
5	ISABELLA	34386t	89	21.5k	169.4m	2480P	364C	70T	BA	FI
6	MARIELLA	37799t	85	22k	177.0m	2500P	480C	82T	BA	FI
7	ROSELLA	16850t	80	21.3k	136.2m	1700P	340C	52T	BA	FI

ÅLANDSFÄRJAN Built at Helsingør, Denmark as the KATTEGAT for *Jydsk Færgefart* on Denmark for the Grenaa - Hundested service. She was used on this route until 1978 when the service became a single ship operation. She was then sold to *P&O Ferries*, renamed the N F TIGER and introduced as the second vessel on the Dover - Boulogne service. Sold to *European Ferries* in 1985 and withdrawn in June 1986. In 1986 sold to *Finlandshammen AB*, Sweden, renamed the ÅLANDSFÄRJAN and used on *Viking Line* summer service between Kapellskär and Mariehamn.

AMORELLA Built at Split, Yugoslavia for *SF Line* for the Stockholm - Mariehamn - Turku service.

CINDERELLA Built at Turku, Finland for *SF Line*. Until 1993 provided additional capacity between Stockholm and Helsinki and undertook weekend cruises from Helsinki. In 1993 she replaced the OLYMPIA (a sister vessel of the MARIELLA) as the main Stockholm - Helsinki vessel after the OLYMPIA had been chartered to *P&O European Ferries* and renamed the PRIDE OF BILBAO. In 1995 switched to operating 20 hour cruises from Helsinki to Estonia in the off peak and the Stockholm - Mariehamn - Turku service during the peak summer period (end of May to end of August). During 1997 she remained cruising throughout the year.

GABRIELLA Built at Split, Croatia as the FRANS SUELL for *Sea-Link AB* of Sweden to operate for subsidiary company *Euroway AB*, who established a service between Lübeck, Travemünde and Malmö. In 1994 this service ceased and she was chartered to *Silja Line*, renamed the SILJA SCANDINAVIA and transferred to the Stockholm - Turku service. In 1997 she was sold to *Viking Line* to operate between Stockholm and Helsinki. She was renamed the GABRIELLA.

ISABELLA Built at Split, Yugoslavia for *SF Line*. Used on the Stockholm - Naantali service until 1992 until she was switched to operating 24 hour cruises from Helsinki and in 1995 she was transferred to the Stockholm - Helsinki route. During 1996 she additionally operated short cruises to Muuga in Estonia during the 'layover' period in Helsinki. In 1997 she was transferred to the Stockholm - Turku route.

MARIELLA Built at Turku, Finland for *SF Line*. Used on the Stockholm - Helsinki service. During 1996 additionally operated short cruises to Muuga in Estonia during the 'layover' period in Helsinki but this has now ceased.

ROSELLA Built at Turku, Finland for *SF Line*. Used mainly on the Stockholm - Turku and Kapellskär - Naantali services until 1997. She now operates 21-24 hour cruises from Stockholm to Mariehamn under the marketing name 'The Dancing Queen', except in the peak summer period when she operates between Kapellskär and Turku. She also operates as a reserve vessel for the larger ships.

VV-LINE

THE COMPANY *VV-Line* is the trading name of *Västervik – Ventspils Färjelinje AB*, a Swedish company.

MANAGEMENT Managing Director Sven-Åke Ohlson.

ADDRESS *Sweden* Lucernahamnen, Västervik Färjevägen 10, S-593 50 Västervik, Sweden, ***Latvia*** 7 Plostu Iela, Ventspils, LV 3600 Latvia.

TELEPHONE Administration & Reservations *Sweden* +46 (0)490 258080, ***Latvia*** +371 (0)36 07 355.

FAX Administration & Reservations *Sweden* +46 (0)490 258089, ***Latvia*** +371 (0)36 07 358.

INTERNET Email office@vvline.com **Website** www.vvline.com *(Swedish, Emglish)*

ROUTE OPERATED Västervik (Sweden) - Tallinn (Estonia) (19 hrs; *(1)*; 3 per week).

1	MERMAID II	13730t	72	17.5k	137.3m	69P	170C	84T	AS	FI

FINNMAID Built at Turku, Finland as the HANZ GUTZEIT and chartered to *Finncarriers* for Finland - Germany service. In 1982 she was sold to *EFFOA* of Finland and renamed the CAPELLA. She continued to be chartered to *Finncarriers* and this charter continued under a number of subsequent owners. In 1986 she was renamed the CAPELLA AV Stockholm. In 1988 she was renamed the FINNMAID. In 1989 she was placed on the *FinnLink* service between Uusikaupunki (Finland) and Hargshamn (Sweden). In 1997, this service was transferred to the Kapellskär - Naantali route. In 1998 she was replaced by the FINNARROW and, after service on *Finncarriers'* Finland - Germany routes, was laid up. In 2000 she was chartered to *VV-Line*. Passenger capacity was raised from 48 to 69. She was owned by *Rederi AB Gustaf Erikson* of Åland but in 2001 purchased by *VV-Line* and renamed the MERMAID II. Sevice to Ventspils withdrawn in 2002.

WAGENBORG PASSAGIERSDIENSTEN

THE COMPANY *Wagenborg Passagiersdiensten BV* is a Dutch public sector company.

MANAGEMENT Managing Director G van Langen.

ADDRESS Postbus 70, 9163 ZM Nes, Ameland, Netherlands.

TELEPHONE Administration & Reservations +31 (0)519 546111.

FAX Administration & Reservations +31 (0)519 542905.

INTERNET Email wagenb@euronet.nl **Website** www.wpd.nl *(Dutch)*

ROUTES OPERATED Holwerd (Netherlands) - Ameland (Frisian Islands) (45 minutes; *(2,3)*; up to 10 per day). Lauwersoog (Netherlands) - Schiermonnikoog (Frisian Islands) (45 minutes; *(4)*; up to 6 per day).

1	BRAKZAND	450t	67	10.5k	50.0m	1000P	20C	-	A	NL
2	OERD	1121t	85	12.2k	58.0m	1000P	46C	9L	BA	NL
3	SIER	2286t	95	11.2k	73.2m	1440P	72C	22L	BA	NL
4	ROTTUM	1121t	85	12.2k	58.0m	1140P	46C	9L	BA	NL

BRAKZAND, OERD Built at Hoogezand, Netherlands for *Wagenborg Passagiersdiensten BV*. The BRAKZAND is now a spare vessel.

ROTTUM Built at Hoogezand, Netherlands for *Wagenborg Passagiersdiensten BV* as the SIER and used on the Holwerd - Ameland route. In 1995 renamed the ROTTUM and transferred to the Lauwersoog - Schiermonnikoog route.

SIER Built at Wartena, Netherlands for *Wagenborg Passagiersdiensten BV*.

Cinderella *(Matthew Punter)*

Superfast X *(Mike Louagie)*

section 7
others

The following vessels are, at the time of going to print, not operating and are owned by companies which do not currently operate services. They are therefore available for possible re-deployment, either in the area covered by this book or elsewhere. Withdrawn vessels not yet disposed of owned by operating companies are shown under the appropriate company and marked '•'.

DIFKO (Denmark)

1	DIFKO FYN	4101t	87	12.7k	95.8m	253P	170C	26L	BA	DK
2	GITTE 3	4296t	87	12.7k	95.0m	300P	170C	20T	BA	DK

DIFKO FYN Built Sunderland, UK at as the SUPERFLEX ECHO for *Vognmandsruten*. She was unused until 1995, when she was renamed the DIFKO FYN (*Vognmandsruten* having meanwhile been acquired by *DIFKO Færger A/S*) and placed on the Nyborg - Korsør service. In 1998, following the opening of the Great Belt fixed link, the service ceased and she was laid up at Helsingborg, initially in the care of *HH-Ferries* and was them to charter at short notice should one of their own vessels be unavailable; this arrangement has now ceased. In summer 2000 operated by *DIFKO* between Langeland (Denmark) and Kiel (Germany). This was not repeated in 2001 and she remains laid up.

GITTE 3 Built at Sunderland, UK as the SUPERFLEX DELTA for *Vognmandsruten*. In 1990 this company was taken over by *DIFKO* and she was renamed the DIFKO STOREBÆLT. In 1998, following the opening of the Great Belt fixed link, the service ceased and she was laid up. In 1999 she was chartered to *Easy Line* renamed the GITTE 3 and operated between Gedser and Rostock. Laid up after August 1999 except for brief periods on charter to *HH-Ferries*.

Eidsiva Rederi ASA (Norway)

1	ANJA 11	4101t	88	13k	95.0m	253P	170C	42T	BA	DK

ANJA 11 Built at Sunderland, UK as the SUPERFLEX KILO for *Vognmandsruten* of Denmark. In 1989 sold to *Mercandia* and renamed the MERCANDIA I. In 1990 she began operating on the *Kattegatbroen* Juelsminde - Kalundborg service. In 1996 this service ceased but it has not proved possible to use her on the *Sundbroen* Helsingør - Helsingborg service. In 1997 chartered to *Litorina Line* to inaugurate a new service between Öland and Gotland. In 1998, sold to *Eidsiva Rederi* and renamed the ANJA 11. She inaugurated a new service for subsidiary *Easy Line* between Gedser and Rostock. In December 2000 the *Easy Line* service ended and she was laid up. Note she initially carried the name 'ANJA #11' but the '#' character did not form part of her registered name. This character was subsequently removed. Service ended at end of 2000 and she was laid up.

Elbe-Ferry (Germany)

1	HINRICH-WILHELM KOPF	5148t	64	16k	104.6m	450P	124C	18L	BA	GY
2	JOCHEN STEFFEN	5293t	60	17k	104.6m	450P	157C	18L	BA	GY
3	WILHELM KAISEN	1553t	67	12k	87.9m	250P	55C	12L	BA	GY

HINRICH-WILHELM KOPF Built at Aalborg, Denmark as the PRINSESSE ELISABETH for *DSB* for the Århus - Kalundborg service. In 1986 transferred to the Helsingør - Helsingborg service. In 1998, sold to *E H Harms GmbH* of Bremen. In 1999 she was renamed the HINRICH-WILHELM KOPF and inaugurated a new service between Cuxhaven and Brunsbüttel by subsidiary *Elbe Ferry*. Laid up spring 2001.

JOCHEN STEFFEN Built at Aalborg, Denmark as the PRINSESSE ANNE-MARIE for *DSB* for the Århus - Kalundborg service. In 1986 transferred to the Helsingør - Helsingborg service, generally as a relief vessel. Following the withdrawal of the REGULA and URSULA she became a regular vessel with a

Swedish crew. Withdrawn in 1997. In 1998, sold to *E H Harms GmbH* of Bremen. In 1999 she was renamed the JOCHEN STEFFEN and inaugurated a new service between Cuxhaven and Brunsbüttel. Laid up spring 2001.

WILHELM KAISEN Built at Århus, Denmark as the NAJADEN, a vehicle/train ferry for *DSB* for the Helsingør - Helsingborg service. In 1987 converted to a vehicle ferry and transferred to the Fynshav - Bøjden service. In 1997, transferred to subsidiary *SFDS A/S*. In 1998 she was sold to *E H Harms GmbH* of Bremen. In 1999 she was renamed the WILHELM KAISEN and inaugurated a new service between Cuxhaven and Brunsbüttel. Laid up spring 2001.

Estonian Shipping Company (Estonia)

1	GEORG OTS	12549t	80	20k	136.8m	1200P	107C	15T	BA	ES

GEORG OTS Built at Gdansk, Poland for *Estonian Shipping Company (ESCO)*, then of the USSR, to operate between Tallinn and Helsinki. Later chartered to *Tallink* (which was at the time partly owned by *ESCO*). Rebuilt in 1993 to increase car capacity from 14 to 110 and bring up to modern standards. In 2000 charter ended and she was returned to *ECSO*. Currently for sale. An agreed sale in 2002 to Norwegian owners fell through.

Far Eastern Shipping (Russia)

1	MIKHAIL SHOLOKHOV	12798t	86	20k	139.6m	412P	344C	22T	A	RU

MIKHAIL SHOLOKHOV Built at Szczecin, Poland for *Far Eastern Shipping* of the Soviet Union and later of Russia. In 1999 started a service from Stockholm to St Petersburg; service ceased at the end of the year. In 2000 began operating for *Mono Line* between Stockholm and Riga (Latvia). In 2001 service ceased. Laid up.

section 8

prospective new services

Ballycastle (Northern Ireland) - Campbeltown (Scotland) The Scottish Executive have invited bids from operators to restart this service. If the project goes ahead it is likely to resume in spring 2003 but it could be earlier.

Greencastle (Co Donegal, Republic of Ireland) - Magilligan (Co Londonderry, Northern Ireland) It is planned to start a new service between these points in spring 2002. The service is to be operated under tender to authorities in Northern Ireland and the Irish Republic. The project is being managed by the North West Region Cross Border Group, a joint NI/IR body. At the time of going to press, the tender process is not completed and we therefore have no information on who the operator is to be and what vessel will be used.

Arendal (Norway) - Bremerhaven (Germany) A Norwegian company called *Viking Seaways* has announced an intention to establish a cruise ferry service between these ports. No timetable has been stated and no orders placed for new ships.

Lysekil (Sweden) - Sandefjord A Norwegian company called *Lysekilslinjen* is planning to establish a car and freight ferry service between these ports. A start date of December 2002 is currently planned. No other details are available.

section 9 changes since ferries 2001

british isles and northern europe

DISPOSALS

The following vessels, listed in the *Ferries 2001 - British Isles and Northern Europe Edition* have been disposed of - either to other companies listed in this book or others. Company names are as used in that publication.

ABEL MAGWITCH *(White Horse Fast Ferries)* In 2001 chartered to *Collins River Enterprises.*

ALLASDALE LASS (*Comhairle Nan Eilean Siar)* In 2001 charter ended. Passenger service replaced by vehicle service in March 2002.

BAZIAS *(Cobelfret Ferries)* Incorrectly listed. Actually called the BAZIAS 1. In 2002 charter ended. Chartered to *Dart Line* to operate between Dartford and Dunkerque.

BOOMERANG *(Polferries)* In 2001 sold to Tallink and renamed the TALLINK AUTOEXPRESS II.

CCTL HAMBURG *(CCTL)* In 2001 charter ended. Chartered to *van Uden RORO* operating from Western Europe to the Mediterranean.

CELTIC SUN *(P&O Irish Sea)* In 2001 charter ended and renamed the LEMBITU; chartered to *NorseMerchant Ferries.* In 2002 charter ended and returned to *ESCO* service in the Baltic.

CITY OF CORK *(Swansea Cork Ferries)* In autumn 2001 charter ended. In 2002 sold to *CTMA* of Canada. Renamed the LE VACANCIER.

CONTENDER *(Orkney Ro-Ro Services)* Withdrawn in 2001 following the ending of the service. In 2002 sold to a Dubai based company.

COTE DES ISLES *(Emeraude Lines)* Operation of this vessel in conjunction with *Emeraude Lines* has now ceased.

CUPRIA *(Finnlines)* In autumn 2001 chartered to *Cobelfret Ferries.* In winter 2002 chartered to *SeaWind Line.*

DANIEL QUILP *(White Horse Fast Ferries)* In 2001 withdrawn and laid up for sale.

DART 3 *(NorseMerchant Ferries)* In 2001 charted ended; returned to *Dart Line* and placed on the Dartford-Dunkerque/Vlissingen service.

EBENEZER SCROOGE *(White Horse Fast Ferries)* In 2001 withdrawn and laid up for sale.

ELK *(P&O Ferrymasters)* In early 2001 sold to *DFDS Tor Line.* Continued to operate for *P&O Ferrymasters* until May when their service ceased. She was transferred to *DFDS Tor Line* services and renamed the TOR BALTICA.

EUROPEAN TRADER *(P&O Irish Sea)* In 2001 sold to *Taygran Shipping* and renamed the TAYGRAN TRADER. Operated between Ullapool and Stornoway (Lewis). Later sold to *El Salam Maritime Company* of Egypt and renamed the LINA TRADER.

FELIX E *(Scandlines (Sweden))* In 2002 sold to *Mediterranean Shipping Company* and chartered to *SNAV Aliscafi* of Italy to operate between Ancona (Italy) and Split (Croatia) in a joint venture with *Sea Containers* and renamed the CROATIA JET.

Quiberon *(Brain Maxted)*

City of Cork *(Gordon Hislip)*

SUPERFAST II

Superfast – a new generation of ferries for Europe – Superfast II *(Philippe Holthof)*

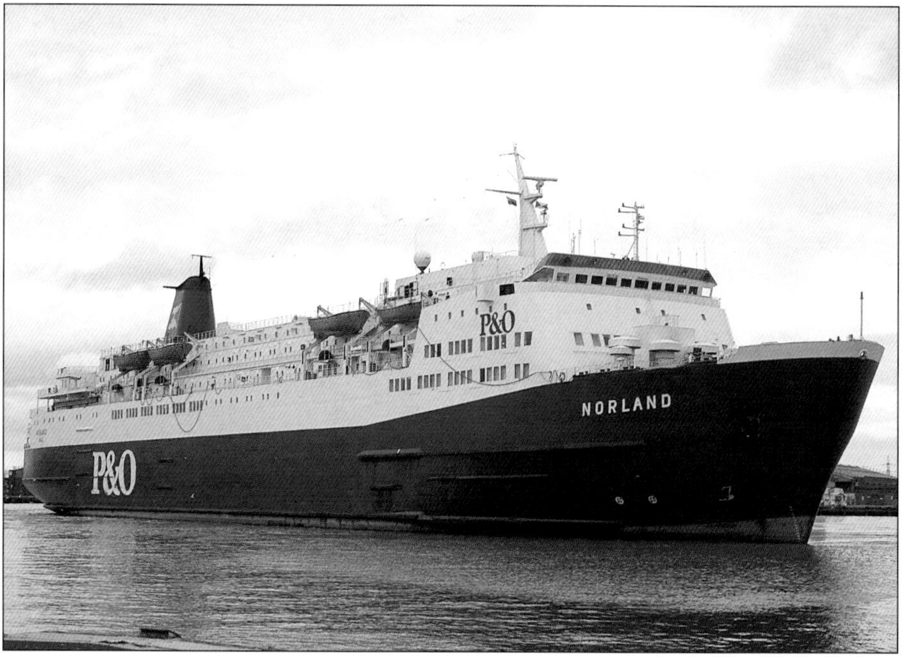

Norland *(Michael Drewery)*

Stena Galloway *(Miles Cowsill)*

FINNFELLOW *(Finnlines (FinnLink))* In 2002 sold.

FINNWOOD *(Finnlines)* In 2001 sold for scrap.

FRANCOISE *(Gulfstream Shipping Irelande)* Service withdrawn during 2001. In 2002 sold to *Aegean Cargo* (*K.Agapitos*) to be used in the Cyclades. Renamed the AEGEAN MELODY.

GALWAY BAY *(Island Ferries)* In 2001 withdrawn.

ISLE OF INNISFREE *(Irish Ferries)* In 2002 chartered to *P&O Portsmouth* and renamed the PRIDE OF CHERBOURG. Used on the Portsmouth - Cherbourg service.

KING OF SCANDINAVIA *(DFDS Seaways)* In 2002 sold to *Marmara Lines* of Turkey and renamed the CESME She did not inaugurate the Copenhagen - Gdynia service as planned.

KONINGIN BEATRIX *(Stena Line)* (Irish Sea Service in Section 1) In 2002 transferred to *Stena Line's* Scandinavian service in Section 6 and renamed the STENA BALTICA.

LØBEREN *(Scandlines (Denmark and Germany))* In 2001 sold to *SNAV* of Italy and renamed the SNAV ALFA.

MARTIN CHUZZLEWIT *(White Horse Fast Ferries)* In 2001 chartered to *Lower Thames & Medway Passenger Boat Co Ltd.* She continues to operate the Gravesend - Tilbury route.

MIKHAIL SHOLOKHOV *(Mono Line)* In 2001 service ceased. Vessel returned to owners and laid up.

NEPTUNIA *(Falcon Seafreight)* In summer 2001 service ceased. Charter ended.

NORBANK *(P&O North Sea Ferries)* In 2002 transferred to *P&O Irish Sea* and operates between Liverpool and Dublin.

NORBAY *(P&O North Sea Ferries)* In 2002 transferred to *P&O Irish Sea* and operates between Liverpool and Dublin.

NORDHAV *(Nor-Cargo)* In 2002 sold to *Cargoferry* of Norway to operate between Moss and Århus.

NORLAND *(P&O North Sea Ferries)* In 2002 sold to *SNAV* of Italy and renamed the SNAV SICILIA. Operates between Naples and Palermo.

NORSTAR *(P&O North Sea Ferries)* In 2002 sold to *SNAV* of Italy and renamed the SNAV CAMPANIA. Operates between Naples and Palermo.

ÖRESUND *(Scandlines (Sweden))* In 2001 sold to *Sea Containers Ferries* for conversion to ro-pax ferry for *SeaWind Line.* To be renamed the SKY WIND.

ØRNEN *(Scandlines (Denmark and Germany)* In 2001 sold to *SNAV* of Italy and renamed the SNAV AURIGA.

P&OSL PICARDY *(P&O Stena Line)* In 2001 sold to *Seaborne Navigation Co Ltd* (associated company of *TransEuropa Ferries*) and renamed the OLEANDER. To operate between Ostend and Ramsgate.

PHILIP PIRRIP *(White Horse Fast Ferries)* In 2001 withdrawn and laid up for sale.

PICASSO *(Sea Containers Ferries)* In 2001 sold to *Aegean Carriers* of Greece, renamed the MARINA and placed in service between Greece and Crete.

PORTO EXPRESS *(RoRoExpress)* In autumn 2001 charter ended after service ceased. Renamed the LOUISE RUSS. In 2002 chartered to *Cobelfret Ferries.*

PRIDE OF SUFFOLK *(P&O North Sea Ferries)* In 2001 transferred to *P&O Irish Sea* and placed on the Liverpool - Dublin service. Renamed the EUROPEAN DIPLOMAT. Later transferred to the Rosslare - Cherbourg service.

ROSEBAY *(TransEuropa Shipping Lines)* Did not go to this company. In 2001 sold to *Rederi AB Engship* of Sweden, renamed the TRANSPARADEN and chartered to *Botnia Link.*

ROSEHAUGH *(The Highland Council)* In 2001 sold to *MacDonald Ferries,* Invergordon.

SAGA STAR *(TT-Line)* In 2002 sold to *Transmanche Ferries* and renamed the DIEPPE.

SEA SPRINTER *(Island Ferries)* In 2001 withdrawn.

SERENADEN (*Transfennica)* In 2001 service reduced to two ships and redeployed on other *Transfennica* routes.

SOLIDOR 3 *(Emeraude Lines)* In 2001 sold to *Förde Reederei* of Germany, renamed the TANGER JET and used on a new service between Spain and Morocco.

SPIRIT OF PORTSMOUTH *(Gosport Ferry)* In 2001 the order for this vessel was cancelled. However, her builders have continued construction and she may yet be sold to *Gosport Ferry.*

SPRINGAREN *(Scandlines (Denmark and Germany))* In 2001 sold to *SNAV* of Italy and renamed the SNAV AQUARIUS.

STENA GALLOWAY *(Stena Line)* In 2002 withdrawn and sold to *IMTC* of Morocco and renamed the LE RIF. She operates between Algeciras (Spain) and Tangiers (Morocco).

SUPERFAST I, SUPERFAST II, SUPERFAST XI, SUPERFAST XII *(SuperFast Ferries)* None of these vessels are to operate between Zeebrugge and Rosyth. The SUPERFAST IX and SUPERFAST X will operate instead.

TALLINK EXPRESS I *(Tallink)* In 2001 sold to *ANES* of Greece and renamed the CATAMARAN PANORMITIS.

TOR CALEDONIA *(DFDS Tor Line)* In 2001 sold to *StradaBlu Srl* of Italy to operate between Voltri, Italy (near Genoa) and Naples, Italy and renamed the STRADA GIGANTA.

TOR HAFNIA *(DFDS Tor Line)* In 2001 sold to *StradaBlu Srl* of Italy to operate between Voltri, Italy (near Genoa) and Naples, Italy and renamed the STRADA CORSARA.

TT-TRAVELLER *(TT-Line)* In 2001 charter ended. Chartered to *Stena Line* to operate between Karlskrona and Gdynia and renamed the STENA TRAVELLER.

URIAH HEEP *(White Horse Fast Ferries)* In 2001 withdrawn and laid up for sale.

VIIRE *(DIFKO Færger A/S)* In 2001 chartered again to *Saaremaa Lævakompanii* of Estonia.

WASA QUEEN *(Silja Line)* In 2001 sold to *Megastar Capricorn Limited,* an Isle of Man subsidiary of *Star Cruises* of Singapore. Not renamed, she now operates a cruise ferry service between Xiamen (China) and Hong Kong.

WHITE SEA *(Taygran Shipping)* In 2001 charter ended.

WILKINS MICAWBER *(White Horse Fast Ferries)* In 2001 withdrawn and laid up for sale.

NAME CHANGES

The following vessels have been renamed without change of operator.

AMAZON *(Mann Lines)* in 2001 reverted to original name of ESTRADEN.

AQUARIUS *(DFDS Seaways)* In 2001 renamed the PEARL OF SCANDINAVIA.

BALTIC STAR *(Ånedin Line)* In 2002 renamed the BIRGER JARL.

CELTIC STAR *(P&O Irish Sea)* In 2002 renamed the NORTHERN STAR.

EUROPEAN HIGHLANDER *(P&O Irish Sea)* In 2001 renamed the EUROPEAN MARINER.

FENNIA *(RG-Line)* In 2001 renamed the CASINO EXPRESS.

FINNMAID *(VV Line)* In 2001 renamed the MERMAID II.

GABRIELE WEHR *(Ferryways)* In 2001 purchased by *Ferryways* and renamed the FLANDERS WAY.

MOUNTWOOD *(Mersey Ferries)* In 2002 renamed the ROYAL IRIS OF THE MERSEY.

European Trader *(Miles Cowsill)*

Norbay and Northern Star *(Gordon Hislip)*

STENA FORWARDER
Stena

Stena Forwarder *(Miles Cowsill)*

NILS HOLGERSSON *(TT-Line)* In 2001 rebuilt to near original specification and renamed the TOM SAWYER.

PETER PAN (1988) *(TT-Line)* In 2001 rebuilt to near original specification and renamed the HUCKLEBERRY FINN.

THOMAS WEHR *(Ferryways)* In 2001 purchased by *Ferryways* and renamed the ANGLIAN WAY.

TOR NORVEGIA *(DFDS Tor Line)* In 2001 sold to *Lisco Baltic Service* renamed the TOR NERINGA. Continues to operate for *DFDS Tor Line*.

COMPANY CHANGES 2001-2002

Elbe-Ferry Service ceased in spring 2001. As ships remain with company laid up they are shown in Section 7.

Mono Line In 2001 service ended.

Nor-Cargo In 2001 formed a joint venture with *Seatrans* of Norway trading as *Sea-Cargo.*

Orkney Ro-Ro Services Service ceased in summer 2001.

P&O Ferrymasters Services ceased spring 2001; traffic accommodated on *DFDS Tor Line* services.

P&O Stena Line (Section 3) As passengers are now conveyed on the Dover - Zeebrugge service, transferred to Section 1.

Philip Ltd Ferry operations now run by subsidiary, *Dartmouth - Kingswear Floating Bridge Co Ltd.*

RORO Express Service ceased in autumn 2001.

Seaboard Marine (Nigg) Ltd Shown as Cromarty - Nigg Ferry as this company may not continue to operate the service following a Highland Council tendering exercise.

Taygran Shipping Service ceased in summer 2001.

White Horse Fast Ferries Service ceased in spring 2001. Tilbury-Gravesend ferry taken over by *Lower Thames & Medway Passenger Boat Co Ltd.*

LATE NEWS

Cetam French company, UK agents: Tel: +44 (0)23 80 223671, Fax: +44 (0)23 330880, Email: r.thornton@wainwrightgroup.com, Web: www.cetam.fr. New freight service started May 2002 Southampton - Santander (Spain) 1 per week, 35/40 hrs. Vessel CETAM VICTORIAE (10171t, 1975) (ex SEAHAWK 2002).

Rigas Juras Lines (new operator) Latvian Company Tel: +371 6540202 or +371 7500412.Email: rjl@rjl.eunet.lv. Route operated: Riga (Latvia) - Nynäshamn (Sweden), 12 hours, alternate days overnight service. Vessel used: MAX MOLS chartered from Mols-Linien.

P&O North Sea Ferries The Felixstowe - Rotterdam and Felixstowe - Zeebrugge routes may close later this year. The three vessels used on the former route may be sold to Stena Line and used on a new service from Harwich or Felixstowe to Rotterdam.

P&O Stena Line P&O may buy out the Stena Line share of the company. The Dover - Zeebrugge service may end by the end of the year and two of the vessels used may be converted to full passenger specification (like the P&OSL BURGUNDY) to replace the P&OSL CANTERBURY and P&OSL KENT on the Dover - Calais service. Renaming of the company and its ships seems likely.

Scandlines (Denmark and Germany) The SÆLEN was in April sold to SNAV of Italy. Renamed SNAV AQUILA.

Shetland Islands Council New vessel ordered for Lerwick (Mainland) - Out Skerries service. To be built in Gdansk, Poland, delivery 2003, 30 pass, 10 cars.

SuperSeaCat Two *(Brian Maxted)*

index | ferries illustrated

Solent Cat and **Pride of Hampshire** *(Chris Randall)*

For the last thirteen years we have produced over 50 books covering ferry operations in the UK and Europe, and are the leading specialists in the history of the ferry industry and current ferry operations. Ferry Publications also produce a quality ferry magazine **"European Ferry Scene"** which is accepted as Europe's leading ferry journal.

Our most recent titles and forthcoming books include:

- **Caledonian MacBrayne - The Fleet**
- **A Century of North-West European Ferries**
- **P&O - The Fleet**
- **Greek Ferries**
- **In Fair Weather and in Foul**
- **Sally Line - The Complete Story***
- **The Townsend Eight**
- **Ferries around Britain (Published June 2002)**

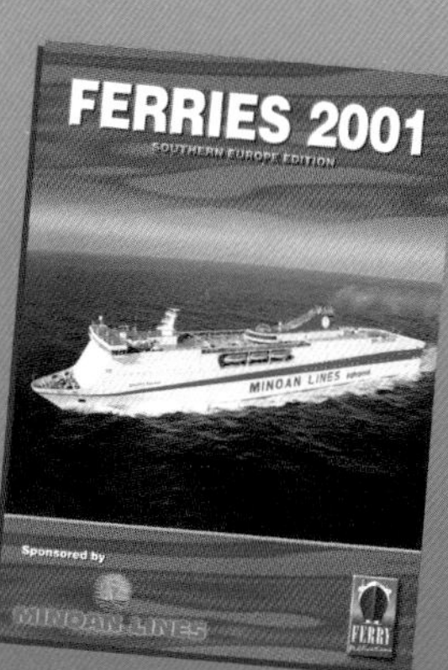

JUPITER

Jupiter *(Matthew Punter)*

index 2
ferries a to z

NORQUEEN

Norqueen *(Miles Cowsill)*

Still Available Back Issues of

FERRIES AND FERRIES OF THE BRITISH ISLES & NORTHERN EUROPE

from

Ferry Publications
PO Box 33, Ramsey,
Isle of Man, IM99 4LP

email: ferrypubs@aol.com website: www.ferrypubs.co.uk

FERRIES 2001 NORTHERN EUROPE

This edition sponsored by Caledonian MacBrayne, including review of Cal Mac's operations. Comprehensive review of ferry industry in Northern Europe. Price £14.05 (European and Overseas orders add £1.00 p&p)

FERRIES 2001 SOUTHERN EUROPE

New publication covering Mediterranean operations, sponsored by Minoan Lines. Full technical details on major ferry operators in Southern Europe. Price £11.40 (European and Overseas orders add £1.00 p&p)

1999

Sponsored by Dart Line. Features include History of Dart Line Europe. Review of the Ferry Industry 1998. Fast Ferry Review. The Rise of the Ro-Pax. Price £10.35. (European and Overseas orders add £1.00 p&p)

2000

This publication was sponsored by P&O Ferries. Reviews of P&O's new ferries - the *Pride of Rotterdam* and *Pride of Hull, European Causeway* and *European Ambassador*. Review of the ferry industry for 2000. Price £10.35. (European & Overseas orders add £1.00 p&p)

1997

Sponsored by Commodore. Features on Commodore Shipping Company, Development of the Fast Ferry Industry. Round Britain and Northern European Ferry Reviews. Price £9.35. (European and Overseas orders add £1.00 p&p)

1998

Sponsored by Ramsgate Port. Features include Round Britain Review, Fast Ferry Industry and Scandinavian Ferry Review. 184 pages. Price £10.35. (European and Overseas orders add £1.00 p&p)

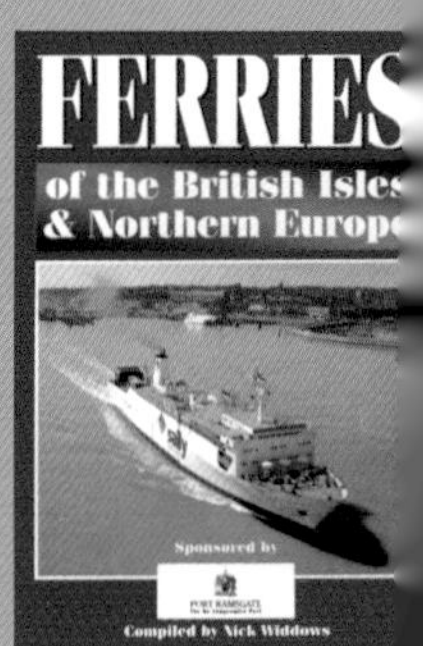